TRANSFORM YOUR LIFE
NOW!

TRANSFORM YOUR LIFE
NOW!
THE SPIRITUAL KEY TO EXCELLING ON ALL LEVELS

LAURIE URI GRANT

Outskirts Press, Inc.
Denver, Colorado

Outskirts Press, Inc.
http://www.outskirtspress.com

ISBN: 978-1-4327-7354-0

Library of Congress Control Number: 2011933705

Outskirts Press and the "OP" logo are trademarks belonging to Outskirts Press, Inc.

PRINTED IN THE UNITED STATES OF AMERICA

Dedicated To

All my children,
who have been my greatest teachers

and

Ku Kahuna Lokahi
for his trust, faith, love and support.

Author's Note

As additional support to transform your life, I have included two audio meditations as part of this book. To receive the optimum benefit, I strongly recommend that you read Chapters 2 through 8 before listening to the first meditation, and read Chapter 9 before listening to the second meditation. This will prepare you to receive and utilize the powerful transforming energies in both meditations. As with all meditations, do not listen to these recordings while driving or operating heavy equipment. You can download both recordings by emailing audio@transformyourlifenow.net.

I have been privileged to work with over 18,000 people. The names of many of my students and seminar participants have been changed to protect their privacy, so that I could share their amazing stories of transformation with you.

Contents

Introduction

Growing up with a learning disability in a family of PhDs caused me to be very creative in order to survive. I had acute dyslexia and I couldn't read or write very well. My parents were world-renowned PhDs in their fields. It really didn't work for them to have a child that couldn't read, especially the oldest child. If you are the oldest child, you know the extra pressure that puts on you.

I had to come up with something fast to survive in my family. I would hold a book in my hand and I would make up what I thought it said. In school, I took tests and made book reports on books I never read. I did not read an entire book all the way through elementary, junior or high school. Not because I didn't want to, it's because I literally couldn't.

Surprisingly, I only got caught twice—once in the eighth grade and once in the tenth grade. Both teachers said to me, "Laurie, you didn't read these books." I said, "You're right, I didn't."

One thing you should know about me is that I have "truth turrets," so truth just comes out of my mouth whether I want it to or not. Growing up, it was not such a happy thing for my parents when I would point out the pink elephant in the middle of the living room.

When I told both these teachers that I didn't read the book, they each said, "Oh, that's okay, honey, we just won't count this one." I decided that my teachers where not very smart because they didn't realize that I was stupid. Much later I learned that educators knew that dyslexics who have discovered ways to compensate for their disability are usually very intelligent, even if they do not see it themselves.

In my family of PhDs, you go on to college. It's irrelevant whether you can read or write. I found it was a little harder to bluff the college professors, but I managed to do all right. I had a C plus, B minus average.

Premonitions

Then one day when I was twenty years old, on a Sunday afternoon I suddenly *knew* that my boyfriend's uncle—who was only thirty-five— was going to have a heart attack at ten o'clock that night and die, and I wondered what to do. I knew if I called the uncle, he would think I was crazy.

What I did first was to call my boyfriend. I told him, "Your uncle is going to die at ten o'clock tonight. What should we do?" After a brief pause, he said, "You know, Laurie, finals week is coming up. You haven't read any of your textbooks; you're just getting stressed out. You've gotta get a grip."

Then I called my best friend, who is supposed to be supportive, right? That's why they're your best friend. I told her what I knew and asked her what I should do. She said pretty much the same thing my boyfriend did. So I allowed them to convince me to do nothing.

Sure enough at ten o'clock that night the man had a heart attack and died. I went through tremendous guilt because I didn't call him and say, "You know you might want to be near some hospital or health care center at ten o'clock tonight, just in case." But I didn't do that.

Two weeks later during finals week, I was really stressed out. I still hadn't read the textbooks. But I *knew* that the next morning at three minutes after eight on the corner of Cherry and Third some acquaintances of mine were going to be in a car accident. Now not only am I getting the time, I'm getting the place. And no, I didn't have their last names, so I couldn't call them up. Again I wrestled with the question: What am I going to do?

I considered going to Cherry and Third the next morning to try and stop traffic, but I didn't know what the car looked like. I told my boyfriend and my good friend who gave me such terrific advice the first time. Their unanimous response was that it was finals week, I hadn't read the textbooks, and I had been obsessing about the "coincidence" that happened a couple weeks before. Pass or fail, it would be over in a couple of days. I just needed to chill out and stop bothering them. Once again I allowed them to convince me to do nothing.

Sure enough, at three minutes after eight the next morning on the corner of Cherry and Third these same acquaintances were in a car accident. It was really hard for me to rationalize these things were coincidences, and that they meant nothing.

I didn't know what to do with the premonitions. They continued and they were always negative. I had them all of the time. I tried many things to deal with them. As soon as a premonition came into my mind, I tried to erase it thinking maybe I could make it go away. That didn't work at all. I tried telling people, I tried *not* telling people. My friends stopped wanting to hang around me—*I* stopped wanting to hang out with me.

I went on to graduate school to get a Masters degree where I found a redeeming quality to these premonitions—I knew all the answers to the test questions! All of them. My professors knew that I was cheating because I got a hundred percent right on their exams. There would be multiple-choice exams, and I would struggle to read the question. And I would struggle to read the answers and I'd hear "b." Then I would start to read the next question and the answers and I'd hear "d." Okay, I thought. Inevitably by the time I got to the third or fourth question, I wondered what was I doing trying to read these things, it had absolutely no relevance to the answer I was being told. So I would just put my pencil on the question, and I'd hear "e." And I'd check e. I'd get done in about five minutes and I'd turn it in to the professors and they marked it all correct. They thought someone was feeding me the answers from the other side of the wall. They were right about the "other side" part, not the wall. There was no physical evidence, so I graduated with honors. My parents were thrilled.

Medical Intuition

I got over my dyslexia through a psychic experience, but I had learned to use my intuition in order to survive. Then I met someone who taught me how to control my psychic ability rather than it controlling me. I became my psychic teacher's "protégé" (her word not mine) and went on to do readings and discovered that I could do medical intuition, which I called body readings. Eighteen years ago I was booked solid for over a year in advance doing medical intuition. My specialty was knowing what was going on that the doctors weren't able to diagnose. The doctors said that I had a hundred percent accuracy rate. I think it was more like ninety-five percent, but the information saved many, many lives.

This led me to also becoming a Reiki master teacher. I saw Reiki create miracles and I thought that was the answer. Then I was in a serious car accident and the meniscus in my knee was torn. For three and a half years I walked around with bone on bone thinking I was going to be able to heal it. I tried doing Reiki on it myself. It didn't work. I tried having other Reiki masters work on me. That didn't work either. Then I tried other kinds of holistic *anything* to get it healed. Nothing worked.

Little did I know that all of this was preparation for the greatest experiences of my life, which would heal much more than just my body.

Hawaiian Kahuna

It all began when I was hobbling around on crutches after flying to Honolulu to teach a Reiki class. Needless to say, it doesn't look good for the Reiki master teacher to show up on crutches touting the miracle healing benefits of Reiki. My knee was so swollen I could barely put my pants on over it. I needed a miracle and I needed it fast.

So in the wee hours of the early morning, I made my way to the Kahuna Healing Stones on Kuhio Beach in Waikiki, of all places. Back then there was a little sign with a legend about four kahuna (Hawaiian word for priest/ priestess) who traveled around the islands teaching their form of healing. Before they left, the sign said they deposited all of their mana or life force energy into the stones.

Standing there in front of the massive boulders that looked like they each weighed many tons, I made my plea, "I don't know if there's any truth to this legend that the kahuna placed all their healing energy into these stones, but if there is, I could use a little bit of help. I have five kids—two sets of twins—that ought to give me some sort of good karma. I'm on crutches, so I need a miracle fast because I'm teaching a class today. If you help me heal my knee, I promise you I will do whatever I can to get your mana out to the world."

Mostly I thought I was venting, but as soon as I made that promise, a column of shimmering rainbow energy came straight down in and around and through my whole body. It was so hot on my hands it felt like I was being branded. All the swelling disappeared. And my knee healed instantly!

The x-rays *before* this experience showed that I had a torn meniscus, which ultimately was cut out leaving bone on bone, and the *after* x-rays showed a basically normal knee.

As I stood within this column of shimming rainbow energy, I continued to feel the heat permeating through my body. Then I had a vision with my eyes open. I saw all these Hawaiian Gods and Goddesses and the Cosmic Mother Uli, who said to me that I had made a commitment lifetimes ago to come back when the time was right to teach the ancient secret wisdom that we were all One. And was I going to honor that commitment?

"Of course," I managed to reply, awestruck by what was happening to me. I then received a huge download of information on how the ancient kahuna healed. Later I found eighty-five percent of that information in ancient writings. Reading this afterwards just verified that was indeed how the ancient kahuna healed.

I then dedicated my life to this spiritual path and I started teaching Ancient Rainbow Conscious Healing or ARCH. As of this writing 18,000 people have taken my seminars, with amazing results in all aspects of their lives—physically, emotionally, mentally and spiritually. The results have included everything from complete body healings, reversing schizophrenia, manifesting abundance to spiritual awakenings. You will find many of these stories in the chapters that follow.

Initiation

Shortly after I began teaching ARCH, I received an email from a kahuna, Ku Kahuna Lokahi, on the Big Island, saying, "Congratulations on accepting your position." I thought, *Who is this guy and what does he know?* He said, "Never apologize for not being Hawaiian. At one point, we knew we were all One. It was only power and politics that separated us."

We corresponded some and I invited the kahuna and his wife to attend my next ARCH seminar as my guests. After the seminar, they took me out to dinner. The kahuna told me that he was trained by his grandmother in the ancient kahuna ways of healing. "The whole time she was training me," he explained, "she kept telling me about a centuries-old Hawaiian legend that there would be a fair-haired woman destined to take a leadership role in the Ku Kahuna tradition, and she thought I was going to meet that woman in this lifetime."

Then Kahuna Lokahi added, "It's a lot of work, a lot of responsibility and not everybody's going to accept it."

I'm thinking, that poor woman. Who would sign on for that?

"It's you!" the kahuna firmly stated.

"Nooooo!" I said.

"It's *you*," he affirmed.

"No!" I repeated.

"You think it's all about your knee?" the kahuna replied.

"Oh," I said, as the understanding slowly dawned within me.

The Kahuna Lohahi hanai (adopted) me as his daughter and became my papa. To be hanai is a huge honor in the Hawaiian tradition. It means you are choosing someone as your child. He then trained me. In 2003 after a four-hour ceremony at Queen Lili'uokalani's Summer Home in Honolulu with fifty-six of my students participating in the ceremony, Papa officially initiated me not only as a kahuna, but as the head of his Order of Ku, which in ancient times was the Order of Ku-Hina.

The reason why Papa said he made me the head of the Order is that in ancient times the Ku Kahuna lineage was a matriarchal society. The masculine (Ku) and the feminine (Hina) were always together—each balanced the other— male and female in equality. Then after the twelfth century, the men took over power and got rid of Hina, and made it about Ku and about war. "It has to go back to love and peace," Papa said, "and the only way that's going to happen is if a woman is in charge." I was given the title of Kahuna Ho'okahi, which means Kahuna of Oneness.

It was during the initiation ceremony into this ancient Hawaiian kahuna lineage that certain secrets were revealed to me. But I was told it was forbidden to reveal these secrets to others. However, when Papa initiated me as head of his Order, he told me that now I could change the rules. So the first thing I knew I would do was reveal these secrets to living an empowered, abundant, joyous, loving, peaceful life that had been hidden for so long. In that same year I had two life-changing experiences that deepened my knowing it was time to teach these long-forgotten secrets of happiness.

The Shock of Developing Stigmata

The first was an experience of stigmata. About a month before Easter, I developed wounds on my wrist, feet and forehead that bled spontaneously. I had no idea what was happening to me. I had to wear three-inch thick gauze bandages at all times.

I went to three doctors—an emergency room doctor, an internist and a dermatologist—who could find no evidence of trauma to my extremities and no physical cause for the bleeding. They all looked at the wounds and said, "You know there is no medical explanation for this."

Then I did my own research and what I found astounded me. This phenomenon mirrors the wounds Jesus suffered during the crucifixion, and they occur at the points where Jesus was nailed to the cross and where the crown of thorns was placed upon his head. There are three hundred and twenty confirmed cases of stigmata and out of them, ten are non-Christian who either watched something or read something about the crucifixion before it happened to them. I then remembered reading a book describing Jesus' crucifixion right before this happened to me. I learned that this little-understood phenomenon has affected individuals throughout history. Some of the most notable figures to have stigmata were Saint Francis of Assisi, Therese Neumann and Saint Pio of Pietrelcina known as Padre Pio.

Still searching, I consulted a Catholic nun and a bishop as most of the recorded cases were Catholic, even though I'm not Catholic. They each told me that the stigmata was "a gift" and that I was blessed. Not only did they both believe that this was the real thing, they both asked me to pray for them!

On Easter Sunday I went to my favorite Hawaiian heiau (sacred temple). Sitting there, I asked, "Just tell me what I'm supposed to do, just tell me. I live my life for the spiritual path; it's really what I've devoted my life to. Just tell me what you want from me. What am I supposed to do with this? And how do I make it stop?"

Suddenly I was lifted up out of my body a mile up in the air, and I could see everything. My body was still down there, but my vision was so expanded, I could see the other islands and everything on them. Then I experienced being lifted higher and higher as wave after wave of unconditional love and bliss permeated every part of my being and I felt myself going into Divine union with God, as God came into me. As this energy of Source came into my body, I felt myself merging in ecstatic Oneness with the Divine.

When I finally came back down into my body, a pure white butterfly came right up to my forehead, and went around and around my head a dozen times like it was making a halo, before it flew off. Then slowly the stigmata stopped.

As I reflected upon what had just happened, I understood that the stigmata had prepared me to move beyond the pain and suffering of human limitation into the utter bliss and limitlessness of Oneness with the Divine. In that moment, it made all the time spent with the bloody gauze bandages understandable. It was a sign of transformation.

There are as many ways for us to wake up as there are people to awaken! For some it is through synagogues and churches, Buddhist temples or other spiritual groups. For others it is through personal prayer, meditation, healing experiences or being in nature. Still for certain people, it may be in classes or seminars, and for particular individuals to truly get it, it may take something as dramatic as stigmata. The universe does have a sense of humor and I was working on keeping mine throughout all of this.

I was discovering that the message of Oneness is also in the Buddhist Sutras, the Kabbalah, the Bhagavagita, and in the Bible. Jesus says, "The Father and I are one." And "The Kingdom of Heaven is within." The translation of the Lord's Prayer from the original Aramaic—Jesus' native language—states, "Father/Mother, make me a vessel. Fill me with it. Let Oneness now prevail."

The Oneness Experience

Six months after having stigmata, I had the most profound experience of my life. In the months preceding this extraordinary event, I felt that I was being offered the Buddha enlightenment test. Buddha was said to have achieved enlightenment by being able to stay centered and spiritually focused while all forms of temptation and discord were going on around him.

At this time, it seemed everyone around me, especially my family, was going through chaos, drama and trauma. I felt my job was to be supportive and have compassion, but to stay in my light and on my path. My friends were surprised that I was so calm, especially when my teenagers were creating havoc and making very poor decisions. My advice to them was, "Know that you have wisdom inside of you, and that you can use that wisdom to make wise choices." I said this to them even when they weren't making wise decisions. The seeds I planted back then must have sprouted for now they are all making very wise choices. The universe must have thought I was passing the test because I was rewarded with a life-transforming lasting Oneness experience.

It happened during a seminar I was teaching in Boston, appropriately named "Over the Bridge and into the Rainbow—The Oneness Seminar." I was working with participants who had taken at least three other seminars with me. This was also the day that the Dali Lama was in Boston, and enlightened beings from all over had come to see him. So the energy was very high in the city and in the class.

I was preparing to give a Breath of I'O (an ancient Hawaiian term for God) initiation. Before I do initiations, I tell my students to go into a meditative state while listening to a chant and then I use that time to clear out any energy that would stop me from giving the clearest, cleanest, purest initiation that I can give. I felt the energy that I usually tap into getting much stronger. Then I stood up and asked for the highest level of Breath of I'O that I could easily accommodate to come through me for the purpose of initiating the participants. Normally it comes down in this nice neat little column. Instead it came forth in a huge expanded field. Suddenly my consciousness extended out to be one with everything around me. I was one with the student I was standing behind, as well as the chair. I was one with all the participants in the room. I was also one with the room. Then I was one with the building. I was one with Boston. I was one with the Dali Lama. And I was one with God, the Divine Source.

There was no limit. I was everything and everything was One. We were all One. I could not feel my body as a separate entity. There were no thoughts and no sense of time. My apprentice had to help move me—and sometimes gently shove me—from person to person, moving my hands to the next person's shoulders. Some of my students said they heard no sound as I moved from one to the other. All of them felt the incredibly powerful initiation they received, most saying they knew it was not just me giving the initiation.

When we were done with the initiation, I still could not feel my body. Initially I could not open my eyes and could barely move; I could only whisper, and some of my students mentioned that the whisper did not sound like my voice. Someone put cashews in my hand, but I could not feel them as separate from my hand. My apprentice gave me a cup of water, but I couldn't feel it either. He helped hold the cup while I tried to bring it to my mouth, but instead I hit my nose. We all had a good laugh. My apprentice then suggested I ask a higher being for help. I sent out the thought: "Is there a higher being out there who can help me integrate this experience into my body?" I heard my own thought come back like an echo, repeating the same request: "Is there a higher being out there who can help me integrate this experience into my body?" This was highly unusual for me because I have always had direct contact with my guides and the Source. I realized then that I was even one with the guides as well as the Source.

Later that afternoon, I was to do another initiation, in which I initiate the participants into the Divine Peace Perspective. When I asked for the highest level of that energy to come through me that I could easily accommodate, there was no separate higher energy. I already *was* it.

I had achieved Oneness—non-duality—with all that is. Since non-duality is only one, in that state I was privileged to experience beyond the illusion of separation. I was All, and All was me. There was no separation between myself, my body and everything else.

This is now my usual state. I experience no separation of anything. I am aware of always being connected and in a state of Oneness, although now I have complete control over my body.

I had no context for knowing what had happened to me. I began to research if anyone else had also experienced this. Dr. David Hawkins, a psychiatrist and author of "Power vs. Force," has done the most research on non-duality in the West. This research shows that only one in ten million people spontaneously experience true non-duality Oneness. No matter what their beliefs, religious background, age, culture, education or socio-economic status, all of them—including me—seem to experience the exact same thing. This includes a loss of awareness of the body, of thought, of time, and is accompanied by a feeling of pure bliss and of being one with everything and everyone, including the Divine Source. There is only the desire to "be" in that state. After this experience, there is no "Source" outside, all is within.

In his book, "Putting on the Mind of Christ: The Inner Work of Christian Spirituality," Jim Marion documents this state experienced by true spiritual teachers throughout the ages. The Buddhists call this state of non-duality Oneness "the highest level of enlightenment" and the Christians refer to it as the "highest level of human consciousness" because you are literally privileged witness to the truth. You *know* that you are One with the Divine.

I now live in a state of non-duality Oneness. I can change my field of vision, like a camera lens, to be in the state of total non-duality or to focus back in the body and to be in this world, but not of it. I see the universe through the eyes of compassion. No judgments, just compassion. I feel blissful, and detached from the everyday drama. I really, truly get it now. We are one with each other, with everything in the universe and with Source! If we all lived our lives knowing that we are one, there would be no war, no poverty, no hunger and no judgments.

It was from this state of Oneness that I discovered the Key to transform our lives that has been hidden for so long.

Part I:
Awakening Your Divine Potential

CHAPTER 1

Finding the Hidden Key

You hold in your hands a book that has the power to transform your life on every level. For within these pages is the Key to end all fear, doubt, lack and limitations that have caused conflict and unhappiness. This Key has transformed the lives of my seminar participants and it can do the same for you.

In this book, you will learn a revolutionary new way to view your life and those around you, and you will discover how to go beyond judgment of yourself and others, and truly transform your life *now*! Finally, you will learn the truth of who you really are and the steps to live in unlimited peace, love, joy and abundance.

What I am about to reveal to you was received in an on-going state of Oneness non-duality or Self-realization. Being a privileged witness beyond the illusion of separation allowed me to see the larger truth affecting each of us and all of humanity. It was from this unlimited perspective that I saw every individual's path, where they had come from and where they were going and the process to get there. I was shown the significance of family and friends and the important role countries play to support our continuous unfolding. And I was shown the extraordinary loving embrace the Divine Source, Mother Earth, all of the Cosmos and the entire universe hold us in on our journey back home.

I saw how everything—down to the very last detail—was created to support us in our growth as human beings remembering ourselves beyond this human mind and body. From this vantage point of being a privileged witness I saw the perfection of every single event and circumstance. And I saw that everything was part of a larger magnificent Divine plan that was perfectly designed to support us to awaken to our true Divine nature.

Suddenly all the questions I had been asking since my Oneness experience when I first realized that *everything is Divine all the time* was answered. I now understood why there are starving babies in Africa, why women are being raped, why slavery still exists in some parts of the world and why we can't always love ourselves. Now it made perfect sense why we don't always see the Divine in ourselves or in others, why we can't easily speak our truth, why we are not psychic all the time and why we can't always see things clearly with the unlimited perspective of the Divine. It was crystal clear why we can't use Divine creativity at the snap of our fingers, why we can't always instantly heal and why we are challenged to live in a state of grace knowing that we are Divine. And I knew why we are here!

The Divine Source as used in this book is the universal creative life force power that we all come from and to which we will all ultimately return. What is the Divine Source for you? Is it the Creator, the Supreme Being, God, Goddess, Divine Mother, Divine Father, Jesus, Buddha, Allah or the Great Spirit? Is it Universal Consciousness or Infinite Intelligence? What is your truth? Every time you see the words, "Divine Source," have that refer to *your* truth that resonates with you.

The End of Karma

I was shown that a single thought has united humanity in limitation—that there is something inherently wrong with us and we need to be punished for our wrongdoing or sin. The idea of karma (law of cause and effect) has been around for thousands of years and has affected millions of people. In the state of Oneness, I witnessed this limited perception of karma *being a thing of the past* as it focuses mostly on punishment and has no built-in system for growth and evolvement now!

I saw that karma worked in the past as a stage of development because of the limited state of consciousness on the planet. Now, as we move into higher levels of vibration as humans and as a planet, it is time for a paradigm shift. We are being given a whole new way of looking at ourselves and others, which brings peace and helps us grow rather than chopping us down and diminishing us.

Instead of thinking about human beings as having "karma"—that we do these bad things, and then we come back and we are punished for them, which is defeating rather than empowering—there is an entirely revolutionary way to understand the challenges and opportunities that are brought to us each day.

From the place of Oneness, it was clear that we come from the Divine and progress through a series of often challenging adventures until we once again return to the full knowingness that we are Divine, and with that awareness we create a life of grace, joy and blessings.

I was shown that we all are in the Universe University of Spiritual Growth and we move through our lifetimes in the order of our body's energy centers or chakras, as we evolve back to complete awareness of our Divinity. And I was told that we choose to be born into families that are set up to learn certain lessons and countries where the vast majority of people resonate with the particular chakra we are learning to master so we can gain wisdom and grow.

When we know that we are simply growing spiritually through the chakra system—moving as if from spiritual kindergarten to spiritual elementary school to spiritual junior high to spiritual high school to spiritual college to spiritual graduate school and finally to getting a spiritual PhD—we know it is a journey of *empowerment* rather than perceiving the events in our life as punishment. As soon as we learn the lesson and change our behavior, we immediately move up to the next level of awareness and our experience dramatically transforms for the better!

I have written this book so that you can accelerate your journey, master the lessons you have come to learn and move through the levels of awareness to create the life you want.

Chakra Lifetimes

Chakra is an ancient Sanskrit word that means wheel. I perceive them as three-dimensional balls or spheres of energy. Each one of these energy balls governs a different aspect of our lives as shown in the Chakra Chart that follows.

When we understand that we go through our lifetimes in the order of our energy centers or the chakra system to grow and evolve and master our lessons—each time revealing more of our Divinity—we get to be an active participant in our own awakening. Looking at where we are and how far we have come and all the growth we have already achieved is empowering. Wherever we are! Then we know what we need to master next. There are actual steps! This book will show you where you are in your growth process, as well as the steps to take to move to the next level.

Just as the illustration on the next page shows the order of the seven chakra centers in the body, so too do we progress through our lifetimes in this same order. As we master each chakra aspect, we go on to the next.

The Chakras

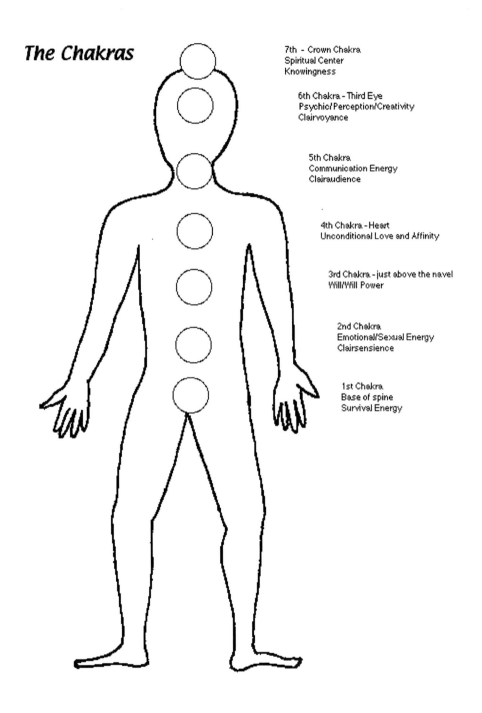

7th – Crown Chakra
Spiritual Center
Knowingness

6th Chakra – Third Eye
Psychic/Perception/Creativity
Clairvoyance

5th Chakra
Communication Energy
Clairaudience

4th Chakra – Heart
Unconditional Love and Affinity

3rd Chakra – just above the navel
Will/Will Power

2nd Chakra
Emotional/Sexual Energy
Clairsensience

1st Chakra
Base of spine
Survival Energy

First Chakra

The *first* chakra lifetimes are all about learning our survival lessons. For instance, being homeless for an entire life or chronically starving because there is not any food and struggling to survive. Many people choose really short incarnations and die before the age of two because they are just trying to learn how to operate in a body. First chakra lifetimes are not prolonged any longer than absolutely necessary as they involve great effort on a physical body level. The children that are starving to death in Africa or struggling for food in Haiti are good examples of this._

Second Chakra

Then you move into your *second* chakra or emotional and sexual lifetimes and you learn about the extremes of emotions and feelings that one can have on this planet. You also get to experience being sensual in a body and how that feels and you have the "not so good" experiences, such as being raped or molested and all the emotions associated with that. As you grow and evolve, the more positive feelings and sensual experiences come, such as "Oh my God, look what this body can do!"

Third Chakra

Next you move into the *third* chakra lifetimes of learning about will and willpower and experiencing being the victim and the persecutor or bully. You have to try both roles to be able to really master self-empowerment and learn how to manifest what you want.

Fourth Chakra

Then you move into the *fourth* chakra lifetimes and you learn to love yourself, which is the foundation of a happy life. You also learn about loving others; yet you cannot really love others if you do not love yourself first.

Fifth Chakra

Next you move into the *fifth* chakra communication lifetimes where you get to discover how to speak your truth clearly and effectively. This can include communicating non-verbally through sign language, facial expressions, body language, writing and singing.

Sixth Chakra

Then you move into the *sixth* chakra lifetimes—mastering your psychic, creativity and healing abilities as well as clearly using every opportunity to see things from a different perspective to help you grow. You get to explore all these amazing gifts that are available to you in a body.

Seventh Chakra

Finally you get to move into the *seventh* chakra spiritual lifetimes where the whole lifetime is about your spiritual growth. To illustrate this, every single thing I do, every hour of the day, every minute of the day is all involved in my spiritual path. Otherwise I do not do it. Well-known examples of those on a seventh chakra lifetime include Gandhi and the Dalai Lama.

Now you may be wondering, "If I'm on a *sixth* chakra lifetime because I'm really interested in opening up my psychic abilities or my healing abilities or changing my perception of the world or expanding my creativity, why have I struggled financially and had emotional depression at times and had sexual issues with people that tried to abuse me sexually? Why have I felt like a victim? Why have I had a hard time learning to love myself and others? And why can't I always speak my truth?"

This is because we have different layers of each chakra. Therefore, we have an opportunity to master the lessons in all of those aspects or layers of that chakra. Then we get to move on to the next.

Chakra Layers

As pictured in the following illustration, we also have seven layers of each chakra. The *first* layer of all of your chakras is the survival aspect of that chakra. The *second* layer is the emotional and sexual aspect of that chakra. The *third* layer is the will and willpower aspect of that chakra. The *fourth* layer is the love and affinity for self and others aspect of that chakra. The *fifth* layer is the communication aspect of that chakra. The *sixth* layer is the psychic, perception of things, creativity, and healing abilities of that chakra. Finally, the *seventh* is the spiritual aspect of that chakra.

Rainbow Layers of the Chakras

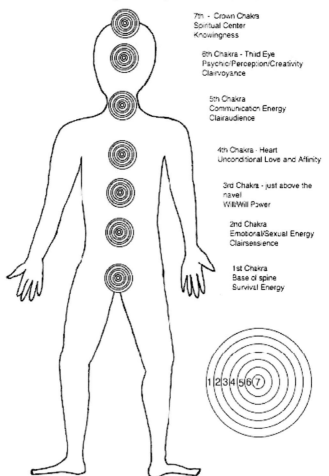

7th - Crown Chakra
Spiritual Center
Knowingness

6th Chakra - Third Eye
Psychic/Perception/Creativity
Clairvoyance

5th Chakra
Communication Energy
Clairaudience

4th Chakra - Heart
Unconditional Love and Affinity

3rd Chakra - just above the navel
Will/Will Power

2nd Chakra
Emotional/Sexual Energy
Clairsensience

1st Chakra
Base of spine
Survival Energy

1|2|3|4|5|6|7

First Layer

For example, if you are working on a *sixth* chakra lifetime, you are here to demonstrate mastering your psychic, creativity and healing abilities as well as your unlimited perception of things on the *first* layer level, which is survival. You get to discover how to use your survival aspect of your psychic ability to keep you safe and take good care of yourself. If you walk into a place and you get a creepy feeling that *something is wrong and might not be safe*, paying attention and turning around and walking out is using the first layer of your sixth chakra.

Second Layer

On a *second* layer level of your sixth chakra, you are here to master the emotional and sexual aspect of your psychic ability. If you are with someone and you apply your emotional clairsentience to learn what their feelings are for you *or* you are feeling psychically that they are sexually attracted to you, you are using the second layer of your sixth chakra.

Third Layer

In the *third* layer of the sixth chakra, you are mastering the will, willpower and manifesting aspect of your psychic abilities. You are realizing psychically that you are not a victim in any situation, and that you can use your energy to change whatever is not working for you.

Fourth Layer

Then you move into the *fourth* layer of the sixth chakra, your love and affinity aspect of your psychic ability. Here you master loving yourself by using your intuition to know *who you really are* that you get to love! What a great gift it is to tune into who you truly are and all those amazing aspects of you.

The next step is to use your intuition to love somebody else. Everyone has had the experience of looking across the room and immediately liking someone or not. They have not said a word to you, and you are not even in earshot of anything that they have said. Yet you already know whether this is a person you can connect with by using your intuition.

When my hairdresser met her husband they were twenty years old. He walked into a room and saw her across the room and said to a friend, "I'm going to marry that woman." She had not said a thing. He was not even anywhere close to her, so that connection on a psychic level was already speaking to him. They have been together for many years, and undoubtedly will continue to be.

FIFTH LAYER

On the *fifth* layer of the sixth chakra, you have an opportunity to master the communication aspect of your psychic ability by using your intuition to know the right thing to say. Then the perfect thing comes out of your mouth that you could not have designed better if you spent an hour or two or even a week thinking about it. It just falls right out of your mouth.

SIXTH LAYER

Next on the *sixth* layer of the sixth chakra, you can master the psychic, healing, creativity and perception aspects of your psychic, creativity, healing and perception abilities. Using your sixth sense just as much as your other five senses or using your healing abilities if it is called for, trusting your clear perception of things and automatically using your creativity to solve problems are all examples of using the sixth layer of your sixth chakra.

SEVENTH LAYER

Finally, on the *seventh* layer of the sixth chakra, you move into the spiritual aspect. Now you use that psychic evolvement to reach the point where it is not just about psychic energy anymore, and you move into the bigger picture of the spiritual part of life and begin to awaken that within you. You ask yourself: *What is it that I believe? Why am I really here? What is the bigger purpose of my life? Is there a Divine? Am I part of it?* And you start to pursue the answers to those spiritual questions.

When you master all of those layers of the sixth chakra, then you get to move to the seventh chakra, which is all about the spiritual path. *Isn't that Divinely designed!*

One of my seminar students said that when she learned about the layers of the chakra lifetimes and having to master that chakra on all those levels, it explained her entire life and she stopped judging herself for those times when she was not being the spiritually evolved person she thought she was. It just wiped out all of that guilt.

Celebrate Your Mastery

The really beautiful thing about this journey is not only do you get to experience yourself as someone who has mastered *all* the lessons of these aspects and *all* of these chakra lifetimes to reach wherever you are right now, you have the benefit of all the qualities of the Divine you have reclaimed along the way. You ought to be singing your praises for growing to wherever you are right now. Look how far you have come!

You started in spiritual kindergarten as *first* chakra survival lifetimers, just working on how to run a body in this world. Your focus was on food, shelter and clothes, or lack of them as the case may be.

Then you got into spiritual elementary school as *second* chakra emotional and sexual lifetimers, and you learned how to *feel* about yourself and other people, discovered your sensuality and that there is a difference between boys and girls.

Next, you moved into spiritual junior high as *third* chakra will, willpower and manifesting lifetimers. And you started to learn about cliques and who was better than who, who the bullies were, who the popular kids were and who the unpopular kids were and all of the dynamics of power. Also, you began to discover that you could create more of your reality than you thought you could when you were in elementary school.

Then you move into spiritual high school as *fourth* chakra love of self and others lifetimers, and you learn your lessons about love—self-love. Then you get to explore being attracted to somebody else and having love for another, whether it is your best friend or a potential partner.

Next, you move into spiritual college as *fifth* chakra communication lifetimers. You are beginning to ask: *What is it that is truth? What knowledge and wisdom do I want to share and communicate to the world?*

Then you move into spiritual graduate school as *sixth* chakra psychic, perception, healing and creativity lifetimers, learning about the bigger perspective of things and mastering all of those wondrous intuitive, creative, healing abilities.

Finally you get your spiritual PhD as *seventh* chakra spiritual lifetimers. Learn your spiritual lessons and then you have mastered it all!

Most people take at least seven lifetimes to go through each chakra lifetime, and others take many more. Some get attached to particular chakra lifetimes, such as the third chakra and they experience third chakra lifetimes over and over and over to really make sure they get that lesson of not being a victim or victimizing others any more before they move on to learning to love themselves. One easily leads to the other—just like the third chakra of learning that you are not a victim or victimizer naturally leads to the fourth chakra to fulfill the need to learn to love yourself. All by Divine design.

Discovering Your Chakra Lifetime

Remember that those working on mastering first chakra lifetimes will experience intense survival lessons. In a second chakra life there will be great opportunities to learn emotional and sexual lessons. Those working on third chakra lifetimes will draw to them increased will, willpower and manifesting lessons.

How do you identify the chakra lifetime you are currently living? Look at which one of the chakras reflects the most overriding picture of your life. Everybody has elements of all of them, but what is the major one that is your biggest focus?

Rest assured if you are reading this book, you are working on either a fourth, fifth, sixth or seventh chakra lifetime. You will not be experiencing as much current drama and trauma as first, second or third chakra lifetimers. Fourth chakra lifetimers will be learning self-love and to love others. Fifth chakra lifetimers will be discovering effective communication. As a sixth chakra lifetimer you will have the opportunity to use your psychic, creativity and healing abilities, as well as to expand your perception. And as a seventh chakra lifetimer your major life focus will be your spiritual path.

Many of you are here to help the planet raise its vibration during this time. You are at the level to help others see new perspectives, heal old wounds and create harmony in their lives—yet you must first work on doing that within yourself. Remember, you have come to help balance out all of the negative doom and gloomers and assist others in moving into higher states of enlightenment. You have an important role to play.

Discovering Others' Chakra Lifetimes

My seminar students weep with understanding when they discover that their parents may not be working on the same chakra lifetime that they are, and everyone is exactly where they need to be for their own growth.

We are all at different development levels. Piajet discovered that if children up to the age of five or six see you pour a tall glass of water into a short wide glass, they cannot tell that it is the same amount of water. Even if you show them, they will always say that the taller glass has the most water in it, until they reach a certain developmental level, and then they understand.

In the same way, people are all at the developmental level that they are meant to be at right now. If you were in college or graduate school, you would not expect somebody in junior high to be able to understand things in the same way you do. Yet if you are frustrated by a third chakra lifetimer and you are annoyed at them that they cannot see it the way you do, you are doing the same thing—expecting somebody at an younger developmental stage, who is exactly where they are meant to be, to see it from a perspective that they are not going to see until they have moved through their wondrous growth and evolvement process.

When you feel frustrated by people who do not see things the way you do, I encourage you to stop, tune in, and ask yourself: *What chakra level lifetime are they working on?* For example, if you think it is the third chakra, instead of judging them for being there, support their growth and awareness as they go through their learning. Just as if you are a parent of a junior high school child, you would support them through those years of angst because you have been there yourself. You have already had a third chakra lifetime.

The next time you are disturbed by someone's behavior:

1. Ask yourself: *What chakra lifetime is that person operating from?* That will enable you to see if they are in spiritual kindergarten, getting their spiritual PhD or somewhere in between, which will give you a more realistic view of where they are in their journey.

2. Then remind yourself that all of us start out with first chakra lifetimes, that you have been there, and have done at least second and third chakra lifetimes and will continue on and on in your growth process, just as this person will. Realize that everyone is doing exactly what they need to be doing.

3. Next look beyond the situation and observe: *What is the lesson they have an opportunity to learn here? What is the reason why they are in this situation?*

4. Then hold the image for them that they can learn that lesson as easily and effortlessly and enjoyably as possible.

5. Finally, give the ultimate gift that will be the greatest benefit to them. Hold the vision of the Divine within them. It is there in them as surely as it is in everyone and everything.

If you truly practice this, if this is the way you live your life, there is never any judgment—for yourself or others—because you understand you are exactly where you are meant to be right now for your own growth and so are they.

This book will speed up your evolutionary journey by light-years! Not only will you know what chakra lifetime you are on, but also what layer you are in the process of mastering. You will have a map of where you have been as well as the steps to progress forward from here. And you will see where your partners, children, friends and associates are, without judgment or trying to make them different, so you can encourage them to take the next step. Even bigger than that, every situation can be used to take you closer to fully reclaiming your Divinity.

Think of the people who annoy you and ask yourself:

What chakra lifetime are they on?
What does that trigger in me?
What layer of the chakra I am on is being reflected back to me by the other?
What is my opportunity here for learning and mastery?

Then it is all about growth and moving forward, rather than it being punitive.

This is a whole new way of perceiving ourselves, our world and our growth towards higher levels of consciousness. Karma is a thing of the past, as it is a third chakra understanding of victimhood. You are now ready to move into empowerment—self-empowerment and opening to receive the unlimited support from the Divine that is waiting for you, and empowerment of others as you support them where they are.

When you truly get this, there is such an incredible peace within yourself because you are not trying to change people that are not ready and meant to be exactly where they are.

If you tune into this in everything you do, you will begin to attract relationships with people who are working on the same chakra lifetime you are so you can help support each other's growth. If you are working on a sixth chakra lifetime and you are attracting somebody who is on a second chakra lifetime, then probably you are working on the second layer of your sixth chakra. They are giving you an opportunity to master that layer in an even more amplified way to help you learn and grow....

Relationship Suddenly Transformed

Brenda, one of my students, is working on her sixth chakra lifetime and had great frustration with one of her children who constantly seemed to be in victim mode. She did not understand how this child could possibly continue to see himself as less than. He was handicapped when he was born and did not have full use of his body. In her eyes, he was no different than her other children. Her attitude was "Just suck it up! I'm not treating you any differently." She knew he was missing full use of his body, but he was not missing who he is. He was not missing his spirit, which was what she was working on. But he continued to play the victim card throughout his life and he is now in his late teens.

Suddenly she realized, "Oh, my gosh! This is a third chakra lifetime for him. He has to learn how to stop being a victim and he has to deal with that, not just suck it up. He has to experience that—that's why on a spirit level he needed to have the experience of being handicapped."

Immediately it shifted her from annoyance at him to compassion. Then she could support him where he is—rather than have unrealistic expectations of who she thought he should be. It instantly changed her perception of the situation, and changed her ability to love and nurture and encourage him in a way that was right for him.

Then she had to look at her third layer (the victim and the persecutor) of her sixth chakra. She realized she had moved into being overbearing and telling her son, "Just deal with it!" She took the opportunity that her son's behavior was giving her to learn the lessons of the third layer of her sixth chakra. And just like that, it changed the relationship—because she now understood where he was.

The more triggered we are by somebody else's behavior, the more we have an opportunity to learn the lessons that are being triggered within ourselves.

If you really lived this understanding that we are all students of Universe University (U.U. or *You You*) and looked at everything from this point of view, how would this change your life? *Would you be judging other people? Would you be judging yourself? Would you be questioning why events are happening?*

Life-Changing Results

When my seminar students really get that we are all moving through our lives in the order of the chakra system, it is life-changing. One of the participants, Kim, reported:

"The minute I got that, I stopped judging everyone in my life—everyone. And it totally transformed my way of being in the world because I didn't have to expect this person to do it the way I think it ought to be done. I could see that they were doing it in their Divine way, learning what they needed to learn. I realized that my job was to try to assist them in knowing that. Whether they are on a first, second, third, fourth, fifth or sixth chakra lifetime, I can now focus on how best to support them, like my children, in their growth. It is life changing!"

Epiphany of Understanding

Another student, Rebecca, had always felt like she had to be the adult with her alcoholic mother and had to take care of her in many ways. She was very annoyed throughout her life that she had to take on the parenting role with her parent. When Rebecca suddenly had an epiphany that her mother was working on a third chakra lifetime, she said, "Well, of course!"

When Rebecca looked at the benefit of having a mother who was working on a third chakra lifetime, she realized it had facilitated her stepping into her own self-empowerment at a young age in preparation for doing all the things that she has successfully accomplished in this lifetime.

From Outrage to Laughter

Margaret, one of my older seminar participants, described her experience of watching an old western movie that violated her code of ethics:

"First the sheriff and his girlfriend were having an intimate relationship. Then the bad guy kidnaps the sheriff's girlfriend and runs off with her and takes her down to the river and the next thing you know she is having sex with the bad guy. At first I was outraged! 'Oh what a hussy,' I thought. 'She's just a whore!' Then I caught myself and realized, 'Oh my gosh, she's working on first chakra issues. She is just trying to survive.' When she's with the sheriff, she's trying to survive cause that's the best way to exist in that town, and then when she's with the bad guy the best way to survive and not be killed is by sleeping with him. She's just on a survival lifetime. I totally got it and couldn't stop laughing."

Although my student saw this as a first chakra lifetime, I feel that it is probably the first layer of a third chakra life.

Judgment Turned to Love

Anita, another of my students who was working on her fourth chakra layer of love and affinity for self and others, felt like she was losing her friends and family. When she looked at the chakra lifetimes they were on, she realized she had been judging them instead of realizing she had outgrown them. A butterfly cannot hang out with a caterpillar—they just do not have much in common anymore. The caterpillar always sees the ground or the leaf in front of it, whereas the butterfly can soar through the air with unlimited horizons. Anita also saw the opportunity for her own learning in this situation. She decided she was going to master her fourth chakra layer by allowing herself to be full of love and gratitude for her family and friends and to accept them as they are.

Instead of making others bad and wrong, realize that whatever chakra lifetime they are working on, you are working on the same chakra layer yourself. Use this as an opportunity for your own growth. None of us would be here unless we still had something to learn. Even the Dalai Lama and those who believe that they came back for the benefit of others have an opportunity to learn and grow even more while they are here.

Know that the people you are attracting into your life are your greatest teachers. If they are working on a lower lifetime than you, than that is certainly an indication you have magnetized them into your life to give you an opportunity to work through that layer and to see it more clearly.

If you are drawing people who are working on a higher chakra lifetime than you, you are working on the higher end of that chakra lifetime. For example, if you are drawing a seventh chakra lifetimer to you to interact with, then you are moving toward the seventh layer of whatever chakra lifetime you are working on. Isn't that beautiful! What a Divine plan!

That is why it really is Divine all the time, whether you realize it or not. You are exactly where you are meant to be.

"It all makes perfect sense!" Ted told me with great excitement after a seminar. "It's perfectly designed to allow for our growth on all levels. Now I understand why everything is the way it is."

Chakras of Countries

Another level of the Divine plan that supports our unfoldment is the chakras of countries. All countries carry the frequency of the particular chakra that the vast majority of people living there are working on. We can choose to be born into the country that has the same chakra vibration that we are in the process of mastering so we have a supportive environment for learning and growing. Or we may choose to move there.

When people start growing and evolving, they start moving around, often leaving their birth country. You have probably noticed that when you have moved to a different country or different area of the country, you can open up to your next level of growth in a much more rapid way.

No matter where anyone is on their evolutionary journey, there is a place on Earth that has the appropriate vibration to support their growth.

Here are some examples of different chakra countries at the present time— that does not mean that it cannot change:

First Chakra Countries

When a country or an area is resonating at a *first* chakra level, that being, soul, spirit can count on experiencing survival struggles there. Survival chakra lifetimes are very hard since the body is being taxed and the ability to survive is being pushed, so it is not a comfortable or easy lifetime. As a result, they tend to be shorter because spirits want to learn it and move on.

Parts of Africa are *first* chakra as evidenced by the many children who are starving to death as well as the children whose parents have died of AIDS and they also are going to die of AIDS at a very young age or of malnutrition.

A good example of a *first* chakra country is Haiti. That does not mean that every single person living in Haiti is working on a first chakra lifetime—it means the majority of the population. The country is resonating at a level that offers the greatest opportunity to learn survival lessons there. Many spirits will choose to go there who need to learn their first chakra lessons. In the past Haiti has given spirits the opportunity to learn those survival lessons rather quickly and that also means that children are probably going to die fairly young.

Of course, there are those that are drawn to be in Haiti to help people learn their survival lessons—sometimes in challenging ways and sometimes very positive ways, such as what happened when a major earthquake struck the country and people struggled to obtain food and survive.

The really wonderful thing that happened after this devastating earthquake is that it gave a good percentage of the population there the opportunity to move into second chakra lifetimes. Why is that? Because the world responded with such an outpouring of support and compassion that Haiti had never seen before. All the people who came from all over the world to help, for the most part, were working on their fourth chakra lifetimes, their love and affinity for themselves and others. As the fourth chakra lifetimers mixed with the first chakra lifetimers, it increased the frequency resonance there. And the common denominator of the vibration of the spirits in Haiti went up! As the helpers held the vibration of compassion, it created an energy field for the Haitians to move into gratitude and being thankful, realizing that they were cared about and people were there for them. As they were lifted up into that energy, they moved into their *feelings*—not just the struggle for survival—the *feeling* state of having received and being able to feel that gratefulness. It set the stage for the people of Haiti to grow.

People ask: *Why do bad things happen? How can the Divine allow this to occur?* This is a really good example of why it happens and the good that can come from great challenges. It gives the population an opportunity to grow and evolve. Not only did it give the Haitians an opportunity to grow, but it gave the fourth chakra lifetimers who came to help the opportunity to demonstrate that they were learning their fourth chakra lessons of love and compassion for themselves and others, so they can move on. Isn't that Divine?

SECOND CHAKRA COUNTRY

Africa is an illustration of a *second* chakra country. It is true that there are parts of Africa that are still working on first chakra lifetimes and many children die before the age of two. Yet, the overriding energy is second chakra. It does not mean that everyone in that country is working on a second chakra, but that is the overriding essence of the lessons that have an opportunity to be learned there. AIDS, which comes from sexual contact, is an epidemic right now and rape of young girls and female genital mutilation is a fact. So much of Africa—not all—but much of Africa is stuck in second chakra lifetimes as they are dealing with all of that.

Again, there are people who are moving in to help, which raises the vibration of the country. For example, the glorious Oprah Winfrey who started a school to educate girls is the perfect one to help the Africans evolve to their next level and begin to move out of victimhood of being raped, sexually mutilated and not knowing their value and finally learning to speak up and find a better way. What better role model than Oprah who herself survived being raped and not being treated with value by her own family, and then later found her voice and is now an international spokeswoman for ending violence against women and treating all humans with respect. When she learned that one of the people in charge of her school was sexually abusing the girls, she used this as an opportunity to teach the people of Africa, as well as the whole world, that this is not to be tolerated and how to put an end to it. And in so doing, she made a major contribution to the people of Africa and the rest of the world. Even though the perpetrator was acquitted and no criminal charges were filed, the awareness that this is something not to be tolerated has begun.

As people move into Africa to help with AIDS and to educate people how AIDS is spread, this energy of compassion gives the country an opportunity to then begin to move up into higher levels of the second chakra, that ultimately may move them up into the third chakra. Remember the lower layers of the third chakra focus on victim mentality, which moves up out of the raw emotions and sexual state, so dealing with all of that is a way to learn lessons in the third chakra. Then as people move through that, they become more self-empowered and they move into the dominating state. So Africa has an opportunity to begin to move more into the third chakra lifetimes.

Third Chakra Countries

The majority of the Middle East is an example of a *third* chakra lifetime area. Not all of the Middle East, but most of the Middle East where there have been dictators, victims and power struggles throughout history. Those working on third chakra lifetimes are pretty much guaranteed some third chakra experiences there.

The dynamic of the third chakra is victim and persecutor, will and willpower, control and submission. In third chakra countries there is almost always a dictator type of regime. Just as in a pack of wild dogs, which is very much third chakra, wild dogs always have an alpha dog that is in charge. This is how the pack functions, how it works, and what makes that community able to survive. In the same way, the majority of the Middle East—again not all of it—has tended to have a dictatorship structure where the dictator is the alpha dog.

However, that too is beginning to change and evolve. Of course, the war in the Middle East is not contributing to uplift and change that state. If anything, it is lowering it. However, because some of the higher ideals of democracy are affecting some of the Middle Easterners, those people do have an opportunity to begin to move up from their third into their fourth chakra lifetime.

Fourth Chakra Country

A great example of a *fourth* chakra country is the United Sates. By and large the people here are working on fourth chakra lifetimes. It does not mean that there are not some people working on higher chakras and some people are working on lower chakras, it means the majority of the U.S. is working on fourth chakra lifetimes. This is an ideal environment to learn the lessons of love and affinity for one's self and others.

There is an epidemic in this country of people not loving themselves. The evidence of this is the huge percentage of the population that is clinically depressed, feeling unworthy, not good enough, low self-esteem, unmotivated and feeling like they have nothing to give.

The lesson of depression is learning to love one's self. From my vantage point, no matter how many anti-depressants people take, that is not the answer. Yes, it does allow people to be able to function, and sometimes that may well be necessary for people to learn to move into the real solution and the real answer, which is to love themselves. In the past, the vast majority of people have been taught that they were not good enough. As we grow, we learn *that is not true!* You are doing exactly what you need to be doing in exactly the way you need to be doing it to gain the wisdom and grow. Once people have learned to love themselves, they can begin to love and have compassion for others. Then they have the motivation to help others.

Different sections of the U. S. are working on different aspects of the fourth chakra. In the cities, there are a greater number of people who are depressed, and who are working on loving themselves. Across this country there are many wonderful loving families as well as a high divorce rate as people learn to master this chakra. Yet, the heartland of America is all about love and an example of the higher level of the heart chakra. They already have evolved to being truly loving and having community consciousness to be able to take care of the people around them, as demonstrated in the heartland tradition of "barn raising." When someone needs a new barn, the community comes together and in a weekend they build a barn for their neighbor by all joining together and working together and making it a community event, complete with food and celebration at the end when it is done.

The exceptions to the U.S. mainland being a fourth chakra country are the areas of Sedona and Mt. Shasta, which are *six* chakra regions within the U.S.

In Europe, there are many countries where the population is also on fourth chakra lifetimes.

Fifth Chakra Areas

The Antarctica and the Arctic are examples of *fifth* chakra areas. These places have the greatest concentration of PhDs of any area on the planet because they are all scientists there. They are working on doing research, which is a very mental aspect of the fifth chakra (the fifth layer of the fifth chakra) and they are working on finding ways to effectively communicate their research.

Sixth Chakra Areas

A really good example of the *sixth* chakra is Hawaii. It is said that the Hawaiian islands were the tips of the lost continent of Lemuria. The native Hawaiian culture embraces the psychic and intuitive knowing that we can receive messages directly from the Divine to help guide our journey. Hawaii gives people an opportunity to move into their intuitive states, to really use their psychic, healing and creative abilities as well as to expand their perception of things. Many people in Hawaii are stepping into those higher areas of their self-development and exploring in bigger and bigger ways who they are.

When I was at the doctor's for a routine test, I told him the list of vitamins I was taking and that I was very holistic and very much into preventative medicine. He had just recently moved here from the mainland. He looked at me and replied, "Of course you are, you live in Maui." And there you have it—out of the mouth of a physician. Obviously I am not the only person in Maui that is telling him the list of vitamins and minerals and preventative things that they do. And he sees a whole array of individuals walk through his doors. Hawaii gives people an opportunity to open up to their intuition and explore that in ways that perhaps they have not done before.

As mentioned earlier, both Sedona and Mt. Shasta are sixth chakra areas of the U.S.

Seventh Chakra Countries

An example of a *seventh* chakra country is the original Tibet where the leader of the country is also the spiritual leader, the Dalai Lama. For thousands of years, the ruler of the country was the spiritual leader. The whole focus of the original Tibet was for spiritual growth and understanding. It was one and the same, and that was the focus of the entire population.

What a wondrous Divine design we find ourselves in: We come to Earth where there is the perfect environment, even the country and the population, that will stimulate our growth in any particular chakra so we can release whatever blocks our Divinity as we go through our evolutionary journey back to knowing we are Divine. And it all is good.

Our Divine Destination

The hidden key is knowing that we are all mastering chakra lifetimes. The point of going through all of these chakra lifetimes is to return to Source, return to the awareness that we are Divine. That is our destination.

When I was first doing professional readings in my early twenties, a twelve-year old girl came to me. I wondered what a twelve-year old was going to ask me: What is she going to be when she grows up? When is she going to get married? How many children? Or about the fight that she had with her friend? Instead her question was: *What is the meaning of life?* Obviously, she was a precocious young lady.

The Divine Source through me used this analogy: Just like all the water on this planet is essentially the same water, so too are all humans' essence the same. When you look up in the sky and you see the beautiful majestic cloud forms, those clouds are like the Divine. Maybe the thunderclouds are the Buddha, the stratus clouds are the Christ, the cumulus clouds the Great Spirit and the wispy clouds are Allah. The clouds put a piece of themselves out in the form of rain or sleet or snow, just like the Divine puts a piece of itself out in the form of each of our beings, souls, spirits. The water particles' job is to go through the streams and the waterfalls and the lakes and the rivers until they empty out into the ocean where they are evaporated back up in the clouds again. This recycling process is the way that the water on this planet attempted to keep itself clean, clear, pure and not stagnant.

In the same way, it is our beings, our souls, and our spirits' job to go throughout lifetime after lifetime becoming cleaner, becoming clearer, becoming purer, and becoming more conscious until we are absorbed back into the Divine again. This is the way that the Divine prevents itself from becoming stagnant and ensures continuous evolvement.

We go through our first chakra lifetimes, then our second chakra lifetimes, third, fourth, fifth, sixth and seventh until we are evolved enough—we have mastered the highest level of consciousness—and then we return back to the Divine Source.

We are All Divine All the Time

Some of my seminar participants have asked: *Does that mean that if we are on a first chakra lifetime we are not Divine?* No! *We are all Divine all the time.* Just like a baby when it is born is Divine. Everybody knows that. You look at it and you see what an incredible miracle this child is! All of us were that child. No one would argue that child did not come from the Divine, whatever your definition of that is.

Yet that baby still needs to learn its lessons—it needs to learn how to walk, it needs to learn how to talk, it needs to learn how to share, it needs to learn how to play well with others. So even though it is Divine, it is still growing and learning and evolving, figuring out how to operate that baby body. First it cannot do much but eat and sleep and poop in its diaper. As it grows and evolves, it figures out more. It figures out how to roll over, how to sit up, how to crawl, how to walk and talk.

So even though we have lessons to learn, even though we have growth that we can achieve, the core of us is the Divine. The more we can honor that in ourselves—regardless of where we are—and the more we can honor that in others—regardless of where they are—the more we will be living in the Divine flow and experiencing the inner peace that all is Divine all the time.

Even when we see that another is not in that awareness, if we adopt this expanded perception we then see them through the eyes of the Divine, thereby encouraging their growth as well as our own in the maximum way possible.

As you do the exercises in this book, you can help move yourself along your path to the next level. First, you have to give yourself credit for where you have been. Again, you would not be reading this book if you were still on a first chakra lifetime. You probably would not be reading this book if you were on a second or third chakra lifetime. You have survived the three hardest ones. Good job!

Now the question is: What are you going to do with that awareness which is the greatest gift that allows *you* to live your life in the Divine flow, and to support others living in their Divine flow?

The Ancients Knew We Are All Divine

The Hawaiian kahuna knew that not only are we One with the Divine, *we are all Divine,* all the time. The ancient Hawaiians *knew* that we were all One with the Divine Source, as is everything and everyone.

It is not just the ancient Hawaiians who believed that everything is part of the Divine. What the Hawaiians called the "aka grid," the Navahos refer to as the "web," the Tibetans the "net," and modern science terms the "quantum hologram." Some people call it the "Divine matrix." Everything is literally one with that.

The ancient Hawaiian kahuna knew that since everything was made up of Divine Source energy, that their spiritual path was to honor that Divinity in everyone and everything—in all of the animals, all of the plant life, in the earth and the sky and the sea—including themselves. They knew that if they did that, it would be a planet of peace and harmony and love.

The idea of "aloha" comes from treating *everything* as if it is Divine, and knowing that everything is one with God. To this day, before most Hawaiians pick a fruit or a flower, they ask permission from the tree—to honor that Divinity. If we all did that, if we all honored the Divine in everything and everyone, would there be war on this planet? No! Would there be children going hungry? No! Would there be poverty? No! Would there be abuse? No! Everyone would come together to help each other all of the time.

Knowing this aspect of the Key and implementing it transforms everything. We would naturally be honoring the environment. We would be honoring the air, the land and the sea. We would be honoring the animals. We would be honoring all people if we truly were awakened to the fact that everything, everyone—including ourselves—is made up of Divine energy.

If you honor the Divine within, then you also have to treat yourself with respect, dignity, honor and love. Whether you are aware of it or not, you are all Divine. Regardless of whether you are conscious of it or not, whether you believe it or not, whether you have experienced it or not, regardless of whether it is your truth or not, *you are made of Divine Source energy, which makes you Divine.* Your entire body is made of Divine Source energy. If you embraced that as your truth, you would naturally awaken to your Divine potential.

All the great spiritual teachers throughout time have told us this. In the Hindu tradition of India Krishna said, "Everything is God. *Everything is God.*" Buddha said, "Everyone has Buddha nature." Jesus said, "Even the least amongst you will do all that I have done, and even greater things." *Even the least amongst you will do all that I have done and even greater things!* As Wayne Dyer, the bestselling author of "The Power of Intention" says, "Who does that leave out?" No one. When did we think that would be? We have waited over 2,000 years. How about now!

Once you become consciously aware of it, this part of the Key can allow you to live your life without limits, and achieve your heart's desires. For if you know that you are Divine, it automatically eliminates any feelings of unworthiness or not deserving or limitation of any kind—for *we know the Divine Source is unlimited!*

Understanding that we are *all* Divine, not just a select few, allows us to dissolve any feelings of arrogance or superiority and open our hearts and minds to everyone around us.

Practicing this aspect of the Key naturally allows you to tap into your limitlessness. For if you knew, if you truly knew that you were One with the Divine, you could not hold on to limited thinking. You cannot be One with the Divine and be limited. It is an oxymoron. It is not possible. You would *know* that you are limitless.

As you live this part of the Key, all addictive tendencies and behavior naturally fall away. Once we realize we are Divine, it stops the craving for drugs and alcohol to try and make us feel better about who we are. The knowledge that we are Divine immediately lifts us to the supreme realization that we are unlimited in every way and can create the well being, abundance and happiness we desire, for we all know the Divine is limitless and can manifest anything—including a new world.

Imagine how the world would be if we all lived as if we were one and honored the Divine Essence in everyone! At this time when the old way based on fear, greed, control, manipulation and misuse of power is in the process of crumbling, the way to thrive is to align with this Key, which honors the highest in everyone and everything. This is the new way that is beginning to blossom. By practicing this Key and making it a part of your life, you will be perfectly positioned to excel on every level now and in the future.

Since I have been teaching this Key in my seminars around the country, I have seen truly remarkable results—including reversing financial ruin and reversing a death-sentence diagnosis. You will read about these miraculous transformations, starting in the next chapter.

I believe that you don't have to have a Oneness non-duality experience to begin to live your life as the Divine. And it is my hope that through this book you will experience your own Divinity and your Divine birthright of love, happiness and Oneness.

How do you transform your life now? By remembering—or changing your perspective back to the truth—*you are a Divine being* and so is everyone else.

This perspective shift can happen in an instant, and allow you to transform your life *now!*

You now have the big picture that I was privileged to witness beyond the illusion of separation. You now know why you are here and why events have unfolded as they have in your life. As you proceed through the chapters that follow, I will guide you into a deeper understanding of where you are, and take you step-by-step through each layer of each chakra so that you can clear them and access the qualities of the Divine that each center holds. You thereby return to your true essence, able to manifest the life of your highest dreams and live in the Divine flow of grace, so that peace, joy and abundance are yours in every area of your life.

You are now ready to move on to Chapter 2 and uncork your ability to excel.

Uncorking Your Ability to Excel

What if you *knew* that you were Divine? Is the Divine limited in any way? Would you—knowing that you were Divine—live a limited life? Would you still have physical body problems? Money struggles? Emotional turmoil? Sexual issues? Feel like a victim? Search for love? Unable to speak up for yourself? Lack intuition, creativity, or healing abilities? Feel abandoned by God?

Of course, not! You would know that your body was Divine. You would have health, financial abundance, emotional balance, fulfilling sexuality, limitless manifesting abilities, unconditional love for yourself and others, able to speak your truth perfectly, gifted psychic, creativity and healing abilities, and true oneness with your Source.

All spiritual and religious traditions tell us that we are children of the Creator, which not only makes us Divine with the ability to create, but all one family, connected to each other and the Source. And just as the Source affects us all, so too can we positively affect our own lives and those around us. Intellectually we know that we are all one. But when you experience it for yourself, it's like a drop of water in the ocean suddenly realizes it is one with the ocean. And that every time the ocean is affected, it also is affected and visa versus. So every time there is a tsunami somewhere or every time the tides make the waves, or every time a chunk of the polar ice cap falls off into the ocean, it is affected. And it can never go back to seeing itself as a separate water particle when it knows it is one with the ocean.

When you are blessed to have that peek, your life will never be the same again because you will know you are one with everything. Not just intellectually, but all the way down to the core of your being, you will know.

Since you are reading these words, you have the opportunity to experience Oneness non-duality in this lifetime. You have the opportunity to become one with the Godhead. Just holding that frequency changes you and everyone around you in wonderfully positive ways. Knowing that you are an aspect of the Divine Source creates love, bliss and joy. Not only does your life get better, you are more loving, more flexible, wiser, more understanding, more compassionate, more joyful, more empowered, healthier and definitely more abundant.

As I guide you through this book, you will go from a peek to the highest state of enlightenment that you are ready to achieve right now. I witness my students who have taken my I'O (Infinite Oneness Enlightenment) 1, II, III and Mastery seminars, and their lives are never the same again—they are just walking bodies of bliss.

The First Step: Creating What You Want

Your brain is like a computer. It does exactly what you tell it to do. If you go around saying, "I never have enough energy. I'm always sick. I don't have any money. I only have relationships with jerks. My boss hates me." If that is true for you, pat yourself on the back. You are getting exactly what you are putting out there. If you want a different life, you have to put a different message in your computer.

You want to start saying, "I am healthy and full of energy. I now have wonderful relationships with people who love me and support me. I always have enough money. My boss loves me." Or "I'm going to quit that job and I'm going to start doing what I really love and I'm going to make lots of money doing it this year."

This is not wishful thinking, this is not woo-woo; this is scientific fact.

Scientifically speaking, at a molecular level matter does not exist. It is just energy. Science also knows that when they are looking for the building blocks of atoms—neutrons, electrons and quartz—they are there. They also know when they are *not* looking for them, they don't exist. Think about that! *They don't exist*. What does that mean? It means, scientifically speaking, *we create our own reality*. When? *All of the time*.

Any time you find yourself thinking a negative thought, or even speaking it—which gives it more power—cancel that order because the universe is going to serve you up whatever you are thinking and feeling. It is just like when you go to a restaurant and you give your order to the waitress. Whatever you order is exactly what you are going to receive. If you realize, "Oh, no, I don't want bacon and eggs, I want granola and strawberries," you have to communicate that change to the waitress who then tells the chef; otherwise you are going to get bacon and eggs. From this moment on, cancel those limiting orders and request what you really *do* want. *You can do that!* Everybody can do that.

This is the beginning of living the Key: knowing you have the Divine power and ability to create your life exactly the way you want that brings you peace, abundance and joy.

If you are reading this book as part of a book club, which I heartily recommend, support each other to create the life you want. If you hear anyone in your group saying something disempowering about themselves, their lives, their friends, this country or the universe stating what they don't want, say to them, "Excuse me, is that what you're ordering today? Is that what you want? The chef of the universe is going to bring you whatever you order. Wouldn't you rather order something better?"

Did you know that science has proven that your brain does not know the difference between you imagining something occurring and it actually occurring? It acts as if whatever you are imagining or you are experiencing as reality is one and the same.

This enables you to change your view of how you perceive your life and create a new message or a new life script of living your Divine life in every aspect of your life.

Reveling in the knowledge that you are the one who is creating your reality is the first step to embracing the truth of your Divinity. You can create the life you want, with every thought you think and every word you speak.

The Second Step: Embracing Your Highest Truth

Living your own truth leads to inner peace and happiness. Attempting to live someone else's truth leads to dis-harmony and dis-ease. If you have tried to live someone else's truth, you learned that it didn't work.

That also applies to what you will read in this book. Probably 95 to 100 percent of what I will share with you is going to work for you, but if there is something that is not your truth, put it aside. Don't throw it away; it might work for you later. Your job is to run everything through your truth filters. Ask yourself: "Is this my truth? Does this work for me? Is this correct for me?" If not, then do not use it or act upon it.

Living your highest truth begins with *not* listening to outside "authorities" who told you that you were not okay. This includes parents who unconsciously planted seeds of doubt within you or ex-spouses, or so-called friends, who projected their own fears and doubts onto you.

Most importantly, embrace the highest truth of who you are. Know *"I am Divine. I am One with the Divine."* This essential second step is vital because it literally affects your physical, emotional and mental well being. For oneness with the Divine Source creates love, bliss and conscious healing. The ancient kahuna knew all dis-ease—whether it was on a body level as some kind of physical ailment, whether it was on an emotional level as some sort of emotional dis-ease, whether it was on a mental level or whether it was on a spiritual level—came from a disconnect or separation from the Divine, and forgetting that we are One with the Divine.

I also know this to be true, for as I have been teaching this Key in my seminars, a powerful transformation technique has emerged and miraculous healings have occurred over and over again. When I first received the epiphany to teach this, I thought it was about helping people reach enlightenment and Oneness. A side benefit was that my seminar participants were having these incredible transformational healing experiences. As my students have taken this out into the world, the healings on all levels continue. Some have incorporated this Divine I'O healing technique in their existing practices, while many have quit their jobs to become full-time I'O practitioners. I found that I'O is the bridge back to Oneness with the Divine Source where unconditional love and conscious healing can occur.

Here are two of my favorite I'O healing examples:

Cancer Disappeared

One of my students, Kristi, had a stepfather with two different kinds of throat cancer. It was so bad that he was sent to the Mayo Clinic. This student had just completed the I'O I seminar and gave her stepfather only one I'O treatment. He then went back to the Mayo Clinic and they did another scan to look at the cancer again, and they thought it was the wrong person. They thought the information that they had from previous tests showing two different kinds of cancer must be a different person because there was absolutely no evidence of cancer there at all anymore. And two years later, there is still no sign of cancer.

Healing the Almost Dead

Stacey, my office manager, called to tell me her mother was dying, and could I heal her mother. I asked what was going on.

"My mother's in the hospital," she tearfully explained, "she's in kidney failure, heart failure, she's on a respirator, and they've already given her the last rites and the doctors estimate she only has two to three hours to live!"

"You waited until now to tell me this?" I replied. Two to three hours, kidney failure, heart failure, on a respirator—not looking good, I thought.

"You've gotta heal her," she pleaded.

"First off, that's not up to me," I quickly replied. "I've got to ask her higher self for permission and if her higher self says 'yes' and only if her higher self says 'yes,' then I will do an absentee treatment on her. But even if her higher self says 'yes,' we don't know if she's going to use the treatment to help her passing be more gentle and easier or if she's going to use this energy to turn it around. I'm just the radio that's broadcasting this energy. It's entirely up to her how she uses it."

And quite frankly, it didn't look good to me. But I did just what I said I would do. I asked her higher self for permission and her higher self said "yes" and I did an I'O absentee treatment.

A couple of hours later I got a call from Stacey, "Oh my God, she's out of heart failure, out of kidney failure, they took the respirator out of her mouth, she sat up in bed. And my mother said, 'Why did you bring me back?' And I said, 'I didn't do it, Laurie did it!'"

So it can bring people back from almost being dead, I can tell you that. The doctors had no explanation for either of those cases. And it can revitalize people's lives even when their house has burned to the ground and they have lost everything.

TRANSFORMING LOSS INTO ABUNDANCE

Sara, one of my students, literally saw her entire house and everything in it burn completely to the ground right before her eyes. She lost everything. Sara and her family barely got out with their lives. She, her husband and four children huddled in the freezing cold car in the below zero December night air clad only in their pajamas, as they watched their house burn down.

Then Sara remembered she was Divine and that she had God-given qualities to survive even in the midst of disaster. Almost immediately help came as neighbor after neighbor brought them warm clothes and blankets and food and warm beverages. And the abundance began to flow back into their lives.

They were blown away by the kindness of their family and friends who provided food, clothing and shelter and took care of all their needs. The people in the community provided assistance and saw that everything they needed was provided. The outpouring from the community was so great—more than they could use—Sara and her family started a fund to help other families in need so they could share the abundance and have others also experience not only surviving, but thriving during what seemed like the very worst of times.

The Fire Department told her there was nothing left and the bulldozer was scheduled to level the property. On the appointed day, Sara took a bunch of my students there and they did blessings on the land and she cried her tears and did transformational work and let go of everything. Then just as the wrecking company was getting ready to bulldoze the property and remove the wreckage, a workman came over to her with a little box. "We found this box," he said putting it into her hands. In the box were all of her most valuable little treasures—that probably didn't have a lot of value to somebody else, but did to her—things her mother had given her and things that had special memories that she had stored in this little box. That was the only thing that was saved.

Before the fire, Sara had been very attached to material things, especially her home, and valued her things more than she valued herself. It was a huge lesson for her to lose everything. She was brought face to face with her own survival and that of her family, and the truth of what was really important. Remembering that she was Divine—even while her house was burning down—allowed her to handle the situation with amazing grace and draw to her whatever she needed on every level, and even enough to share.

TURNING JOB LOSS INTO TRIUMPH

Remembering that you are Divine can also allow you to move beyond your fears and find a new career when your job has been downsized.

Another student, Patricia, was always concerned about money and never seemed to have enough. She had not been able to manifest a job that she enjoyed that met her salary requirements close to home and utilized her skills, talents and interests. Patricia kept getting stuck in jobs that she really didn't want and as a result, she worked with people who were not likeminded. She was not happy or fulfilled by what she did for 40 plus hours a week.

Not having enough money kept her from doing the things that she truly enjoyed. The amount of overtime that she had to work to make ends meet kept her from her personal and spiritual pursuits. Patricia felt worthless and stuck. She was angry that she kept trying to manifest a better job and wasn't able to find what she needed.

After doing the steps in this book, her life transformed. Patricia now has a new job that is very stable, provides good benefits, and grants her the time for personal and spiritual pursuits. And she feels good about what she does. "Focusing on being more of my Divine unlimited self was the key," she told me. "I now know and trust that I am capable of doing whatever I feel led to accomplish!"

I have included many of my student's stories about emotional and financial transformations in the next two chapters.

The Third Step: Developing the Divine Characteristics Within

By choosing to focus on the Divine characteristics always within you, these qualities begin to develop and expand. Science has shown us that whatever we focus on expands. If you have placed your focus on what is limited, lacking and not working, that is what has expanded in your life.

The very first characteristic of the Divine is limitlessness. We all know the Divine Source is unlimited in every way. When you realize that you also are Divine and have the same Divine essence within you, you begin to discover the truth of you and your unlimited nature. By shifting your focus to your unlimitedness, unlimited abundance, love, harmony and health can manifest in every area of your life.

Seven Energy Vortexes

These Divine characteristics are held within the *seven* energy spheres or chakras in your body. Refer to the Chakra Chart in Chapter 1.

All of the chakras are your connection to the Divine. It doesn't matter which chakra lifetime you are working on, these Divine qualities are located in each of these energy vortexes within your body.

- Your Divine ability to survive and excel emanates out from the *first* chakra located around the base of the spine for a man or between a woman's ovaries, or that general vicinity. Mine is at the base of my spine and I'm a woman this lifetime, I checked! It is wherever it is for you. You never need a chakra transplant, it's exactly where it's supposed to be for you.

- Your Divine emotional and sexual energies are in the *second* chakra, located a few inches below the belly button, or where you *feel* the energetic of sensuality, and emanates out from there.

- Your Divine will, willpower and manifesting energies are in the *third* chakra located in your solar plexus.

- Your love and affinity from the Divine for yourself and others radiate out from the *fourth* chakra at your heart or in the center of your chest. The bottom half is love and affinity or unconditional love for yourself. And the top half is your love and affinity for others.

- Your Divine communication on all levels radiates out from the *fifth* chakra in your throat.

- Your Divine psychic ability, perception of things, creativity and healing abilities emanate from the *sixth* chakra located in your third eye or your pineal gland in the center of your head.

- And your Divine or spiritual connection with the Divine radiates out from the *seventh* or crown chakra on the top of your head.

Seven Different Layers

All of these seven chakras are major energy centers that govern the main aspects of your life. However, because you have influences of all those various facets going on all the time, they are affecting each one of your energy centers. So each energy center has *seven* layers to it. Refer to the Chakra Layers Chart in Chapter 1.

- *1st layer* - Starting from the outside in, the layer on the outer most edge of your chakra, or the one that is furthest away from your body's center, is your Divine survival and thriving aspect of each energy center.

- *2nd layer* - The next layer in is your Divine emotional and sexual part of each chakra.

- *3rd layer* - The following layer in is your Divine will, willpower and manifesting portion of each chakra.

- *4th layer* - The subsequent layer in is your Divine love and affinity facet of each chakra.

- *5th layer* - The next closest layer in is your Divine communication characteristic of each chakra.

- *6ᵗʰ layer* - After that, the next layer in is your Divine psychic, perception of things, creating and healing abilities aspect of each chakra.

- *7ᵗʰ layer* - At the very core or the center is your Divine spiritual part of each chakra.

Not only do these chakras and their layers hold the abilities of the Divine to create a life of freedom and abundance, these energy centers also carry all your false limited beliefs and feelings that have kept the Divine from manifesting in your life. When you block your connection to the Divine in any of these areas, you experience lack and limitation.

The good news is you can clear out all the blockages that are in each layer of each chakra, so that you can have the Divine flow in all areas of your life and create unlimited abundance. Transforming the false beliefs that block your Divine qualities and abilities and focusing on the unlimitedness of your essential nature allows you to live your true destiny as the Divine here on Earth.

You will discover in this book what chakra and what layer of that chakra you are working on in this lifetime. I will guide you through opening them up and cleaning them out so that you can access the Divine qualities of each one.

No matter what chakra lifetime you are working on, you still have seven major chakras operating within you all the time. There is a need for the spirit to reinforce what it has already mastered throughout its past lives in other chakra lifetimes. Even when you have mastered your first chakra lifetime, you still need to make sure it is cleaned out so the energy is flowing smoothly in that energy center, that you are doing your best to keep it open and that you have all the energy in that center available for your use. Just like we may learn our multiplication tables in elementary school, we still continue to use them for the rest of our lives. In the same way we are still continuing to use those lessons we have mastered in other lifetimes in this lifetime.

Levels of the First Chakra

In this chapter, we will be transforming every level of your *first* chakra, your survival chakra, which carries the ability to not only survive, but to thrive. It also holds the Divine characteristic of unlimited continued existence. We know that the Divine is eternal and exists continuously throughout all time. This center holds the energy of survival on all levels.

Remember, this is where we all start out. In our first chakra lifetimes we learn how to run a body, experience how to survive in a body and usually experience the struggle of survival. In a lesser way, when we are working on the *first* layer of the first chakra, there are elements of that.

- The *first* layer or outer most layer is the protection or survival aspect of the survival chakra. This has the most mass or energy of any of the layers. Why is that? These energy centers are connected to the body and being protected or surviving is the most important thing to the body.

- The *second* layer is the emotional and sexual energy part of your survival. This relates to how you feel about your life as well as procreation, which is the survival of the species.

- The *third* layer is the will, willpower and manifesting facet of survival. Having the will to live and manifesting what you need to live.

- The *fourth* layer is the love and affinity portion of survival. Love of life or trying to save somebody else because you love them, such as your child.

- The *fifth* layer is the communication characteristic of your survival. Asking for help, talking yourself out of a dangerous situation, or giving somebody a warning.

- The *sixth* layer of your survival center is the psychic or perception, creativity, healing and clairvoyant aspects of your survival. Perceiving when there is danger.

- The *seventh* layer of your first chakra is the spiritual quality of your survival, which is living your soul's purpose.

What Blocks Your Divinity

When these unlimited God-given energies and abilities are blocked by our limiting beliefs, fears and doubts accumulated from our personal experiences or by watching or listening to the experiences of others, this literally creates a block around each layer of our energy centers, keeping them under wraps and its Divine spiritual power inaccessible to us to positively affect our lives.

When you are no longer able to access the unlimited eternal power of the Divine, when you no longer feel safe and protected by the Divine and you feel your survival on some level is at risk, you know that some aspect of your first chakra is blocked.

This becomes increasingly important to transform when you are experiencing a health, safety or financial crisis since these areas are affected by your first energy center.

What Holds These Blocks in Place

There is always a perceived payoff or a life lesson that you haven't been ready to learn until now that keeps these blockages firmly in place. Here are two examples to illustrate how this works in the case of disease, which threatens the very survival of the physical body.

Perceived Payoff

The only time when an oldest child, who is expected to be superchild and do more than a normal child would, gets excused from that over-responsibility is usually when they are sick. Then what happens is when they grow up and life gets overwhelming, that perceived payoff kicks in. For me, it was when I had a two-year old and newborn twins and my husband was on call twenty-four seven. My body personality responded with, "I know there was something I used to do when life was overwhelming, what was that? Oh yeah! I got sick!" Then my body tried getting sick. Well, all that happens then is you're sick and you still have to do everything!

Blind Result

My friend's husband decided that since the kids were grown he was joining the Peace Corps. She was a "get her hair done, manicure, pedicure once a week at the hairdresser" kind of gal, and they don't have pedicures in the Peace Corps. So she told him she did not want to go.

"You stay here and I'll go," he replied.

Well, that wasn't okay with her. Then she got a job, a very prestigious job at a private university.

"Now you've got something to do with your time," he said. "So you stay home and I'll go to the Peace Corps."

That still wasn't okay with her. And she decided to get laser surgery, which works for most people, but it made her virtually blind. And she called me up and told me that she couldn't see.

"I'll be right over," I said, "and I'll do healing work on you."

"No, you can't come," she quickly replied.

"I can't come?" I couldn't believe my ears.

"No, no, no, I'm busy."

"You're virtually blind. What the heck are you doing?"

Why didn't she want me to come? Her unconscious perceived payoff was that if she was virtually blind, her husband had to stay home from the Peace Corps and take care of her, which he did.

Growth Disappeared

A student in one of my ARCH classes had this great big growth on the side of her neck. It was the size of half a grapefruit. She couldn't figure out what the perceived payoff was. On the last day of the seminar she said, "I figured it out."

"What is it?" I asked.

"My husband waits on me," she replied. "He takes care of me."

"Are you willing to let go of that?" I asked.

"Yes," she said. And before our eyes, we watched the growth disappear.

By that time in the seminar she had already had numerous treatments, so when the perceived payoff became conscious to her and she made a decision to let it go, it left immediately.

Life Lesson

My mother's closest friend had cancer and her entire torso was filled with cancer. Her doctors had removed every single organ that they could remove and still have her breathing. First it was ovarian cancer and they removed her ovaries and her uterus. Then it went into her breasts and they removed her breasts. It went into her lymph nodes and they removed her lymph nodes. And it went into her stomach and she had part of her stomach removed and part of her intestines removed and one of her kidneys removed. Meanwhile, she's doing multiple rounds of chemo and radiation. This was over a three and a half year period. Finally her entire torso, every single cell in her torso or what was left of it, was filled with cancer.

Her doctors said, "There's just nothing else we can do. You have maybe three to six months. You just have to go home and get your affairs in order. We're really sorry."

About that time I went to visit my mother and I did a full body healing treatment on her friend and the next day I followed it up with a chair treatment. During the chair treatment I said, "This is a lesson. You have a classic Type C personality."

The medical model has labeled people who don't allow themselves to receive as Type C personalities. When we allow ourselves to receive, there is an endorphin excreted in the brain that is a cancer prohibitive. When we don't allow ourselves to receive, we have less of that endorphin and we are literally more pre-disposed to cancer. So if you need a reason to learn to receive, how about so you don't get cancer.

If you are a recovering caretaker and you have learned really well how to take care of everybody else except yourself, here's your job: Every time someone says to you, "Can I help you?" You make yourself say "Yes." The harder that is for you, the more you need to do it. Even if the first thing that comes out of your mouth is "No, no, that's okay, I can take care of that myself." They are not saying you can't do it, they are just offering to help you do it. They get to learn their lesson to give, as that is the life lesson for many, and you get those endorphins that are cancer prohibitives.

Start now to practice this. Every time someone offers to do something for you, say "Yes." Even if the first thing that comes out of your mouth is "No, no, no, that's okay, I can take care of it myself." Instead say, "On second thought, I'd love to have you help me with this." And again, the harder that is for you, the more you need to do it.

My mother's friend was a classic Type C personality and I told her, "If you are going to get over cancer, every time somebody says, 'Can I help you with this?' you have to make yourself say 'Yes.' I understand it's not going to be easy, but you have to do it. This is your life lesson."

To her credit, for the next month, every single time someone offered to do something for her, even though it was really, really hard, she made herself say "Yes." Then she went back to the oncologist and they did a full body scan, and all the cancer was gone, except for a spot on her spine that was the size of a pea. And the oncologist said, "My God, what did you do? And how can I help my other patients do this?"

Then this woman decided she had learned her lesson since all the cancer was gone except for the spot that was the size of a pea. And she went right back to not letting people help her. What do you think happened? All the cancer came back and she died. She'll have another lifetime where she'll come back as a quadriplegic or some kind of disability to have the opportunity to receive.

Here's what happens: If the universe sets it up so you have the opportunity to learn a lesson, and you refuse to learn it, then you decide to make it a "have to" thing in another lifetime. So most people that are quadriplegics or paraplegics have lessons to learn about receiving, and they are being forced to do that.

She will just have another opportunity to come back and learn it and it will probably be harder than having learned it the first time.

Letting the Blocks Fall Away

You will be amazed just how creative you have been to keep this essential awareness of your true nature hidden from yourself. To give you an understanding of how you are not allowing your Divinity to be your truth, the following exercise will help you spot the blockages you have placed in your first energy center so they can begin to fall away, revealing your Divinity.

Once you have had a chance to look at all the blocks, we will then do a meditation so that you can transform them.

Identifying All the Ways You Have Kept Yourself From Being Divine in the First Chakra:

This exercise will show you how your Divine nature is being blocked and what you would like to transform in your first energy center.

As you answer the following questions, make a list of everything you would like to release and transform:

- Has survival been a struggle?

- How do you feel about your life?

- Are you angry about how your life has been?

- Were you physically abused or molested?

- Have you feared for your life?

- Do you have a satisfying, on a body level, sexual relationship?

- What is your will to live?

- How easily are you manifesting on a survival level?

- Are you surviving or thriving?

- Are you manifesting abundance or are you manifesting scarcity?

- Are you enjoying your life or are you resenting it?

- Do you hate your life? Or do you love your life?

- How do you communicate your survival needs to others?

- Do you understand other people's communications to you about how your life and your survival affect their survival?

- Are you communicating easily in the survival aspect of your life? Or is it challenging for you?

- How much do you use your psychic abilities to survive?

- How much of your clairvoyance are you using to help you survive?

- Are you using these abilities to help get the best job for you?

- Are you using your psychic abilities if you are playing the stock market? Did you use it to get out before you experienced any loss?

- Did you use your clairvoyance before you got the major loan for your house? Did you tune into whether it was going to be easy for you to make the payments or not?

- Do you use your psychic abilities if you are in a challenging situation and you get that feeling that something is just wrong, and you need to get out of there, or this person is not a good person for you to be hanging around?

- How do you use your perception of things for your survival? Do you see the glass as half empty and constantly putting energy into trying to create abundance?

- Or are you really looking at the glass as half full and assisting that abundance and manifesting to come to you more easily?

- Are you using your creativity to help you survive better? If your company is having financial challenges and your job is in jeopardy, are you being creative to expand how you can make money in a different way?

- Are you using your healing abilities to heal problems with your body, with your emotions, with your mental aspect, and with your spiritual connection?

- Is your religion or your spiritual path an important part of your life? Or do you put your energy into other things and then don't put any energy into why you are really here?

- Are you willing to transform all of the old energies that you have pushed into this area of your body, that perhaps have caused you lower back pain?

- In the areas that you identified as being limited, what is your perceived payoff? What is the benefit your body personality is getting out of it?

- Are you willing to let it go?

- Has this been a recurring theme in your life? Is it a life lesson?

- What is the lesson you have the opportunity to learn here?

- Are you willing to completely transform this area of your life that is stopping you from thriving, and allow yourself to honor your own Divine nature?

Releasing the Blocks

Now that you are aware of how you have kept yourself limited, it is time to release everything on your list so that you can begin to transform the nature of your survival reality to thriving and living the Divine life.

This mini transformation experience is simple and easy to do.

1. Close your eyes and go into a relaxed state.

2. Create a big bubble out in front of you and put everything from your list that you no longer want into the bubble.

3. Release the bubble out to the sun. Watch it evaporate.

4. Now envision what you do want on a thriving level, and see and feel that clearly.

5. Create a powerful statement of transformation that captures you experiencing how you want to thrive easily, effortlessly and enjoyably. Repeat this statement to yourself throughout the day until this is your reality.

Returning to Your Divine Essence

You can come back to the way that you were Divinely designed by bringing your attention to activating the Divine within every layer of your first chakra and moving out any emotions that stop you from *feeling* your connection with the Divine on all those levels.

Begin by centering yourself. Just like a tree draws nutrients from the earth and receives the rain and the sun from the sky to blend within it to create photosynthesis so it can grow and evolve to its fullest maturity, you too can draw energy from the earth and the universal energy from the cosmos to blend within so you can grow to your fullest level of consciousness.

Sit with your feet flat on the floor so you can feel that connection with the earth, your hands uncrossed on your lap, and imagine bringing that earth energy up through you, drawing it up through your feet, filling every cell in your body. I see earth energy as molten gold, but you may see it, sense it, feel it differently. If you feel it as a temperature, it would be rather warm; if you hear it as a tone or vibration, it would be in the medium range; if you see it as a color, it would be a warm color.

Imagine it flooding every cell of your body, down the arms, out the hands. Then fill each chakra center and move it out to the edge of the skin, all the way up to the top of your head and fountain out the top. Feel the connection with the earth.

Turn your hands palms up on your lap and ask for the highest level of universal energy that you can easily accommodate to gently come down into the crown of your head. Then imagine it going into every chakra center, mixing with the earth energy, spreading out to the edges of the skin, especially the heart chakra, which is where your own special blend of earth and cosmic energies is created, so it is mixed really well. Next send it down your arms out the fingers, down the legs and out the feet, and any excess universal energy goes down into the center of the earth. Then experience your connection to the earth and to the universe.

Next use your intent to fill the first chakra back up with the Divine, which you can see as white, you can see as golden energy, you can feel it as a warmth, you can hear it as a tone, you can just feel it as a particular vibration, or you can just know that you are filling up every one of those layers. Activate the Divine in every layer, *until you can feel those feelings in your body* and establishing:

> *"I am safe, I am secure.*
> *I am One with the Divine.*
> *I **feel** that connection at all times.*
> *I emanate that Divinity out into the world*
> *through my feelings of love and joy and bliss*
> *and harmony and peacefulness and gratitude."*

Remember, the Divine Source energy is available all the time. Whether you are in touch with it or not, it is there all the time. It is what everything in the universe is made of. By placing your focus on each one of the layers of the chakra with the intention to activate, to stimulate, to turn it on in a way that you can sense at greater levels, you can know that you are filling up every one of those layers with the Divine that is already within you.

If you are about to begin a busy day and want to reconnect with these Divine feelings of joy and peace and harmony, go into that centered meditative state that I just described and connect with the earth energy and the universal energy and then bring your attention to your first chakra, and activate the Divine in every layer until you can feel it in your body.

Returning to Divine Feelings Throughout the Day

Anytime you want your body to automatically be conditioned to return to this Divine state, you can decide on two fingers to place together. Perhaps for the first chakra, it is the thumb and index finger on your right hand. Then once you have gotten in that state where you are feeling the connection and the Oneness with the Divine in the first chakra, and it is flowing through every layer—you are feeling peacefulness, contentment, bliss, love—when you are there and you are connected with the earth and you are connected with the universe and it is exactly where you want to be, then take those two fingers and put them together and say to yourself:

> *Every time I think Divine peacefulness in my first chakra*
> *and I place these two fingers together,*
> *my body will automatically go into this state.*

And then place those two fingers together.

Throughout the day if you start to lose that connection and feeling, you have a way to return to this state. I suggest you go into the bathroom. The great thing about restrooms is nobody asks you what you are doing in there. Shut the door and get centered and say to your body:

> *When I count to three and place these two fingers together,*
> *I'm going to go into that Divine peacefulness in my first chakra.*
> *One, two, three, Divine peacefulness.*

And put those two fingers together.

Remember which fingers they are. If you do this with each chakra, you will have seven different hand and finger positions associated with each one. You may want to write them down so you have it firmly established in your consciousness.

It is important to know that you are not pretending to be something you are not. You are being who you really are—the Divine!

You are now ready to move on to Chapter 3 and activate your feelings of well being.

Activating Your Feelings of Well Being

In every moment, you have the choice to live as the Divine essence that you are or as the limited personality that you have identified yourself to be. This choice is always available. Do you choose to live as your Divine Self feeling harmonious and at peace, enjoying your sensuality and sexuality? Or do you choose to continue feeling fear, guilt, depression, distress, disowning your sensuousness and sexuality?

These are the gifts and issues of your second energy center, located a couple of inches below the belly button and where you *feel* the energetic *feeling* of sensuality. This is your emotional and sexual center. It is also your center for clairsentience, your *feeling* nature. People who are empaths use the abilities of this center. Do you feel chicken skin or get goose bumps when you hear the truth? That's using your second chakra, your feeling center.

You were designed to be at peace, to *feel* love, harmony, bliss, oneness and to trust your feelings and your clairsentience or gut feelings that guide you in harmony with the Divine.

Developing the Divine Characteristics Within

When the blockages of limitation are released, here are the Divine qualities available to you in the *seven* layers of the *second* chakra:

1. You will *feel* total connection with the Divine and use that connection to make your daily life safe and protected.

2. You will feel your connection with the Divine and be guided to the best and the highest way to honor your emotions and your sensuality. You will feel the emotions of gratitude, bliss, harmony, peacefulness and the Divine sensuality of being in a human body and all of its higher form.

3. You will manifest the emotions of love, bliss, joy, harmony and peacefulness easily, effortlessly and enjoyably.

4. You will have the emotions of true Divine love of yourself and others.

5. You will communicate those feelings from the Divine to yourself and others.

6. You will use your clairsentience or clear feeling of exactly what the Divine is guiding you to and where to be and when.

7. You will experience the feeling of Divinity within the body. *How much more Divine can you get?*

Is this truly possible for you? Oh, yes! Over the years since I have been using the energy of the Divine in my work, I am always inspired by the complete transformation that occurs when people return to their spiritual essence. And the stories from my students and practitioners continue to pour in. I'O and ARCH practitioners are trained to help facilitate Oneness with the Divine Source by assisting the person in removing blockages that stop them from allowing healing to take place on unconscious, conscious and Divine levels.

Depression Disappears

One of my ARCH practitioners, Anne, sent me the following story:

"A woman I have known for many years was chronically depressed and came to me for help. Though I am a psychotherapist, I was afraid this wouldn't be fast enough and suggested we try ARCH. After the treatment, she described her experience to me:

'I was doing my best to keep my head above the waters of grief that rose relentlessly no matter how hard I tried to heal. I had experienced a seemingly endless series of losses over the past six years: the empty nest syndrome, the hormonal roller coaster of menopause, the ending a long partnership, family conflicts, increasing debt, a change of locale, and the deaths and disabilities of several dear friends. My life was swamped in waves of sadness.

'I had tried many approaches to regain my life's momentum, among them meditation, yoga, psychotherapy, prayer, walking, anti-depressant medication and bodywork. When these failed, I feared I was becoming a permanent melancholic with no golden years ahead.

'At the time of my ARCH treatment, my father was seriously ill and I was exhausted with worry about him. I had no expectations about ARCH beyond hope for some rest and relief from my current distress. About two-thirds of the way into the treatment, I had a definite sense of being connected with something larger than myself. I was in communion with Divine Light in a union so complete that loss wasn't a possibility.

'I felt unburdened and at peace, knowing all was well and would be well, no matter what the appearance. My immediate feeling was gratitude.

'In the days, weeks and months that followed my ARCH treatment, I had the energy to go through whatever was before me. The gratitude I felt increased steadily. My sense of humor gradually returned along with my faith in the unknown. I learned that the life force itself can reveal more possibilities than I can conceive.

'I am enjoying the unexpected gifts that come my way and passing them along with love. I have a sense of living with an on-going communion with the Divine Source. For this, I am most thankful.'

"The effect of ARCH on this client was dramatic and lasting. My clients and I are rewarded daily by the work and the power of the Divine."

Anxiety Vanished

Another ARCH practitioner, Deni, shared this experience:

"A woman came to me with many problems, Not only did she have her own physical symptoms, she was dealing with the death of her mother and she had been out of work for months. She was 'beside herself' with worry, fear and anger. We talked about payoffs and lessons, and she was not truly present in the conversation. She became angry and blamed everyone else for her troubles. I did the ARCH treatment with the intention of emotional balancing and centering only. During the treatment, I knew she was present again. Afterwards, with tears in her eyes, she said, 'I am back.' She called later to say she was still centered and was feeling waves of bliss."

Suicide Averted

Carol, a student of mine, was offering ARCH treatments at a Body, Mind, Spirit Expo in Seattle. She was doing a treatment on this woman, who unbeknownst to Carol, was on her way to commit suicide. On the way to end her life, she passed by the Expo and felt a sudden impulse to go in. She parked the car, paid the entrance fee and immediately went to my student's booth. Carol did one round of ARCH on her, the woman stood up and her energy seemed very different. She didn't say anything to Carol, but she took her card. She called her the next day and told her that she was on her way to commit suicide and that she was led instead to go to the Expo and get this treatment from her. And now she realized that she is God; she is part of God, and has absolutely no desire whatsoever to end her life. This complete transformation happened in a 10-minute treatment of just one round of ARCH.

What Blocks *Your* Divinity

When our inherent Divine qualities and abilities are blocked by our limiting beliefs, fears and doubts accumulated from our own life experiences or what we have learned from others, blockages form around each layer of our chakras, stopping us from creating the life we want. Again, it doesn't matter what chakra lifetime we are on, we still have to clear any limitations that are blocking us from our own Divinity. Then the powerful Divine life force energy can create lasting healing emotionally and spiritually no matter what the problem.

Grief Gone

Another ARCH practitioner, Diane, wrote:

"A woman came to me on the suggestion of a friend. For the last year, she had been helping her mother battle cancer. Her mother had died three weeks before, and in the last week the woman also had lost a good friend to cancer. She was overwhelmed by loss and experiencing grief and depression, crying every day and unwilling to be around people. She felt herself falling into 'something very deep and dark.'

"We spoke about processing her loss. After the ARCH treatment, she seemed happier and at peace. She called me two weeks later to report that the ARCH *healing had changed her life.* During the letting go process, she said she felt like she was vomiting all the ugly stuff out and that she was able to 'remember her forgotten hopes and dreams.' She said she felt she was out from under a dark cloud. She has now taken up a new hobby with a friend and is experiencing her limitless possibilities."

Schizophrenia Transformed

My student of thirty years, Alice, has a son who was labeled schizophrenic. When he was twenty-five, he tried to kill somebody and he was institutionalized for everybody's safety as well as his own. He was in a mental institution for ten years. On his thirty-fifth birthday, Alice went to see him and brought a cake.

"Mom, can you rub my back?" her son asked.

"Oh, I can do more than that," she replied, "I just learned this great new technique."

Alice was one of my first ARCH students and she did an ARCH treatment on him in the middle of the day room with all the other mental patients around. Instantly, it flipped a switch in him and he become unschizophrenic. Within a week or two, he was out doing things in the community, and then he was out of the hospital. It was instant transformation.

When you are no longer able to feel well being or feel clear guidance or enjoying your sensuality and sexuality, you know that some aspect of your second chakra is veiled.

What Holds These Blocks in Place

As mentioned in the last chapter, there is usually a payoff or a life lesson being learned that keeps these blocks to your Divinity in place.

Fear and Fibromyalgia Gone

Another ARCH practitioner, Diane, had this experience:

"My client called and asked how I could help her with fibromyalgia. After some discussion, she came to my office, still hesitant, but willing to work on her condition with the help of ARCH. During our dialogue, it came out that her perceived payoff was a fear of moving forward.

"When I asked her where the pain was greatest, she said, 'It hurts everywhere.' She stated that she was willing to let go of the dis-ease, and we went to work using ARCH. One hour later, I asked her, 'How do you feel?' She touched a spot on her arm that had been extremely painful earlier and said with surprise, 'I don't have any pain—anywhere!' She left the office smiling, skipping down the walkway with a new view of her limitless possibilities."

Letting the Blocks Fall Away

Most of us have been raised with fear, believing that trusting that fear was going to keep us safe. "Do not run out into the street, you're going to be hit by a car. Don't climb that tree, you're going to fall down and break your neck." So we have a hard time just instantaneously giving up the fear because our unconscious belief is that we will run amuck and run out in the street into traffic or climb that tree and be unsafe.

You may be thinking, "*If* I don't have that concern and I just let my little one go do whatever she wants . . . I keep on hearing these screech of brakes in my ear and then I run out and find that my two-year old has been run over! So those fears are a healthy thing."

Do not confuse clairsentience with fear. It is your clairsentience that allows you to *feel* that your two-year old is going to run out in the street and get hurt. Trust that feeling and make sure she is playing safely where you can keep an eye on her. This is about *using* your clear feeling, not getting rid of it.

There are obsessive fears or paranoid fantasies, meaning that these are worries that you are putting a lot of time and attention into. The law of the universe is that the more you focus on anything, the more attention you put into it, the more energy you are giving it, *the more likely it is that it is going to happen*. So rather than focus on the paranoid fantasies, trust your instincts. Do not let your fears rule the day.

If you are thinking, "Fear is what keeps me in check so I don't have an affair with my business partner's spouse," decide who you are going to be. Are you going to be a person of integrity? Are you going to be a person that lives their life in the Divine flow and feels that Divine Oneness within you? I guarantee if you are having an affair with your business partner's spouse, the second chakra is not going to be filled with the Divine, it is going to be filled with lust and fear of being found out! And that's certainly not living the highest that you know.

How can you tell the difference between fear that something *could* happen and clairsentience about it happening? Clairsentience has a quality of truthfulness. You will *feel* it in your body. When it is something real, you might get chills or goose bumps, which I call truth bumps. Whereas the fear pictures are just reoccurring, it is not a clear image or a clear thought or a clear feeling. It is an illusive thing that cannot quite be pinned down. The more you work with these energies, the clearer it will be for you to know which is which.

One way is to close your eyes and go into a centered state and imagine that fearful picture. If you can make it go away by dissolving it into neutralized energy, it is just your imagination. If you cannot make it go away or if it goes away and instantly comes back, then there is probably something there for you to look at.

Dissolving Fear

I suggest the best thing to do when the fear comes up is to acknowledge it. "Thank you, fear, I understand that you're attempting to keep me safe. I really appreciate that you're trying to protect me in this way. But right now, I think I have the situation handled, and I'd like you to step aside." And literally imagine putting it over to the side. "And I promise you, fear, that if I need you, I'll call upon you."

You are acknowledging the fear, you are being grateful that it is attempting to protect you, and then you are asking it to step aside. This is going to help clear out and stop any automatic fear response that was programmed into you as you were growing up.

Once you let go of your fear, you then can make choices from love, which will give you positive outcomes.

ARCH practitioner, Diane, related the following experience:

"A client came to me in a state of shock after having been diagnosed with cancer. He was confused and overwhelmed. He said that when he got the news, he felt himself walk away from his body. I felt the first step was to bring his spirit back and to get him grounded and centered. After the ARCH treatment, he said he felt his spirit was back. He felt blissful and in a state of peace. He was now ready to heal.

"He came back a week later to work out the issues that had burdened him on many levels, at first emotional, mental and spiritual, and now physical. We spoke about letting go on all these levels. He told me he could actually feel heavy weights being lifted from him. He felt more confident and peaceful and felt his choices were now being made not by fear, but with love."

Happiness is Your Birthright

Realize you are here to be truly happy. What have you used to stop yourself from being fully happy?

It might be your body. You are here to feel good about yourself and your body. Acknowledge this precious vehicle that you are privileged to inhabit to move through this grand adventure called life. Honor yourself for exactly who you are.

Make sure that your happiness is not dependent on what someone else does or does not do. Since you have no control over what another does, it only sets you up for unhappiness if they do something that does not please you.

Find what it is that you use to stop yourself from being happy. Let go of it. Make peace with it. Decide to stop beating yourself up with it. In every single moment of every single day you have a choice about how you feel.

There is no such thing as a wrong feeling. There are happy feelings and there are sad feelings—it's your choice what you do with them. You can use those feelings to know your Oneness with the Divine. Or you can use those feelings to feel miserable and depressed and wish that your life were different. Just like a knife can be used to cut up your vegetables or it can be used to hurt somebody, it is the same with your feelings. How are you choosing to use your feelings?

What are you using to stop yourself from being happy? Make peace with it. In every single moment of every single day you have a choice of how you feel, how you respond, and how you react. Does that mean that challenges will not come our way? No. When you are faced with a challenge, I strongly encourage breathing. That is the first step. You take a breath. It gives you a moment. And then you decide what your choice will be. *Okay, this is the situation. What are my options here?*

When our hot water heater broke down, my housemate was upset because the hot water heater was broken. I took a breath and said, "It seems to me we have two choices—we can either shower and bathe in cold water or we can get a new hot water heater. Now we know we're not going to shower and bathe in cold water, even though it's Hawaii, we're going to get the new hot water heater." Instead of complaining, my choice was to skip right to the solution and get the new hot water heater.

You can do this with every situation:

- What are my choices?
- Out of the choices, which one do I want?
- Do I want to complain along the way?
- Or do I just want to skip ahead to the solution?
- What is the best option that will ultimately make me feel happy and grateful?

As many spiritual teachers have said: We can choose love or fear. And it's always a choice. Always ask yourself: Is this choice being made out of fear or allowing me to feel more loving to myself?

Many people say, "Don't die with regrets." I say, "Don't live with them!" *How is that going to help you?* You did the best that you were able to do at that moment. Everybody is doing the best they can, with the knowledge and wisdom that they have right now. If we make a commitment to live by the highest we know, then it is always by Divine order. Honor yourself for the growth you have made and know that you will do better tomorrow. Instead of judging yourself, say, "I will do better next time." And let it go.

Identifying All the Ways You Have Kept Yourself From Being Divine in the Second Chakra:

This exercise will show you how your Divine nature is being blocked and what you would like to transform in your *second* energy center.

As you answer the following questions, make a list of everything you would like to release and transform:

- What challenges or old stagnant energies are you still holding onto in your 2nd chakra that is stopping you from transforming your life to the way you want it to be and living the life of the Divine in the area of your emotions and your sensuality?

- What are the major areas where you are holding yourself back with regard to your emotions and your sensuality?

- Are there old relationships from the past that you are still living with?

- Are there ways in which you are stopping yourself from truly being happy because you are not in the relationship of your dreams?

- Are there old emotional wounds that you have carried forward with you since childhood?

- Are there any emotional scars about your sensuality—messages you got from your parents or other authority figures?

- Are their emotional wounds that you have carried forward that you are still holding onto in terms of your sensuality or sexuality?

- Were you emotionally abused or molested?

- Are you willing to give up the feelings of being a victim to be able to truly transform your life and live in the Divine flow?

- Are you willing to know that all of your emotional, sensual and sexual experiences were for a purpose, even though you may not have known that at the time?

- Are you willing to forgive? Are you willing to forgive others? Are you willing to forgive yourself?

- Are you willing to transform all of the old energies that you have pushed into this area of your body, that perhaps caused you intestinal problems, bladder problems, fibroid tumors, ovarian cysts or even uterine cancer or maybe fear of intimacy?

- In the areas that you identified as being limited, what is your perceived payoff? What is the perceived benefit you are getting out of it or secondary gain?

- Are you willing to let it go?

- Has this been a recurring theme in your life? Is it a life lesson?

- What is the emotional/sexual lesson you have the opportunity to learn here?

- Are you willing to completely transform this part of your life that stops you from being truly happy, and allow yourself to honor your own sensuality and Divine nature?

Releasing the Blocks

Now that you are aware of how you have kept yourself limited, it is time to release everything on your list so that you can begin to transform the nature of your emotions and sensual reality to feeling well being and living the Divine life.

This exercise will help you do that.

1. Close your eyes and go into a relaxed state.

2. Create a big bubble out in front of you and put everything from your second chakra list that you no longer want into the bubble.

3. Release the bubble out to the sun and have it be evaporated.

4. Now envision what you do want on emotional and sexual levels. See and feel that clearly.

5. Create a powerful statement of transformation that gives you the feeling of experiencing what you want emotionally and sexually easily, effortlessly and enjoyably. Repeat this statement to yourself often every day until this is your reality.

Returning to Your Divine Essence

You can return to the way you were Divinely designed by placing your attention on activating the Divine within every layer of your second chakra and moving out any emotions that stop you from *feeling* your connection with the Divine on all those levels.

Begin by centering yourself. As described in the previous chapter, you can draw energy from the earth and the universal energy from the cosmos to blend within so you can expand to your highest level of consciousness.

Once again, sit with your feet flat on the floor so you can feel that connection with the earth, your hands uncrossed on your lap, and imagine bringing that earth energy up through you, drawing it up through your feet, filling every cell in your body. See it, sense it, feel it or hear it.

Imagine it flooding every cell of your body, down the arms, out the hands. Then fill each chakra center and move it out to the edge of the skin, all the way up to the top of your head and fountain out the top. Feel the connection with the earth.

Turn your hands palms up on your lap and ask for the highest level of universal energy that you can easily accommodate to gently come down into the crown of your head. Then imagine it going into every energy center, mixing with the earth energy, spreading out to the edges of the skin, especially the heart chakra, which is where your own special blend of earth and cosmic energies is created, so it is mixed really well. Next send it down your arms out the fingers, down the legs and out the feet, and any excess universal energy goes down into the center of the earth. Then experience your connection to the earth and to the universe.

Next use your intent to fill the second chakra back up with the Divine, which you can see as white, you can see as golden energy, you can feel it as a warmth, you can hear it as a tone, you can just feel it as a particular vibration, or you can just know that you are filling up every one of those layers. Activate the Divine in every layer, *until you can feel those feelings in your body* establishing:

> "*I am happy and joyful.*
> *I am a sensual being.*
> *I am One with the Divine.*
> *I **feel** that connection at all times.*
> *I emanate that Divinity out into the world*
> *through my feelings of love, joy, bliss,*
> *harmony, peacefulness and gratitude.*"

Since the Divine Source energy is available all the time, whether you are in touch with it or not, place your focus on each one of the layers of the second chakra with the intention to activate and turn it on, so you can sense and know at greater levels that you are filling up every one of those layers with the Divine that is already within you.

Before beginning a busy day, reconnect with these Divine feelings of joy, peace and harmony. Go into this centered meditative state and connect with the earth energy and the universal energy and then bring your attention to your second chakra, and activate the Divine in every layer until you can feel it in your body.

Returning to Divine Feelings Throughout the Day

Anytime you want your body to automatically be conditioned to return to this Divine state, decide on which two fingers you will place together. Then once you have gotten in that state where you are feeling the connection and the Oneness with the Divine in the second chakra, and it is flowing through every layer—you are feeling peacefulness, contentment, bliss, love—when you are there and you are connected with the earth and you are connected with the universe and it is exactly where you want to be, then take those two fingers and put them together and say to yourself:

> *Every time I think Divine peacefulness in my second chakra*
> *and I place these two fingers together,*
> *my body will automatically go into this state.*

And then place those two fingers together.

Throughout the day if you start to lose that connection and feeling, you have a way to return to this state. Get centered and say to your body:

> *When I count to three and place these two fingers together,*
> *I'm going to go into that Divine peacefulness in my second chakra.*
> *One, two, three, Divine peacefulness.*

And put those two fingers together.

Remember which fingers they are. You may want to write them down for future reference until you have it well established in your awareness.

This is a quick way to return to your Divine nature anytime.

You are now ready to move on to Chapter 4 and unleash your ability to manifest abundance.

Unleashing Your Ability to Manifest Abundance

What would your life be like if you *knew* without any question or doubt that you were the Divine? What if you knew that you could manifest your greatest dreams? What would you manifest?

If you doubt that you could truly manifest what you want, in Biblical scripture—John 10, verse 34—Jesus reminds us: "Ye are gods." That means *you*!

If you no longer wish to live in drama and trauma and are ready to give up any last vestiges of feeling like a victim or giving your power away to others or feeling unable to manifest the abundance you desire, this chapter will transform your life like no other.

Your will, willpower and manifesting ability are contained in your *third* energy center. This is huge! No other chakra carries the range of power that this one does—from misusing your power, feeling disempowered and like a victim to correctly using your power and totally aligning with the will of your Divine self and being fully empowered, manifesting the life of your dreams.

How can you do that? First, by realizing and releasing what is keeping you from aligning your *third* chakra of will and willpower with your Divine nature and manifesting as the Divine being that you are. Second, by returning to your Divine self and creating the life you want. This chapter will show you how to do both.

Developing the Divine Characteristics Within

When the blocks that keep you from aligning with your true nature are released, here are the Divine qualities available to you in the *seven* layers of the *third* chakra:

1. You will thrive easily, effortlessly and enjoyably, manifesting your life in a harmonious way that is in the Divine flow.

2. You will feel self-empowered emotionally and manifest sensuality in the highest way.

3. You will truly *be* self-empowered and able to manifest *anything you want* with ease, and with enough will and self-esteem to allow yourself to receive all the joyous things that you want to manifest on all levels.

4. You will enjoy balanced partnership relationships and manifest love of yourself and others in a harmonious, mutually empowering manner.

5. You will easily and effectively communicate what you want to manifest in the best possible way so that it is clearly received and understood.

6. You will use your psychic ability, perception of things, creativity and healing abilities to manifest whatever you want and need, easily drawing to you what is beneficial and for your highest good. And you will use your healing abilities to manifest healing within yourself and others.

7. You will easily manifest your perfect spiritual path that allows you to be fully aligned with your Divine will, and manifest the steps that are the best for you to take to open up to higher and higher levels of

consciousness. You will *know* that the Divine guidance within you has the best answers for you.

Levels of Consciousness

There are four different levels of consciousness as you move through your chakra lifetimes:

1st level: It is done *to* me. This is the victim mentality.

2nd level: It is done *by* me. As depicted in the movie, "The Secret," I *make* it happen.

3rd level: It comes *through* you. You are co-creating with your Divine nature.

4th level: It *is* you.

It is done *to* you, it is done *by* you, it comes *through* you and it *is* you. When you are experiencing Oneness with the Divine, it **is** you. It does not mean that you do not have moments of all the others. Which of these places do you live in the majority of the time?

Everyone is exactly where they are meant to be in their own growth cycle. The new souls are still working on "it is done *to* them," and they are experiencing being victims all the time. As you grow, you learn that you can have a say-so in how that occurs.

Most of what stops you from truly evolving and growing is stuck in your third chakra. You do not want your ego, which is your will and your willpower, trying to sabotage you returning to your Divine nature.

What Blocks Your Divinity

This energy center is where you stuffed all of your victim mentality—every time you thought you could not do something, every time you were told that you were not able to, that you were incapable, that you could not, that you lacked any sort of abilities; anytime you took that on and lived your life in a way where you thought bad things in the world happened *to* you, and you stayed stuck in that thinking. Many people get stuck in the feeling that they do not have what they want and they go into victim mentality.

Or on the other hand, this chakra is also where the other extreme of the pendulum occurs—people get stuck in their ego issues and act "better than" everybody else. Although most people that act out in egotistic ways are really coming from low self-esteem. However, there are people who believe they are truly God's gift to the planet over and above everyone else. Those limited beliefs and feelings get stuck in the third chakra.

This is also your power struggle center, where you experience conflict within yourself and with others. In order to live a harmonious, balanced life, and to manifest easily, effortlessly and enjoyable, you need to clear out that old rubbish.

I strongly encourage you to pay attention to clearing each layer as you do the exercises in this chapter, for your life will be so much better. You have been carrying around this stuff for a very long time and when you release the blocks, your life will be so much more in a harmonious manifesting flow that you will be amazed.

Will and willpower can be used for destructive reasons or for positive reasons to create whatever you need or want in your life. I am here to assist you in getting rid of the ways you have used it inappropriately, and to help you develop correct and balanced will and willpower, and establish ease and flow in manifesting.

Issues that are stuck here are really core blockages about victim mentality, feeling like you have given up your power to other people, or the overcompensation of coming on like a Mac truck because you are afraid that you are going to be taken advantage of or that you were told that you will never amount to anything, or people have invalidated your dreams and invalidated your visions and what you thought you were here to do. To sum it all up, the core issues that are stuck here are blocks that have to do with your will, your willpower, victim mentality, feeling manipulated or being the persecutor and manipulating others, as well as feeling lack and the inability to manifest. Blockages in this chakra can manifest as ulcers or l-pylori (bacteria in the stomach).

You Are Born With Manifesting Ability

The truth is you are born with access to the energy of will and willpower so you can use it to manifest whatever you desire, and of course without taking anything away from anybody else. If you return to the knowingness that you are the Divine—and so is everyone else—then you realize that the Divine is *the* creative energy; it is *the* energy that is used to manifest. It is infinite and your Divine ability to tap into that energy is limitless—not only for what you want and what is in alignment with the Divine, but also what is for the highest good of all concerned. *It is literally without limits!*

Most people were raised with unworthiness issues—feeling like they do not deserve it, feeling like they are asking for too much, feeling like they are not entitled to abundance on many levels. These feelings produce scarcity consciousness. The Divine is not scarcity; the Divine is the antithesis of that. It is *total abundance.* If you know that you are the Divine, *why would you limit yourself in any way, shape or form?* As long as what you want is aligned with the Divine plan and for the highest good of all concerned, then whatever is your true heart's desire and whatever you will allow yourself to have is what you can draw to you.

What keeps us from using our Divine-given right to manifest what we want and pervert it into being the victim? Most of us were raised with not only scarcity consciousness, but the victim mentality of it is done *to* you. Because we know that in the bigger picture we are in co-creation with the Divine, we are also responsible for what we are co-creating with the Divine—the good, the bad and sometimes the ugly.

How do we get stuck in the belief that we are victims? We get stuck because our parents were stuck and because their parents were stuck and *their* parents were stuck. The idea that "it is not my fault"—victim mentality—is simply not taking responsibility for what one is putting out there.

You may be thinking, "Yeah, but it isn't my fault. I was abused as a child." Or "My parents really didn't have any money, so I took on their poverty consciousness." If that is true for you, then that is part of your lesson to overcome in this lifetime—to realize that if you are the Divine, you can transcend those early childhood experiences, which I believe we all draw to ourselves to learn and grow and overcome so we can move into higher states of awareness.

First, become aware that was a *taught* pattern, that was something you learned as a child and that you have the ability to decide to go beyond that. Then, understand that if you are the Divine, you certainly are *not* a victim—unless you choose to be and you allow that to happen. Now is the time to begin acknowledging yourself as part of Divine consciousness, along with acknowledging others as all part of the Oneness. Catch yourself in those times of seeing the world as a victim and ask:

Am I really a victim in this?
What can I do differently?
Is this the mindset that I want to hold?

Know that if you are in that state, it means that you are not putting out your Divine intention. Why would you want to settle for limiting the Divine? This is really what you are doing when you relegate it to that limited consciousness.

What Holds These Blocks in Place

1. LIFE LESSONS

Is your present situation a life lesson you are being given the opportunity to learn? What if you have just lost your job and your home has just gone into foreclosure and you are wondering how to feed your kids? I believe that all of our challenges in life are lessons that we have designed before coming into this lifetime to learn. The ancient Hawaiians believed that we get together with what they call our highest council before coming into our lifetime and we plan what our major lesson is going to be, what our major purpose is going to be, and what are the most likely ways that we are going to accomplish both learning the lesson and accomplishing the purpose. Then at the end of our lifetime they get together with us on a soul, spirit level and review: *Did we learn our lesson? Did we accomplish our purpose?*

I think that our major challenges are self-created or self-imposed and are chosen by our being, soul, spirit as a way to learn our lessons. The majority of people who are losing their homes or losing their jobs are having this experience to learn a major life lesson or lessons. For instance, it can be a lesson of learning to take responsibility for their own and their family's financial well being and not giving that responsibility to somebody else, such as a bank or an employer. Many people who have gone into foreclosure borrowed more than they could pay back. This situation is giving them an opportunity to learn to be realistic about their finances.

If you are in foreclosure because you lost your job, I believe you probably have survival lessons that you are working on. What I recommend is—in the words of Jiminy Cricket—pick yourself up, dust yourself off and start all over again. Take advantage of the support systems that are in place, and ask yourself: *What is the lesson from this? What can this crisis teach me?*

I believe all situations in our life, especially the challenges, are opportunities for growth. Ask yourself: *What can I learn from this and use to grow?* Then put those challenges behind you and figure out: okay, now what? Time to get re-centered and re-focused.

Every single moment of every single day we have a choice about how we feel, how we respond and how we react. Our *attitude* about all that has happened is what we can control. If we choose to get stuck in the victim mode, we get stuck in feeling like it is a conspiracy of the universe, and then we are never going to move beyond that.

Moving On After Divorce

When my ex-husband asked me for a divorce, I said, "Are you sure? Is that exactly what you want?"

"Yes," he answered.

Four months earlier I had seen him in a dream in which he said, "Divorce." Later that day I asked him, "Are we okay? What does this mean?"

"We're fine, we're fine, we're fine," he replied.

Then four months later, he said, "I want a divorce."

Fortunately, I had a little bit of a heads up, but I did exactly what I am suggesting to you. I said to myself: Okay, given this, in this situation, what are my choices here? I can rant, rave, yell, scream, cry—that does not mean do not get your emotions out—but then pick yourself up and figure out: *Okay, given this, what are my choices? What are my options? What is the best direction for me to move forward?*

Then use your will, your life force energy, and take action to manifest what you need or want. You can either do that in a destructive way, imposing your will on somebody, or you can use your will in a way that is in harmony with the Divine. You need to put energy into whatever you need or want to draw back to you.

Transforming Your Job Being Downsized

I did a session with an M.D. whose job is in question because the medical center is downsizing. After listening to her describe the situation, I told her, "The problem is you are focusing on all the lack and limitation that could happen to you. As a result, this makes it really hard for you to put energy into creating what you want because your fears and feelings that this is out of your control have closed down your manifesting abilities. From this state of lack, you are not able to put energy out there to create either your employer finding new funds to keep you or finding a different position elsewhere."

First acknowledge: Yes, this is the situation. Yes, this is not what I want. *Now what can I do to envision things being better and imagine what I really want?*

Then align your will with action to create what you do want. We all know that whatever we put our focus on is what is most likely to occur. If you are placing your attention on fear, lack, limitation and all is lost, then you are going to create more of that. Begin by stopping that downward spiral and start to put your energies out there in a positive way by seeing it, sensing it, hearing it, feeling it and knowing it differently.

2. Misusing Your Power

We can misuse our personal will and power by engaging in addictive behavior, by choosing to give up our power or by abusing or manipulating others. An aspect of the third chakra is abuse on any level—forcing your will on another, or feeling victimized by giving away your will. *How are you using your personal will and power? Are you using your willpower to transform your life?*

Giving Away Your Power

There are many ways you give away your power every day. Each time you are afraid to take responsibility for your actions or do not take seriously that you are a powerful creator creating constantly with your thoughts, your words and your actions, or fear the consequences of your actions or think that it is someone else's fault, you have given away your power. Every time you give your power to another, you have chosen to not create the life of your choosing.

VICTIMHOOD TRANSFORMED INTO EMPOWERMENT

Wendy, one of my seminar students, felt that she could not stand up for herself at work and felt abused by her boss and unable to manifest the support and working environment she needed. "My boss constantly stole my ideas and presented them as her own," she said. "I did all of the work and she took all of the credit. When I spoke up about it, she made my life a living hell so I learned to stay quiet.

"I let people walk all over me," Wendy continued. "I also didn't listen to my gut. I knew that I had made a mistake going to work for this company, but I ignored it. In addition, I gave up my personal life for this job and my personal relationships suffered. I also didn't have time for spiritual pursuits.

"I was angry and hurt. I didn't understand why she treated me the way she did or how she got away with her behavior. I felt like I would never get out of that situation and that I didn't have anything to offer another employer.

"In my work with Laurie, I learned that this situation was giving me the opportunity to learn a major life lesson, which was to listen to my intuition and to always stand up for myself. I let go of all of the anger that I had towards my boss. It wasn't serving me and was preventing me from growing and moving forward. I have learned a valuable lesson—I will never give my power away again. I feel at peace since I let it all go."

During the seminar Wendy reclaimed her power by aligning her will with the will of the Divine and saw the unlimited possibilities before her. She promptly found a better job where she felt empowered and was paid and acknowledged for her ideas.

"I recognize what I did in my last job and will not allow that to happen again. I speak my mind now in a very professional manner. I will never work somewhere that is managed by fear and intimidation."

Every time you give your power to someone or something outside of you, you have given up control over your own life.

ADDICTIONS

When you give up your will to something outside yourself—such as drugs, cigarettes, alcohol, food, sex or violence—you are choosing self-abuse. Addictions are a lack of using your will in a healthy, nurturing, supportive way and not effectively using your will to control you and your behavior, instead of letting it control you.

You may think that your addiction is genetic, but you chose your parents because of who they are, not in spite of who they are. And you choose them because they are the perfect catalysts to set into place your life lessons. If your life lesson is in the third chakra or this is a third chakra lifetime, then there are probably addiction opportunities.

Addictions are looking for something or using something outside yourself to fill a place inside that you feel is empty. All addictions are about trying to find something *outside* to feed you, rather than being whole and One with the Divine and feeling that Oneness inside you. Addictions actually numb out the true nature of the physical body, which then sets up a cycle of trying to find a quick fix somewhere outside yourself.

Addiction occurs when you are trying to fill up that *lack of* peace or *lack of* love or *lack of* wholeness. The peace, love and wholeness we are searching for is inherently what we feel when we are One with the Divine. If you are experiencing addiction of any kind, you are not aligning your will with your true Divine nature, and trying to use something external to fill up that hole.

All problems stem from not being aligned or connected with our Divine nature, and the way to transform all addictions is to align with the Divine within. The ancient Hawaiian kahuna knew this to be true. They believed that all dis-ease came from anxiety or stress and that all stress came from forgetting that you are the Divine and One with the Divine. Their whole healing focus was helping people reconnect with that truth of *we are all Divine.*

Stopped Smoking

Karen, one of my students, had been smoking for fifty years. It had become so much a part of her life that she did not think she could ever quit. Yet once she did the exercises that are in this chapter and realigned with her Divine nature, she stopped smoking after fifty years. *After fifty years!* Karen told me, "After smoking for all of my adult life, I was able to stop much more easily than I thought I could. Once I reconnected with the Divine inside, the constant stress I had always felt was replaced with such a sense of peace that I no longer needed to reach for a cigarette."

Abusing Others

Another way we misuse our power is by trying to manipulate or force others to do what we want rather than honoring their own path and choices. Even if our manipulation is subtle, we are attempting to take away the free will of another. When we recognize the Divine in them and respect their decisions, we strengthen it in ourselves.

If you find yourself being the recipient of misuse of power, you can use your willpower to overcome being abused by another.

Learning the Correct Use of Power

When I was nine, my mother divorced my father and married an alcoholic. By the time I was twelve until I was sixteen, he would come into my room naked, drunk and sexually aroused in the middle of the night and try to molest me. I spent much of my adolescence discovering my spiritual life force energy and bringing it through me when my stepfather tried to force himself on me. I would literally blast him with energy and scream at him, which threw him off and he would stagger out. So he was never successful in molesting me.

In my early twenties, I realized that we are never a victim, we are always a volunteer, at the very least. Therefore, if I volunteered for that, what was that about? While we are going through these things, we question the perceived payoff and lesson. Some things seem really harsh. Why in the world did I choose on a being, soul, spirit level to learn whatever it was I was learning by my stepfather trying to molest me and by my mother, even when she saw it, invalidating it?

During a meditation when I was twenty-one, I realized that I had to learn to never abuse my power by being the perpetrator like my stepfather and never allow my power to be abused by being the victim. I realized that on a being, soul, spirit level I had created that experience before coming into this lifetime as part of my life script.

It is helpful to remember that everything occurs for our growth. We consciously or unconsciously choose it to be so. And we always learn more from the challenges in our life. We create our own reality, including the hard times, because we need to learn something. By my stepfather trying to sexually abuse me, I learned that I had to be strong to not allow myself to be the victim. I also learned to not ever be in his position.-

Even though that was a very scary time for me, I believe that on a soul, spirit level, I chose to have that experience to learn very clearly to never abuse my power and to never give up my power to another to be abused. Since that time, my whole focus of whatever I am doing is always with the intent of empowering others. My focus for over thirty years of teaching is to teach people to be self-empowered. I might not be so clear about giving the power back to my students without that powerful learning experience of knowing what it feels like to have someone try to take your power away.

Once I had this realization, I wrote my stepfather a letter forgiving him. I told him that I had to learn that lesson and somebody had to play that role, which must have been hard for him. I never received a response. I forgave him and I moved on. I didn't think about it any more.

About seven years ago, I had this impulse to write my stepfather another letter. Even though I had already done that years before and felt complete, I trusted my clairsentience. I wrote him a letter once again saying that not only did I forgive him, I thanked him for playing that role so I could learn to never abuse my power or to give my power away and be abused. I told him that I understood it must have been really difficult for him and thanked him. Then I mailed it.

I soon got a call from my mother that my stepfather had a heart attack. He was driving and went over a cliff. He had to be cut out of the car with heavy machinery. My mother received a call to come to the emergency room, which was about an hour away.

On the way to the emergency room to see her husband, my mother stopped at her mailbox to get the mail. What are the chances of that happening? Who stops at the mailbox and gets the mail on the way to see your husband who may or may not be alive when you get there? Then she put the mail in her purse rather than leaving it in the car.

When she got to the emergency room, they were doing ex-rays and cat scans. While she was waiting to find out the results of how critical he was, she looked at the mail and found the letter from me addressed to him. My stepfather then became conscious, she read him the letter and he died.

Now you cannot orchestrate that! If you do not believe in a higher power, what does that tell you? Who gets the mail on the way to the emergency room? Who puts it in their purse? Who looks at the mail when you are waiting to find out if your husband is alive or dead? Who does that? Only if you are led by the Divine to do that.

Not only did my stepfather hear my letter right before he left, but my mother heard it too. My biggest issues with her all my life had to do with her not protecting me from his abuse. *She got to be the one who read the letter to him.* By doing what she wasn't able to do before, she received a healing as well. What an incredible gift! Divinely orchestrated.

Since we all have a chance to rewrite the script as the subconscious mind does not know the difference between you imagining something and it actually happening, we all can "redo" any experience where we felt victimized, disempowered or lacking an ability to manifest what we want. By rewriting the script, we recondition the subconscious to the experience of empowerment and abundance. In my redo, I created some wonderful personal member of the family who did not exist in real life come and protect me—because I cannot take my mother's lessons away from her about marrying an abusive, lecherous alcoholic. I cannot take my stepfather's life lessons away from him of whatever he was learning by playing that role. I did not take away my learning to never abuse my power and to never allow my power to be abused.

Was I a victim in all of that? On a body personality level, surely there were times when it felt like it. But on a higher level, on a spiritual level, I chose that situation to learn that lesson. When we look at little kids who have been abused and who have experienced all kinds of horrific things, know that on some level their spirit agreed to that situation to learn something. At the same time, have compassion for them, love them and try to protect them.

The villains in our lives are actually angels that have decided to take that role in our play. They signed on for that role and we hired them to play it. In the process, they are being given the opportunity to learn their own lessons. My stepfather trying to take advantage of me certainly was abusing his power as my stepfather. When we are abusing power and using our power *over* others, we have disconnected from our Divinity. Abusing power is obviously not being One with the Divine.

What is Your Lesson?

What is your main lesson that you have an opportunity to learn regarding your will, your willpower or your manifesting? *What is the main lesson you have an opportunity to learn here?*

Your lessons may be learning not to take things personally and that you are never a victim, at the very least you are a volunteer because you have a lesson to learn from the situation. What an amazing life you would live in the Divine flow if you got these two major lessons:

1. Make a commitment to yourself to learn not to take it personally because it usually is almost never about you; it is about the other person and their issues. It becomes about you and your lesson when you take that on, and you take it as a personal assault to you.

2. Make a commitment to realize that you are never a victim. You are the incredible powerful one that *created* this lifetime and created these opportunities that manifested everything around you, so you have a wondrous chance to learn and to grow.

Remember that before this chakra lifetime, *you* wrote the script and you chose these lessons to learn. First, you tried drama and trauma as the mode to learn your lessons. Fortunately, then you realized somewhere along your journey that did not work very well. The more consciously you decide to learn your lessons, the easier it will be to live in the Divine flow.

Moving from Victim to Manifestor

What are the steps to go from victim consciousness to be able to manifest at One with the Divine in an unlimited way?

1. Put it in the Divine Perspective

Obviously, if you know that you are One with the Divine, you know that on a higher level it is all Divine all the time—even when it does not look like it. Then live in faith in the Divine rather than fear. Live in trust. Live in *I know that I am going to be okay. I need to open up to being Divinely guided to the actions that are for my and everybody's highest good.*

If you are living in fear—and not trusting in the wisdom of the Divine and not living in faith—then that fear will create more drama and trauma in your life and draw more challenges to you *rather than solutions*. Put whatever has happened into the Divine perspective and then begin to rebuild from there.

2. GRATITUDE

Being grateful for what you have will help you find the energy within to put out into the world to create what you want. It changes your mindset from lack to gratitude for what you **do** have. Then that feeling of abundance for the things you are grateful for begins to draw more things to be grateful for. The feeling of gratitude for what you do have is what creates external abundance. *Find it within yourself first.*

How does that work? If you are operating on lack and limitation, you are not going to create abundance either internally or externally. *First,* being grateful gives you a sense of the abundance of love in your life or the abundance of health in your life or the abundance of connection with Spirit or feeling the love of your pets. Find those riches within as a way of filling yourself back up, instead of operating on empty. *Then* once you are saturated and filled up with them internally, flow that out from you into creating the external riches. Begin by going within and look at what you are grateful for. Write it down. Make a list such as:

> *I am grateful for my family.*
> *I am grateful for my health.*
> *I am grateful for my pets.*
> *I am grateful for breathing.*
> *I am grateful that the sun is shining.*
> *I am grateful . . .*

Totally go into a complete state of gratitude and honor all that you have. Then look at the truth of your current situation. For example, if your house is in foreclosure, ask yourself, "Is it the house that gives me joy and happiness and spiritual connection and love?" Of course not! That only comes from the Divine, which is within you *all the time.*

Next figure out what you truly *need.* Maybe what you want isn't the first step. Figure out what you truly need. You truly need food, shelter and clothing. Surrender how that manifests through the Divine by saying: *I trust that I will be clothed and I will be fed and I will be sheltered and so will my family.*

Then envision your family sitting at the dinner table with food. Envision having adequate shelter and clothing. And ask the Divine to allow that Divine energy to flow through you to create those things.

Then that may lead to the house being saved. To master this lesson, ask yourself: *What is the real attachment?* Is your attachment to the house or is it to the love and the family and well being of everyone? What's really important?

The good news is that seemingly devastating things often happen when we have been putting our focus in the wrong place—on the external things rather than the internal things that would give us spiritual and lasting joy and success. These events allow us to reposition our focus to what is really important—our *true* abundance.

When you learn that, when you really get that, and you are willing to demonstrate that you have learned it, then the external abundance will flow. The way you can know if you have learned that lesson is that the abundance you feel on the inside has now shown up on the outside. It's not about *not* having material things. It's about realizing they are not the reason for living. And the material goodies are not controlling you; rather you are sourcing them through your own Divine nature. Ultimately, all fears of lack and not having enough are a result of disconnecting from our Divine Source or our own Divinity.

TRANSFORMING LOSS INTO ABUNDANCE

My student Sara felt having material things gave her power. Then her house caught on fire. It took four hours for the entire four-story house to burn to the ground. "It was indeed devastating to watch your home where you and your family had lived for thirty years with all your possessions that you had taken years to accumulate be wiped out in a matter of hours," she remembered quietly.

"The next morning watching the sun rise from my neighbor's living room window across the street and seeing the birds flying and singing, I knew that if I adopted the Divine perspective, I and my family would be alright. As a student of Laurie's work for six years, I knew I had been given all the tools I needed to start this new chapter of my life.

"I realized that we had been given the opportunity of a whole new perspective—whereas it sometimes takes people years to clean out their basements and attics and garages, we had a giant clearing in the space of four hours.

"That four hours completely changed my perspective—to see what was truly important and what was really inconsequential. Within forty-eight hours, my son said, 'I think the fire did us a favor.' For it brought us together to experience the Oneness with people over and over again. From the limited personality perspective, we had nothing, and from the Divine perspective, we had everything.

"Over the next days, weeks and months, everyone rallied around us to provide whatever we needed—homes were offered, clothes, food and gift certificates for food—all our needs were taken care of. And we got to see the beautiful generous hearts and kindness of everyone in our community and people we didn't even know. People as far away as Hawaii had fundraisers for us; people from other communities sent us donations. So much so that we began to give what we didn't need to others who were less fortunate than us. Then to see their gratitude was amazing, as we felt the wondrous love and generosity of everyone around us.

"This was a major life lesson for me on multiple levels, for I felt for many years that I had to struggle and work hard to manifest what my family and I needed. I was a trained nurse first working night shifts for a children's hospital and then working full time in private practice as well as raising four children and making a home for them and my husband. And here with seemingly nothing, everything we needed was brought to us easily, effortlessly and joyfully. I began to see that there is a whole other way to manifest through the grace of the Divine.

"I used the tools Laurie had taught me to move out of the trauma and drama of the fire and into alignment with the Divine allowing myself and my family to be lovingly provided for by Divine grace. I also was able to move from feeling devastated to being peaceful and calm by clearing the chakras as Laurie had taught us.

"I had been used to *making* things happen by controlling the events and people around me. With the fire I was able to see that nothing was in my control. It facilitated me learning to let go and trust a higher power, the Divine, which created a much better outcome than I could even imagine.

"I was used to manifesting things by using my personal will to *will* things into being, but after the fire I soon saw that it simply didn't work—it would just create a mess. It was only by letting go of the way I thought it should be done that I began to see the unfolding of Divine grace which allowed everything that was needed to manifest with ease. It was then that I moved from self-doubt to certainty and began completely listening to and following my inner guidance.

"Before, I freely gave love to others, but didn't totally allow that love into my own heart. This experience has allowed me to open up and feel my own Divine nature and bask in the love of that connection.

"As I look back, I realize that before the fire I had gotten stuck, afraid to step into my full power and knowingness and share my wisdom. I had stopped growing; I was holding back and playing safe. The fire was the catalyst to move me forward—for that was the only direction to go. I knew that if I tried to hold onto the past or dwell on the loss, I would be digging my own grave and that of my family. It was the springboard that moved me forward and allowed me to pole vault into a new more expanded, exciting adventure as a spiritual teacher, sharing what I have learned with others. I am now being asked to speak to groups to help others with what I have learned from being able to get through this experience with such love and grace.

"When the fire happened, I realized I had been given all the tools I needed to turn this whole thing around and create a new and even better life than I had before. And that's what I have done. Now my family and I are enriched by this experience—far beyond what we had before on all levels—physically, emotionally, mentally and spiritually. For now we are whole, connected to our Divine nature, following the guidance of the Divine and living in the beauty, grace and love of life."

This apparent disaster brought Sara and her family so many gifts. Not only were they able to manifest a new home, with their new understanding of what was truly important, their family realized a closeness and love for one another on a much deeper level than ever before. They learned that material things do not bring you happiness. Happiness is internal and our birthright as part of the Divine.

Everything and everyone—as the ancient Hawaiians and all great spiritual teachers have said—are part of the Divine. You are One with the Divine matrix. This understanding first happens intellectually. As you allow yourself to open up to this possibility, it happens much more easily. Then as you bring this awareness down into your body, you can feel it. Through the exercises in this book you will begin to experience that you are indeed One with the Divine matrix that science calls the quantum hologram. The more you do that, the more you are expanding your energy that can be put out through the energetic web to create what you need and want.

3. Focus on What You Want

Since you are reading this book, you have had the experience of wanting something *or* not wanting something and putting energy into it and then creating it. It is important to remember that even when we focus on something we do *not* want, we are putting energy into it and we will, therefore, draw that to us.

When I was in my early twenties, I really wanted this blouse that I saw in Macys shortly before Christmas. It was very expensive, much more that what I wanted to spend. I kept going back to look at it and each time it was still there. Finally, I said, "I'll just eat beans and rice for the next few weeks" and I bought the blouse. Then both my mother and my stepmother who had no idea that I wanted that blouse gave me the identical one for Christmas, so I had three of them! That's because I was putting out all this energy into wanting that blouse, so much so that my mother and my stepmother without even knowing anything about it on a conscious level bought me the blouse.

When this happens to you, take it as acknowledgment you are aligned in a harmonious fashion with the Divine and that you can draw back to you whatever you want.

Early Lessons in Manifestation

When I was in my very early twenties, I read a book about how to manifest. I got very excited because there were lots of things that I wanted. I had just finished graduate school and gotten a job in a little community where most people were married. I had already decided that I wanted a date with Tom who was the only single available man about my age that I felt I could connect with. I wanted Tom to come to my house for dinner on Saturday night. So I did my little manifestation visualization that he would come over for dinner. Then I called him up and said, "Hey, Tom, it's Laurie, do you want to come over for dinner Saturday night?" He said, "I'm not sure what I'm doing. Can I get back to you?"

I was shocked. I hung up the phone and thought, "Well, this stuff doesn't work!" So Saturday came. I had no hot date, I had not washed my hair and I was in my old jeans when about 6 o'clock there was a knock on the door. I opened it up and it was Tom.

Tom jogged about one to three miles every night and he was standing there looking all hot and sweaty and said, "I was out jogging and I suddenly remembered that I was supposed to come over here for dinner."

Here is poor Tom jogging his one to three miles when my energy I had put out earlier comes and grabs him, drags him ten miles to my house because I had done a visualization that he was supposed to be there for dinner. I learned my first invaluable lesson regarding manifestation—that you never, ever, ever manifest something with somebody else in it. I had actually manipulated that into being. So, of course, the outcome was not what I wanted with Tom.

Next, I decided I wanted a bigger house. I was living in a one bedroom little cottage. I decided I wanted a two-bedroom house. So I imagined where the living room, kitchen and bedrooms would be in my new home. I could not quite figure out where I was going to put the bathroom, so I kept seeing it out there somewhere.

I saw an ad for a two-bedroom cottage in the paper and I went to look at it. The front of the house was exactly like I envisioned it—living room, kitchen and two bedrooms. But I couldn't find a bathroom. I asked the woman showing me the house, "Where's the bathroom?" "Oh, she replied, "You have to go outside the house. It's about 10 feet out behind the house." It was "somewhere out there," just where I had put it in my visualization. Then I realized that I had to be really specific.

My next lesson occurred when I was moving to another town. I decided now I really know how this manifestation thing works, so I envisioned a house right on the cliffs in Northern California. I wanted to have a 300-degree panoramic view of the water and I wanted to have a great big kitchen, as big as the living room, a wood burning stove and a bathroom inside the house with a high shower stall because I am almost 5'10" and I do not like being hit in the chin with water. Then I kept envisioning the bedrooms were attached to the house, since I did not want to have to go out of the house to the bedrooms. And I wanted a bay window and a round table and a couple of chairs.

A friend who also wanted to move and I made an agreement that if she found something she did not want that she thought I might want, she would tell me about it, and visa versa. Soon she called me up and told me about a place she had just seen. "It has a 300-degree panoramic view of the water and the kitchen is as big as the living room and it has a wood burning stove and it has a bay window," she said.

"And a round table with a couple of chairs?" I asked.

"Yeah," she said, "that's the only furniture that comes with it."

So I knew this was the place and I said, "And it has a really high shower stall?"

"Laurie," she replied, "I didn't go stand in the shower. I don't know."

"Well, where are the bedrooms?" I asked.

"They're upstairs," she replied.

"That's fine," I said.

"But they are not yours," she added.

"What do you mean they are not mine?" I couldn't believe my ears.

"They divided the whole house into two apartments," she replied. "The upstairs where the two bedrooms are has been made into a one-bedroom apartment. They turned one of the bedrooms into a kitchen/living room area. And the other one is the bedroom. It has a separate entrance. And then the downstairs is a studio so you would be sleeping in the living room."

Ohhhh! I learned my next valuable lesson in manifesting that you always put yourself and your things in whatever it is you want to manifest. Back then, I manifested many parking places for the car in front of me because I did not see my car pulling into that spot. Now I know better.

I did move into that place and when the renters upstairs moved out, I rented out the whole house and turned it into a healing center and it was wonderful.

My Next Lesson in Manifestation

When I needed $500 for something, I manifested a car accident that was serious enough that I received $500 pain and suffering money. Then I realized you have to ask that the manifestation happen with joyous harmony.

After the accident I needed a new car in a hurry. I called up the Honda dealer and said that I wanted a brand new silver five-speed hatchback with red interior.

"That's really nice," he replied. "There's a three-month waiting list."

"No, I need it tomorrow," I said.

He patiently replied, "As I told you, miss, there is a three-month waiting list."

Since I needed the car immediately, I began focusing on the dealer getting a brand new silver five-speed hatchback with red interior the next day, and that they were going to call all the people on the list ahead of me and in the meantime all of those people had gotten something they wanted *even more* than the five-speed silver hatchback with red interior. And that I was going to be the first person on the list that wanted the car.

The next day the dealer called me and said, "Well, we have your car."

"Of course you do!" I replied.

"Somebody else called you? he asked.

"No," I said.

I learned then that all truly successful manifestations have to be for the highest good of all concerned. I cannot take away something from somebody else. It has to be for the highest good of all concerned.

The Learning Continues

When all of the jobs I had wanted years before actually were offered to me much later, I learned another piece in the manifestation equation. There also needs to be a time, including the year, you are asking for this to happen.

At age twenty-three I wanted to manifest being able to buy a house, as I was making a lot of money working for the California Youth Authority and needed a tax break. The C.Y.A. was like a prison for delinquent kids. I worked on a med psych unit with murderers, rapists and child molesters whose average age was fourteen. The reason they paid me so much money was because three people had been killed in my position before. But at twenty-three I had no fear. I never had any problems with those kids. It worked well for me.

I saved all my money for the down payment of a new house that was being built and planned it down to the carpet and fixtures. Then the loan I had applied for didn't come through, and by that time I had saved $20,000. I quit the job at C.Y.A. and I moved to the place on the coast in Mendocino. And I opened up a Healing Center. I would not have been able to have $20,000 to put into a Healing Center if I hadn't believed I was saving that money to buy a house.

I learned to include in my manifestation exercise *"this or something better"* because we do not know if there could be something better.

This or something better is now manifesting
with joyous harmony
for the highest good of all concerned
on (include the date).

For the Highest Good of All

After being privileged to live my life in Oneness non-duality, I now only ask for whatever is for the highest good of all concerned. I no longer do any of the manifestation steps that I did many years ago. I just ask the universe,

"Whatever is for the highest good of all concerned." That's it. I just send that thought out through the aka grid.

This is even true in situations regarding my children. Instead of deciding that I know best what is for their highest good, I don't put out a particular outcome. I simply ask that the Divine energy create *whatever* is for everyone's highest good, regarding my children. Then I leave it up to the Divine to decide what that is, rather than me think I know what that is. Whatever intention you are putting out in the world, ask that it is for the highest good of all concerned.

Identifying All the Ways You Have Kept Yourself From Being Divine in the Third Chakra:

This exercise will show you how your Divine nature is being blocked and what you would like to transform in your *third* energy center.

As you answer the following questions, make a list of everything you would like to release and transform:

- Have you ever felt like a victim?
- Have you ever felt like you had no options or no choice?
- Have you ever given away your power to somebody else because it seemed easier or because you thought you should or had to in order to survive?

- Have you ever felt like giving up or that you didn't have the will to live?
- Have you ever done anything that you didn't want to do?
- Have you ever given someone else control over your life?
- Have you ever attempted to control someone else's life?
- Have you ever felt like you had to control your life or someone else's life to be powerful?
- Have you ever allowed your power to be abused?
- Have you ever abused your power and bullied others?

- Have you ever felt you were better than everyone else?
- Have you ever been in a power struggle with yourself or another?

- Have you ever felt like you were always the victim in relationships?
- Have you ever felt you had to be in control in a relationship?
- Have you ever tried to control another's love for you or control your love for another?
- Have you ever pushed love away rather than manifesting it?

- Have you ever told other people what to do?
- Have you ever been verbally abusive to another?
- Have you ever allowed yourself to be verbally abused?
- Have you ever felt like a martyr?

- Have you ever disowned your psychic ability?
- Have you ever limited your perception of things and not wanted to see a larger point of view?
- Have you ever felt your creativity blocked?
- Have you ever discounted your healing abilities?

- Have you ever allowed your psychic ability to be manipulated by others?
- Have you ever used your psychic ability to manipulate or have power over others?
- Have you ever allowed another's psychic ability to have power over you?
- Have you ever given your ability to see things clearly over to others?
- Have you ever given another's creativity power over you?

- Have you ever given another's healing abilities power over you?
- Have you ever withheld your healing abilities?
- Have you ever withheld your intuition?

- Have you ever used your will and your willpower to manipulate others in a religious or spiritual manner?

- Have you ever allowed others to manipulate you spiritually or religiously?
- Have you ever given your power away to a religious or spiritual group?
- Have you ever given up your willpower on a spiritual path or a religious path to the leader?

- Have you been holding on to something that you are having difficulty transforming, such as feeling like a victim with your family, your job, your career, with money or lack of it?

- Have you been addicted to drugs, alcohol, cigarettes, food, or a particular relationship?

- Are you willing to transform all of the old energies that you have pushed into this chakra of your body, that perhaps have caused you ulcers or stomach problems?

- In the areas that you identified as being limited, what is your perceived payoff? What is the benefit your body personality is getting out of it?
- Are you willing to let it go?

- Has this been a recurring theme in your life? Is it a life lesson?
- What is the lesson you have the opportunity to learn here?

- Are you willing to completely transform this area of your life that is stopping you from manifesting abundance and allow yourself to honor your own Divine nature?

Releasing the Blocks

Now that you are aware of how you have kept yourself limited, it is time to release everything on your list so that you can begin to transform the nature of your will and willpower reality to manifesting your Divine life.

1. Close your eyes and go into a relaxed state.

2. Create a big bubble out in front of you and put everything from your *third* chakra list that you no longer want into the bubble.

3. Release the bubble out to the sun and have it be evaporated.

4. Now envision what you do want on willpower and manifestation levels. See and feel that clearly.

5. Create a powerful statement of transformation that allows you to experience what you want to be, feel and have easily, effortlessly and enjoyably. Repeat this statement to yourself often every day until this is your reality.

Returning to Your Divine Essence

Once again, you can come back to the way that you were Divinely designed by bringing your attention to activating the Divine within every layer of your third chakra and moving out any emotions that stop you from *feeling* your connection with the Divine on all seven of those levels.

Begin by centering yourself. Just as you have done before, draw energy up from the earth and the universal energy from the cosmos down to blend within so you can grow to your fullest level of consciousness.

Sit with your feet flat on the floor so you can feel that connection with the earth, your hands uncrossed on your lap, and imagine bringing that earth energy up through you, drawing it up through your feet, filling every cell in your body. See it, sense it, feel it or hear it.

Imagine it flooding every cell of your body, down the arms, out the hands. Then fill each chakra center and move it out to the edge of the skin, all the way up to the top of your head and fountain out the top. At the same time, feel your connection with the earth.

Turn your hands palms up on your lap and ask for the highest level of universal energy that you can easily accommodate to gently come down into the crown of your head. Then imagine it going into every chakra center, mixing with the earth energy, spreading out to the edges of the skin, especially the heart chakra, where your own special blend of earth and cosmic energies is created, until it is well mixed. Next send it down your arms out the fingers, down the legs and out the feet, and any excess universal energy goes down into the center of the earth. Then experience your connection to the earth and to the universe.

Next use your intent to fill the third chakra back up with the Divine, which you can see as white or golden energy, feel as warmth, hear as a tone or a particular vibration, or just know that you are filling up every one of those layers. Activate the Divine in every layer, *until you can feel those feelings in your body* establishing:

> *"I am empowered.*
> *I am easily manifesting what I want*
> *for the highest good of all.*
> *I am One with the Divine.*
> *I feel that connection at all times.*
> *I emanate that Divinity out into the world*
> *through my feelings of love, joy, bliss,*
> *harmony, peacefulness and gratitude."*

At this point in your transformation, you know that before beginning a busy day you will want to reconnect with these Divine feelings of peace and harmony. Simply go into this centered meditative state and connect with the earth energy and the universal energy and then bring your attention to your third chakra, and activate the Divine in every layer until you can feel it in your body. Now you are ready for your day!

Returning to Divine Feelings Throughout the Day

Just as you did with the first two chakras, anytime you want your body to automatically return to this Divine state, decide on which two fingers to place together for the third chakra. Then once you have gotten in that state where you are feeling the connection and the Oneness with the Divine in the third chakra, and it is flowing through every layer—you are feeling peacefulness, contentment, bliss, and love—when you are there and you are connected with the earth and you are connected with the universe and it is exactly where you want to be, then take those two fingers and put them together and say to yourself:

> *Every time I think Divine peacefulness in my third chakra*
> *and I place these two fingers together,*
> *my body will automatically go into this state.*

And then place those two fingers together.

Throughout the day if you start to lose that connection and feeling, you have a way to return to this state easily. Go within and get centered and say to your body:

> *When I count to three and place these two fingers together,*
> *I'm going to go into that Divine peacefulness in my third chakra.*
> *One, two, three, Divine peacefulness.*

And put those two fingers together.

Remember which fingers they are. Write down the hand and finger you chose for the third chakra so you can commit it to memory.

You are now ready to move on to Chapter 5 and open your ability to love and be loved.

Opening Your Ability to Love and Be Loved

This chapter will show you how to get what you have been searching for your entire life—unconditional love and complete acceptance. For this chakra holds the sweetness and true riches of life ~ loving yourself, loving others, loving life, and most importantly opening to the love of the Divine and receiving pure unconditional love.

It has been said that when someone is on their deathbed, they never think, "I wish I had spent more time at the office working." Instead they think, "I wish I had spent more time loving, more time with those that I love." This chapter will show you how to do just that. First by releasing whatever is in the way of giving and receiving love, and then by opening to access the unlimited supply of love that is always available to you twenty-four seven! For your true Divine nature is love. This chapter will show you the path back to the love that you truly are.

Developing the Divine Characteristics Within

All the chakras and all the layers are your connection to the Divine, and allow you to access your Divinity. When the blocks that keep you from aligning with your true nature are released, here are the Divine qualities available to you in the *seven* layers of the *fourth* chakra:

1. You will love your life and love yourself on all levels. Your love will thrive in healthy, harmonious, positive ways.

2. You will *feel* love for yourself and others, and feel sexually attracted and attractive to your significant other.

3. You will manifest true love for yourself and others easily, effortlessly and enjoyably. You will draw to you healthy, balanced, loving relationships with true partners.

4. You will have unconditional love and acceptance for yourself and others. You will set clear boundaries to honor the highest good for yourself and others. You will know that you deserve a loving relationship with your soul mate.

5. You will communicate love to yourself and others effectively and appropriately easily, effortlessly and enjoyably.

6. You will be truly loving to yourself and others and use your psychic, perception, creative and healing abilities in ways that enhance and contribute to your love of yourself and others.

7. You will have acceptance and love for all people as they pursue the spiritual paths that are right for them, as well as love your own spiritual or religious practices. You will do the spiritual or religious practices that you love, not just because you were told that was what you needed to do.

When you really love yourself and fill yourself up with that love, then you automatically love everyone else. You are no longer looking for love outside yourself, for you know it is already within you. Then you automatically project that love to everyone and everything else.

What Blocks Your Divinity

1. Putting Yourself Last

In this country, unfortunately, we have it backwards. People are taught to love others and put themselves last, yet then you have nothing within to support that love.

The bottom half of the heart chakra is our love and affinity for ourselves; the top half is our love and affinity for others. If you are loving others more than yourself, instead of your heart chakra looking like a whole sphere, it looks like a valentine heart with a great big bulge of love for everybody else and this tiny little wedge for yourself.

When you are putting so much love out there to others, and you don't have the love within to support that output, it will collapse in on top of you and you will feel depleted. Then you will get sick or feel suppressed or stifled because you have no resources left for yourself. In this chapter, you will transform that.

Wendy had a big realization in one of my seminars: "My love for others has always been more important than that for myself. Loving others is not a bad thing, but because it was to the exclusion of myself it created an out-of-balance in my life. I had an epiphany when I realized that I was crushing the love for myself by the love I felt for others. I am now developing ways to learn self-love and demonstrate my love for myself. The statement I created to remind me is "I nurture and nourish myself with unconditional love."

When you have love and acceptance for who you are, then you are able to be loving and accepting of everyone else. On an airplane you are told that if the oxygen mask drops down you need to put your own mask on first, and then you are better able to assist others. It is the same with love; you have to fill yourself up with your own Divinity, which is your oxygen, your life force energy, and honor the Divine within you. Remember you cannot honor in others what you will not honor in yourself. Loving and honoring yourself and knowing that you are the Divine leads you to being able to hold that vision for others.

2. Feeling Unworthy

When we do not know and experience our true worth as an aspect of the Divine, we cannot access the gifts, talents and genius of our Divine Self.

Then we are easily affected by the limited opinions and judgments of others.

Changing Unworthiness to Self-Worth

Betsy, one of my students, reported: "I felt like I was unworthy of a soul mate and I would never find someone who would love me for who I am. I had made bad decisions in the past about those I dated and I was scared of getting hurt or rejected. I was afraid to let anyone get too close to me, so I didn't go to social events. I gained a lot of weight to keep men away from me. My mom always told me that I needed to lose weight to find a partner. And I let my mom's opinion affect my self-worth. As a result, I never really put myself out there.

"When I did allow someone to get close, I always had to have the upper hand. I was so self-conscious that I didn't want to leave the house or meet new people. I felt like I was unattractive, unworthy of love, and that no one would ever be interested in me. I felt like I needed to weight a hundred pounds to have love.

"It was both a life lesson and a perceived payoff. The life lesson was not to allow others' opinions of me to define who I am and what I can or can't do. The perceived payoff was that I wouldn't get hurt if I didn't put myself out there.

"Now I understand that I am the size that I'm supposed to be right now. My soul mate will accept me in any physical form. I don't need to lose weight to make anyone else happy. I need to be happy with myself just the way that I am.

"I am now going to social events and am not scared of getting hurt or rejected. I'm more in tune to who is physically attracted to me and am now talking to those guys if I am also attracted. I feel happier and more confident. I *know* that I am worthy of love. I am ready to love and be loved."

3. Closing Your Heart

Judgments limit your ability to give and receive love. One of the ways you withhold your love from others is by judging them. As you look for what is wrong with another and criticize them, you close your hearts to them. The Divine within you never judges and only sees you as whole. As you learn to see the Divine in the other, you are strengthening it within yourself.

This doesn't mean that you are not aware of any behavior that feels inappropriate to you. Using that awareness, you then set appropriate boundaries that honor the highest in you both.

The biggest way you close your heart to love is by judging yourself as being unworthy, not good enough or unlovable. Then your giving is not coming from love, but lack and is an attempt to gain love.

Unlovable Changed to Radiating Love
Harold, one of my students, said, "I had a belief that I was not lovable enough. The unspoken, unidentified feelings of being unlovable affected all of my adult relationships, both romantic and platonic. Often the result was me giving away some of my power and trying to take care of them instead of myself.

"Initially, I stayed in relationships longer than would have been best for me because I wasn't confident enough to leave or believe I deserved better. I kept myself closed off to relationships. Once I became aware of my tendency to give away my power and not consider myself equal in order to compensate, I saw that I had looked for relationships with people who I felt were better than me or who didn't match my energy. It made me a giver, caretaker, and made me feel that I had to do extra to earn love from people. This was part of my life lesson to love and nurture myself.

"Working with Laurie, I've cleared the energies that were supporting my old beliefs. I am opening myself to romantic relationships, knowing that I deserve it, and that it will be with someone who is my equal. As I learn to love and nurture myself, I am making choices every day to consciously honor and acknowledge myself. Instead of just assuming that no one would be interested in me, either romantically or as a friend, now I know that I have a lot to offer. And I am getting better at recognizing when someone is interested where before I used to be totally clueless and the last one to realize it.

"I feel so much lighter. The more I love and acknowledge myself and acknowledge the Divine in me, the more Divine I feel, and the more Divine energy I radiate out to others."

4. Forgetting You Are Divine

What transforms all feelings of unworthiness and not being loved is connecting with the Divine and remembering that you are the Divine. The Divine *is* love. You cannot fully embrace that Divine love if you are not willing to see it and feel it and own it within yourself.

My student Toby reported, "I had an issue with not feeling worthy or loved. I held back in relationships. I didn't feel people wanted me or that they loved and appreciated me. I missed out on the fullness of many relationships. I felt sad, lonely and closed. I didn't feel good about myself.

"After doing this work with Laurie, I am now open and loving. I feel accepted and I love and feel good about myself. I now know that my Divine self is love."

Feeling the Connection with the Divine Transforms

Catherine, one of my students, shared this story: "My lack of affinity for myself led to not wanting to be around others. Since I didn't have lots of friends, I spent time alone. However, there were less and less things I wanted to do alone, especially in a group setting or going to an event. I felt very uncomfortable in large, noisy groups and I would leave and go off by myself.

"The perceived payoff was I had been waiting for others to recognize me and ask me to play. I was still the little girl who moved so many times in a short period of time that I never learned how to jump in and meet people. Instead, I stayed at the side of the pool just watching.

"Since doing these exercises with Laurie, I now remember my connection to the Divine and everyone. I take a breath and remember. I now am part of an on-going group spiritual retreat and during the sharing time, I am in my place of personal power and I feel very good about myself. I find that when I am remembering and feeling my connection with my Divine unlimited self, all my reluctances fall away and I am a part of that Oneness and love, and I feel so happy and full."

I am often asked: Is all love—such as love for our cat, love for our spouse, love for our children—Divine love? Absolutely.

5. WITHHOLDING SELF-LOVE

If you do not have love flowing, you get sick or depressed. Why? Because if you are not allowing that loving energy to be there for yourself, then you are not doing nurturing things for you and not having resources available to you on the body personality level. Then the unconscious says, "Wait a minute, what about me? I need some attention. I need some nurturing here. And if the only way I'm going to get that is to break down and get sick to force you to pay attention to me, then I'm going to break down and get sick." The way to prevent all of that is to be loving and nurturing and supportive of yourself, so your body does not have to act like a child having a temper tantrum to get your attention.

Many say that cancer is literally dying for love. As mentioned in Chapter 2, when we allow ourselves to receive, endorphins are excreted in our brain that are cancer prohibitants. When we don't allow ourselves to receive, we have less of those endorphins and we are more predisposed to cancer. If you need a big enough reason to allow yourself to receive, how about so you don't have to get cancer.

Receiving Love Heals

You will remember that when I taught my mother's friend the simple process of learning to receive from others, her cancer started disappearing. When somebody asks you if they can do something for you, instead of just saying, "Oh, no, that's okay, I can take care of it myself," learn to say, "Thank you. That would be lovely."

They are not saying you cannot do it yourself. Women especially have the image that in order to not be vulnerable, they have to do everything. They have to take care of it all—first take care of everybody else, and then if they have any left over energy, take care of themselves. When someone asks if they can help you, they are offering to make it easier for you. Even if the first thing out of your mouth is "That's okay, I can take care of it myself," learn to say, "On second thought, I'd love to have you help me with that."

Stephanie realized in one of my seminars that she was creating so much stress trying to take care of everyone else and all of her children that she was like one of those circus acts spinning all the plates in the air—all of her family's plates—and trying to keep them all spinning at the same time! She is now using the exercises in this chapter to take care of herself, so she can better care for her family. Her new mantra for her life is "I will now serve and be served, love and be loved, learn and teach others."

Then allow yourself to receive from you. If you are doing any kind of healing work, hopefully you are doing healing treatments on yourself everyday and not just doing these treatments for everybody else. Although healers' natural tendency is to save this healing energy as if it is in limited quantity for others rather than realizing that the more healing energy you are using on yourself and filling up your own body, mind, spirit and emotions with well being, the better healer you are going to be for others. Healing others or healing ourselves is all an act of love, whether it is self-love or love toward others.

Transforming Depression

Depression is forgetting about loving yourself. There is presently an epidemic of depression and people not loving themselves in this country. When people stop self-love and sink into the lack of it, the depression continues. Not only do they not feel love coming from outside of them, they certainly are not feeling the love coming from within or knowing that they are the Divine and that love is there all the time.

"Poor Me" Changes to Feeling Fine

"As I began working on the fourth chakra," Jason emailed me after my teleseminar, "I became aware that my feelings were very guarded which resulted in a lack of closeness to others, and no passion. The truth is I was alone with not much of a support system and had a 'poor me' attitude.

"These exercises allowed me to open to new possibilities. Now my life is calmer, more centered, and I feel just fine. I learned that loving myself is the foundation, and from there I can radiate that love to all."

The remedy as well as the prevention for depression is getting in touch with the love within and constantly loving yourself, allowing that love to flow through you and into your life. Begin by doing something for yourself that makes you feel nurtured. It can be as simple as taking a bubble bath or taking a walk in nature. It can be reading an incredibly funny book or watching a really funny movie. Laughter is one of the greatest antidotes for depression. You have to be filled up with love to start to recognize the Divine within, so you can activate it.

Recognizing the Divine Within

What are some of the ways you can recognize the Divine within? Look at a precious child. Everybody can look at a newborn and say, "Oh my, that's a miracle. That is such a blessing. What a gift from the universe. What an emanation of God or Goddess." When we were born, we all had that light around us. We all were that light and the people around us knew it. That radiant precious being, soul, spirit that has blessed this planet with our presence is who we truly are.

Look at an eighteen-month old child—they are full of life. They are so alive, they are curious and creative and spontaneous and filled with laughter and happiness and wanting to do and see and be and try everything. How can you not look at a year-and-a-half-year old and not be smiling at the pure joy they are having of just being in that little body and exploring their world? Of course, everything is about "me," and then they get to be two and see everything as "it's mine." They are in their Divine center.

Then what happens? First people start to tell us limiting messages. I learned when I was getting my Masters Degree in Art Therapy that there are different developmental stages that you can see in children's drawings. It's not about people's artistic ability; it's about what they are expressing. For instance, a five-year old draws his or herself huge on the paper—*huge*, it fills up the entire page—because they are the center of their world. It is all about them. They have this great gift of selfhood, this great sense of presence within themselves and they are sure that they know who they are.

Then the world starts chipping away at that precious child—or we let the world start chipping away at us, and limiting messages are said by our parents, such as "No, you can't do that. You shouldn't do that. You have to do this." And the child takes on those limiting messages.

In the beginning, they are just messages from the outside that start to attach themselves to us. Then the problem is most of us internalize it and it becomes our messages to ourselves about what we cannot do or should not do or must not do. I used to have a sign on my office wall that said, "I will not *should* on myself today" until I stopped that.

Who we really are, our true intrinsic nature is that five-year old that feels wondrous, feels like the center of the universe or that eighteen-month old that is curious and spontaneous and can't wait to get up in the morning and explore what the world has to offer them today! We need to go back to peeling off all the rubbish that is not our true Divine nature and return to honoring the core of who we really are, our Divine essence.

6. Looking for Love Outside Yourself

Many have experienced heartbreak, whether in childhood, as a teenager, or in adult romance, and the heart has then become armored. Heartbreak comes from looking for love outside ourselves. Again, if we are all filled up within our heart center with love for our self and Oneness with the Divine and feeling that love flowing from the Divine, not expecting somebody outside to give us that love, then we would not have the feeling that love has been taken away. We would have the inner support of Divine love and love for our self.

Opening to Receive Love

A seminar participant, Elizabeth, said, "I realized I had closed my heart as a protection from being hurt, but what it was really doing was impeding my ability to receive love freely, interrupting the flow of Divine love. My heart was unbalanced, top heavy from too much inappropriate giving without allowing myself to receive. It was limiting and preventing me from experiencing love for myself and others as well as impeding my progress on my spiritual path.

"As a result of this work, my heart has transformed. My fourth chakra is more evenly balanced. I am now open to receiving love and I am more conscious about acknowledging my love for myself."

From Fear to Joy

"My fear of rejection and being hurt by others made me take fewer risks," Patty shared in a seminar. "I was always looking for love and acceptance from others. I looked outside of myself instead of expressing self-love and self-worth. I never felt good enough. I was always searching for someone or something else to fill the emptiness I was feeling inside. When I switched my focus to loving myself, my spiritual development accelerated. In the Divine flow, life is effortless, easy and joyful."

Love Who You Are

Children are born loving who they are. By teaching our little ones to continue to love who they are and not let that slip away from them, they learn that they are enough just the way they are.

Then we really would not have broken hearts. We may miss that person, we may long for their hug or their touch, but we would not be devastated, we would not be crippled, we would not be incapacitated if our source of love is from within, rather than from another.

Healing Heartbreak

If you have allowed yourself to become debilitated by heartbreak and you have armored your heart, how can you make it back to your self and your own original Divine nature? Since children are in the Divine flow, go find the happy pictures of yourself from childhood. Yes, there are lots of unhappy ones too, but they are not the ones to focus on. Find those happy pictures from childhood and make a list of all the things that you were, that you felt, that you knew, that you relished as a young child. What made your heart sing? What made your heart soar? Realize all that is still within you. Then go back to when you were a child and imagine yourself being that child again, and really feeling all that joy and enthusiasm for life. Then dissolve away anything that isn't that.

One of the ways you can do that is by literally seeing those pictures of you loving your life and loving yourself and envision dissolving away anything that looks like cloudiness, dimness, darkness or anything that is not Divine love for yourself. You can turn it into neutralized energy, which can look like static on a TV screen or the silvery sparkly images you see when you press on your eyelids, and send it down to the center of the Earth. Keep just dissolving away the darkness, and giving the Divine love within the opportunity to be activated. It is already there; it is just a matter of clearing away what is not it.

If you are saying, "There were no happy times from childhood," I guarantee you it is just a matter of finding them. It does not mean that there are not those happy memories; there are. The further back in your childhood you go, the more you will see those happy moments. How can I be so certain? *Children are not born with negative mindsets.* Those happy memories may be buried in there really deep, but I guarantee you they are there. If need be, go back to the time you were growing in the womb when you were still connected to the Divine essence that you are.

Even though many may remember the negative messages that their parents said to them while they were inside their mother's womb, that is all part of our lesson and our growth. Basically ninety-five percent of people have drama and trauma in their childhood and we can focus on that or we can decide, "Okay, that was the set-up for my lessons and for my growth, that is what I am here to overcome."

In the 1980s the psychotherapy profession learned that if you just focus on all of the drama and trauma from childhood, you are never going to get beyond it. Instead the focus shifted to: Okay that happened. Nobody's denying that it was scary and traumatic and horrific. Now, what are you going to do?

As an art therapist, that's what I focused on: *Now what are you going to do? What is it that you want to do with the rest of your life?*

Rewriting Your Childhood
You can also go back and rewrite your childhood story. Some brilliant person said, "It's never too late to have a happy childhood." Your brain does not know the difference between you imagining something happening and it happening. Science knows that time is an illusion; that it is really all happening right at this moment. Science also knows at a molecular level, matter does not exist—it is just energy. In others words, it is all just an illusion anyway. Why do lots of us write the scary illusions and nightmares instead of Oneness dreams and wondrous positive illusions? It is all part of our growth process.

You actually can picture yourself having a different childhood. Imagine people coming along to help you and imagine your life being easier. Your brain does not know the different between you rewriting history and living as if the rewrite is the truth and not going back and telling the old victim story.

I encourage you to stop telling those bad tales, especially to yourself. Then envision yourself having a happy childhood. Even write down what a marvelous happy childhood you had with parents that loved you unconditionally and were loving and nurturing and supportive to you.

Remember, the brain does not know the difference between you putting a new childhood in your brain rather than the old one. So you might as well have a new one that you really like!

Building a Foundation of Love Within

You can also rewrite a heartbreaking relationship without focusing on that particular person, unless you are focusing on it ending in a mutually positive, respectful, harmonious and grateful way. Rewrite the painful feelings that you experienced in that particular relationship into a happy relationship and the subconscious will not know the difference. You have now changed the painful programming in your brain to happiness. Do the rewrite in a general way, not focused around that particular person. For example, you can't change it to make the other person fall in love with you again. "You Made Me Love You" is a song, not a reality.

Instead of being attached once again to getting love from that person, what you ideally want to create, whether it is an imaginary image or what we consider reality, is loving *yourself*, being happy within *yourself* and being able to enjoy that happiness and that love with somebody else—not having to have your source of happiness or love be dependent upon anyone or anything outside of you. First feel that source of love inside you, so that loving foundation is in place. Then you simply share it with another.

If the outside love disappears, then we still feel loved and happy and not devastated if something changes outside because we still have that love and affinity for ourselves and the Divine within us.

Finding Love Within

If you are having a hard time finding where that love is within you, imagine yourself holding a puppy or a kitten and *feel* where you feel that within you. Feel how that awakens your love and compassion. Next, see yourself holding a baby, and feel that love and compassion within. Then see that baby as yourself. Feel yourself holding you as a baby and feel that love and compassion for yourself. Finally, love yourself as you would want to be loved, and would have wanted to be loved as that child.

You don't have to go find love anywhere else. You don't have to go shopping to find it. You don't have to find it in someone else. You carry that love with you always and that is the love you want to have for yourself on all levels because you are as precious as that baby or puppy or kitten. *Is that the way you treat yourself every day of your life?*

If you are a woman, please know that when the Divine feminine or the heart and the loving, nurturing aspect of women was devalued and shut down, as well as your own connection to your Divine nature, it didn't ever go away. It may have become dormant, but it is still there. It doesn't matter if you were a female child or a male child, the place to find unconditional love for yourself is within you. Look for it inside.

The Divine Fills The Gap
My student Roxanne emailed me after our classes, "Having someone to love is not crucial to my happiness. I am happy being alone—all me, at one with myself, the Divine and the universe. It is much different than being lonely. I am free and full of Spirit, full of joy. When there is a connection to the Divine, the Divine fills a gap that people do not, for they cannot fill my inner needs or provide me happiness."

What will happen to us—not only in our own life personally, but in the world—as we begin to reconnect with this precious love that flows from the Divine through our heart? We will go back to what the ancient Hawaiians knew was the truth, which was honoring the Divine in everything and everyone, including ourselves. We will not have war, we will not have poverty and we will not have abuse. You can't abuse the Divine or abuse somebody you see as the Divine. We will know the Divine is in everything and everyone, as well as ourselves.

You cannot give what you do not have. The only way you can truly love others is by truly loving yourself first and being filled up with that love. Otherwise you are coming from a state of lack. If you are looking for a relationship, it will be hard to find if you are expecting that person to make you whole. If you come into a relationship feeling empty and expecting that person to fill you up, it will never happen; at the very least, you will attract another like yourself who is also feeling empty expecting the other to fill them up. The best way to find your soul mate is to find yourself. The best way to find somebody to love you is to love yourself.

You have to totally love yourself and know that you deserve that relationship, for your soul mate to come into your life. If you have a depleted bottom half of your heart chakra and want another to fill up that hole in your heart for you, it is going to be challenging to draw somebody to you that wants to fill it. If you are already filled up with you, then you both can have even greater love for each other and for yourself.

7. WITHHOLDING FORGIVENESS

One of the ways we block our own Divinity is by withholding forgiveness—from ourselves and from others. Until we take this final step, we are not free to love or be loved. As someone once said, "Not forgiving another is like drinking poison and expecting it to hurt the other person." We need to forgive people not primarily for their sake, but mostly for our own.

Transforming Difficult Meetings
"I have been noticing how differently I see things," my student Alexis told me. "People in my life that I have had 'issues' with actually look different to me now and my interactions with them have been much more pleasant and productive. I conducted a meeting at work with several participants that could have been very different had I not shifted my energy to a much more joy-filled place. Before the meeting, I cleared my heart chakra. The other night as I left work, I was aware of how beautiful everything looked and how peaceful I felt for the first time in a very long time."

Forgiveness Sets You Free
A student Diane was invited to work with a retreat group of people with HIV. After the retreat, she sent me this letter:

"I worked with several of the people using the ARCH Forgiveness Technique and they were so touched at the information that came through. One man said, 'Where have you been? You could have saved me thousands of dollars and years of therapy!' The deep core issues were revealed in about ten minutes of talk story as I continued the ARCH techniques.

"I then did a group ARCH healing. Some said they had never been so relaxed and another was so happy with how he felt, he hugged me three times in gratitude. He also said that he came to the healing circle with great resistance, and he was so happy he did. I saw such a shift of awareness and love for themselves—they had glowing faces, bright eyes, smiles and peace. It was a beautiful thing! Thank you for teaching these amazing tools."

What Holds These Blocks in Place
Life lessons, perceived payoffs and belief systems about love, affinity, relationship and unworthiness hold these blockages in place.

Regardless of whatever chakra lifetime you are working on, when the energy in any of the *seven* layers of the *fourth* chakra get stuck and are not expressing the Divine, the result is some variation of the list below, depending on your level of growth:

1st layer (the survival level of love) - co-dependent love; fear that if you are not loved by a certain loved one, that you will die or your life will be over; getting your heart broken and fear of surviving without them.

2nd layer (the emotional and sexual aspect of love) - fearing the one you love, and fear of sexual intimacy with someone you love; fear of loving or fear of not loving and not being loved; hating the one you love—it is often said that love and hate are just two sides of the same coin. You have probably felt at one moment or another like hating somebody that you loved.

3rd layer (the will, willpower and manifesting aspect of love) - being a victim in your love relationship or being the persecutor, the dominator in a love relationship; trying to will someone to love you or trying to will yourself to love someone you don't; as well as trying to win someone's love for you by manipulating them and all the forms of manipulation that come with love, such as manipulating people under the auspices of you love them and it is for their highest good.

4th *layer* (the love and affinity aspect of love and affinity) – heartache and heartbreak of separations, divorce, someone leaving that you love or somebody dying that you love; not being loved the way you loved them.

5th *layer* (the communication aspect of love and affinity) - all the unspoken, unfelt forgiveness of yourself and others that you love; not communicating your love for someone or someone not communicating their love for you; communicating your love or somebody else communicating their love in an inappropriate way. For example, abusive things that are said in the belief that it is loving and for somebody's highest good; or things you said to yourself in an abusive way, such as telling yourself how unlovable you are.

6th *layer* (the psychic, perception, creativity and healing aspects of love and affinity) - intuitive fear about loving someone; negative perceptions of love and fear of loving; someone you love criticizing your creativity and you taking that to heart; withholding your healing abilities from yourself or someone you love.

7th *layer* (the spiritual aspect of love and affinity) - not being able to love someone because their spiritual or religious truth is different from yours or not letting yourself love someone because they are a different religion; holding that programming that was told to you by others and hating other religions or spiritual practices that are different from yours; anything that stops you from really loving your religion or honoring others' religion that are right for them.

When the blockages in the fourth chakra are held in place over an extended period of time, they can result in tachycardia or rapid heartbeat, arrhythmia or irregular heartbeat, heart attacks, closed and blocked arteries, breast lumps and breast cancer.

Letting the Blocks Fall Away

PERSONAL ASSESSMENT

The full potential of the fourth chakra is loving unconditionally.

1. *How are you doing unconditionally loving others?* Remember, unconditionally loving doesn't mean not setting clear boundaries. You don't allow a two-year old to place their hand on a hot stove because you love them. It means setting those parameters and still loving them unconditionally. Loving them for who they are—and wanting whatever is for their highest good and for your highest good. How are you doing with setting boundaries? How are you doing with not judging others? How are you doing with forgiving people that have hurt you on a heart level? How are you doing with having a balance between the top half of your heart chakra, which is the love and affinity for others and the bottom half of your heart chakra, which is the love and affinity for yourself?

2. *How are you doing with loving yourself unconditionally?* Transformation happens when you are not only loving others, but truly loving yourself—exactly who you are right now, knowing that you are growing and learning and evolving and will be more conscious tomorrow than you are today. Loving yourself at every moment as well as forgiving yourself.

Know that what you think of as mistakes are not really mistakes, they are just opportunities for growth. It is just part of being in a human body. If you stay sheltered in your own little cocoon, you are not growing and learning and trying new things. And you won't move toward enlightenment as quickly.

What can you do to forgive yourself, to truly forgive yourself, and to stop judging yourself? What can you do to truly love you for exactly who you are?

Identifying All the Ways You Have
Kept Yourself From Being Divine in the Fourth Chakra:

This exercise will show you how your Divine nature is being blocked and what you would like to transform in your *fourth* energy center.

As you answer the following questions, make a list of everything you would like to release and transform:

- Have you ever felt unloved?
- Have you ever felt unlovable?
- Have you ever felt judged by another?
- Have you ever felt your love for another judged?

- Have you ever taken personally what another has said about you?
- Have you ever felt put down by another?
- Have you ever taken another's criticism to heart?
- Have you ever felt that you weren't good enough?

- Have you ever felt hurt on a heart level?
- Have you ever felt devastated when somebody died that you loved?
- Have you ever felt heartbroken when somebody left that you loved?

- Have you ever left somebody that you loved but you couldn't live with?
- Have you ever felt unloved after being divorced, separated or the breakup of a long-term relationship?
- Have you ever felt unlovable any time your love was not returned?

- Have you ever felt like people would only love you *if* you did x, y and z?
- Have you ever felt that you would only get loved if you did what they wanted you to do?

- Have you ever given conditional love to somebody else?
- Have you ever judged somebody else for any reason?

- Have you ever judged yourself for any reason?
- Have you ever hated yourself?

- Have you ever felt unworthy to be loved?
- Have you ever felt like your heart was broken?
- Have you ever been afraid to love?
- Have you ever been afraid that no one would love you as you are?

- Are you willing to transform all of the old energies that you have pushed into this area of your body that perhaps have caused you physical problems, such as irregular or rapid heart beat or heart attacks or blocked arteries or breast lumps or cancer?

- In the areas that you identified as being limited, what is your perceived payoff? What is the benefit your body personality is getting out of it?
- Are you willing to let it go?

- Has this been a recurring theme in your life? Is it a life lesson?
- What is the lesson you have the opportunity to learn here?

- Are you willing to completely transform this area of your life that is stopping you from giving and receiving love, and allow yourself to honor your own Divine nature?

Releasing the Blocks

Now that you are aware of how you have kept yourself limited, it is time to release everything on your list that you have stuffed in your heart chakra over the years, so that you can begin to transform the nature of your love for yourself and others to manifest your Divine life.

1. Close your eyes and go into a relaxed state.

2. Create a big bubble out in front of you and put everything from your *fourth* chakra list that you no longer want into the bubble.

3.   Release the bubble out to the sun and have it be evaporated.

4.   Now envision what you do want on the levels of love for yourself and others. See and feel that clearly.

5.   Create a powerful statement of transformation that allows you to experience what you want to be, feel and have easily, effortlessly and enjoyably. Repeat this statement to yourself often every day until this is your reality.

Returning to Your Divine Essence

As in previous chapters, you can come back to the way that you were Divinely designed by bringing your attention to activating the Divine within every layer of your fourth chakra and moving out any blockages that stop you from *feeling* your connection with the Divine on all seven of those levels.

Begin by centering yourself. Just as you did before, draw energy up from the earth and the universal energy from the cosmos down to blend within so you can grow to your fullest level of consciousness.

Sit with your feet flat on the floor so you can feel that connection with the earth, your hands uncrossed on your lap, and imagine bringing earth energy up through you, drawing it up through your feet, filling every cell in your body. See it, sense it, feel it or hear it.

Imagine it flooding every cell of your body, down the arms, out the hands. Then fill each chakra center and move it out to the edge of the skin, all the way up to the top of your head and fountain out the top. At the same time, feel your connection with the earth.

Turn your hands palms up on your lap and ask for the highest level of universal energy that you can easily accommodate to gently come down into the crown of your head. Then imagine it going into every chakra center, mixing with the earth energy, spreading out to the edges of the skin, especially the heart chakra, where your own special blend of earth and cosmic energies are created, so it is mixed really well. Next send it down your arms out the fingers, down the legs and out the feet, and any excess universal energy goes down into the center of the earth. Then experience your connection to the earth and to the universe.

Next use your intent to fill the fourth chakra back up with the Divine, which you can see as white or golden energy, feel as warmth, hear as a tone, feel as a particular vibration, or just know that you are filling up every one of those layers. Activate the Divine in every layer, *until you can feel those feelings in your body* establishing:

> *"I am love.*
> *I am easily giving and receiving*
> *unconditional love to myself and others.*
> *I am One with the Divine.*
> *I feel that connection at all times.*
> *I emanate that Divinity out into the world*
> *through my feelings of love, joy, bliss,*
> *harmony, peacefulness and gratitude."*

Before beginning a busy day, remember to reconnect with these Divine feelings of peace and harmony within you. Simply go into this centered meditative state and connect with the earth and universal energy and then bring your attention to your fourth chakra, and activate the Divine in every layer until you can feel it in your body. Now you are ready for your day!

Returning to Divine Feelings Throughout the Day

Just as you did with the first three chakras, anytime you want your body to automatically return to this Divine state, decide on which two fingers to place together for the fourth chakra. Then once you have gotten in that state where you are feeling the connection and the Oneness with the Divine in the fourth chakra, and it is flowing through every layer—you are feeling peacefulness, contentment, bliss, and love—when you are there and you are connected with the earth and with the universe and it is exactly where you want to be, then take those two fingers and put them together and say to yourself:

Every time I think Divine love in my fourth chakra
and I place these two fingers together,
my body will automatically go into this state.

And then place those two fingers together.

Throughout the day if you start to lose that connection and feeling, you have a way to return to this state easily. Go within and get centered and say to your body:

When I count to three and place these two fingers together,
I'm going to go into that Divine love in my fourth chakra.
One, two, three, Divine love.

And put those two fingers together.

Don't forget to remember to write down the hand and finger you chose for the fourth chakra so you can commit it to memory.

You are now ready to move on to Chapter 6 and optimize your communication abilities.

CHAPTER **6**

Optimizing Your Communication Abilities

What if you knew that you could receive communication from the Divine as well as speak the words of the Divine and always have the perfect thing to say in each moment in the most effective appropriate way, would you be interested? Do you think it is even possible? These are the qualities that are simply waiting to be activated within you. In this chapter, you will discover how to do just that.

The *fifth* chakra in the center of your throat is your communication center. We use this center to express the Divine out in the world through various forms of communication—not only verbally, but also through writing, singing, dancing and any form that communicates a message.

In this chakra you can hear the Divine, as well as allow the words of the Divine to flow through you in clear, effective, communication. This is the center for clairaudience or psychically hearing as well as direct voice, which is saying something you did not know you knew until you heard yourself say it.

Twenty-five years ago I was in a metaphysical bookstore and I said to the owner that I was thinking about opening up another center in Parkland, outside of Tacoma, Washington, and I thought it would be a good idea—as I was saying, "I thought it would be a good idea," I had no idea what I was about to say or what words were going to come out of my mouth—"to have a metaphysical bookstore as part of my center and I would be interested in talking to them about having a branch of their bookstore there."

Now, those were not my thoughts. Even as I was saying the words, I was really curious about what was coming out. Direct voice is being able to step aside and just let the Divine speak through you.

Developing the Divine Characteristics Within

Remember, all the chakras and all the layers are your connection to the Divine. When the blocks that keep you from aligning with your true essence are released, here are the Divine qualities available to you in the *seven* layers of the *fifth* chakra:

1. You will be in the Divine flow and easily ask for your survival needs to be met, so that you thrive. You will say loving things out loud to yourself and others about your body and your life.

2. You will communicate your emotions and your sensual desires effortlessly, always finding the best avenue, words and non-verbal form of expression.

3. You will communicate your desires and verbally state what you want to create, as well as set clear boundaries, with ease and grace.

4. You will have a Divine flow of easily, effortlessly and enjoyably communicating your love for yourself and your love for others.

5. You will easily communicate in all ways—verbally as well as nonverbally.

6. You will use your clairaudience (your clear hearing) or your direct voice (saying something you did not know you knew until you said it) effortlessly. You will also express your creativity in all the many forms, such as writing, dance, art, comedy, performance, directing,

photography. You will appropriately and effectively express your perception of things as well as your healing gifts, knowing that your words are very powerful healing gifts and with just a few words you can make someone feel so much better.

7. You will easily have clear communication with Spirit, with the Divine Source, in whatever form you choose.

Utilizing These Gifts

This chakra includes all forms of communication. It can be sign language, artistic creations that have a message or hearing messages from the Divine that are to be passed on, such as hearing, "Tell your parents that they need to pay attention as they are driving home tonight."

If somebody actually gave us a letter and said, "Next time you see your parents, would you give this to them?" Almost everyone would do that. However, when we get a message from the Divine, we do not always decide that it is appropriate to pass it on. Yet if the Divine is speaking to you and saying, "Tell this person!"—maybe because your friend cannot hear it for herself—you are being the receiver and asked to be the broadcaster. That is what we all are; we are just the radio and the Divine is coming through us. Our job is to be the absolute best radio that we can be and to have our channels be as clear as possible so we can broadcast whatever those messages are to others as well as to ourselves.

It is important to honor whatever form Divine guidance comes in for you, and for some people, it is hearing. If you hear the messages, your responsibility is to express them in the best way possible so that they can be heard.

Lets say that you hear that somebody is in danger of being in a serious car accident that night and they need to pay attention. It might not be appropriate to say it in that way because you do not want to illicit and activate their fears, which could create an accident. Instead ask or think to your Divine self: *Give me the best words possible to communicate this message to them.*

Or you can take three deep breaths, center yourself and go into a meditative state and ask the person's Divine self to give you the information that particular person needs to receive right now in the way that they can hear it. Not only are you specifying the specific information that they need right now, but also the form they can hear it in, so the words will be the most meaningful for them. Any message that you receive to pass on to somebody else, ask, "Give me the information in a way that is in the best manner and format to pass on to this person."

For example, when you hear an internal message that a friend is in a very inappropriate relationship for them that will lead to sadness, heartache and heartbreak, how do you communicate that? You know it is probably not going to be welcomed or wanted and perhaps you could lose the friendship.

1. First, step back and ask the source of the inner information if this is their guide trying to get you to give a message to them *or* is it the Divine, that is your super awareness, giving you this information for your own knowledge? The first step is to discern: *Is it a message you are actually meant to tell them? Or is it you receiving the bigger picture?*

Since people choose on a soul level situations in their life to help them move along their path toward higher levels of consciousness, it may be that person has chosen to be in that relationship because they have a lesson that they need to learn there.

For instance, on a soul level I chose to have a stepfather who was inappropriate with me, so I could learn never to abuse my power and never to allow my power to be abused.

Is your friend, who you are getting this information about, creating that situation on an unconscious spiritual level so they can learn to never let their power be abused and learn to cease doing that? Just because you get information about somebody does not mean that it is appropriate for you to pass it on.

First, you have to discern where the source is coming from. Then ask: *Am I to pass on this message?*

2. If you are being asked by the Divine to pass on the message, then the second step is to ask for the absolute best way to communicate that to your friend.

One of the ways that the Divine has guided me to assist people in seeing what is going on in their lives in a way that they can hear it is saying to them: *If this was your best friend,* or *if this was your younger sister or brother* or *if this was your adult child, what would you want for them?* Instead of communicating directly about them, have them look at the expanded picture of how that same situation would affect someone they love.

Lets say I have a friend, Sally, who is in an abusive relationship. And she has a thirty-year old daughter. I could say to Sally, "If this was your daughter Mary, and she was in a relationship like this, what would you want for her? What would you want her to be doing with this relationship?"

It immediately changes the focus, rather than saying directly, "You're in an abusive relationship. You have to get out of it now. It's not doing you any good. I don't like to see you suffer. What the heck are you doing?"

Instead, have them look at it as if this was somebody else that they loved, because people can see it that way very clearly when they cannot see it if they are thinking about it for themselves. Why? Because we are often blinded to our own situation and living in denial.

Say to your friend: *What would you want for your daughter Mary if she were in a relationship like that?* The odds are Sally is going to say, "That would be terrible. I wouldn't want her to allow that to happen." Next you can say: *What changes would you wish Mary to make if she was in that situation?* Sally might reply, "Well, she should think about leaving him and she should think about who she is and that she doesn't deserve that." Then you can say: *You might want to think about making those changes for yourself.*

What Blocks Your Divinity

1. NOT SPEAKING YOUR HIGHEST TRUTH

How many times have we not spoken up, not spoken the truth for whatever reason based on our past programming, and now it has enslaved us and limited us on three zillion different levels. What is it that really keeps us so disempowered? We remain mute when we need to speak up.

From Fear of Speaking Up to Empowerment

My student Suzanne shared in a seminar, "I wasn't speaking my truth. I wouldn't speak my opinion in meetings at work, so I got overlooked. I was afraid of what people would think or that I would be wrong. I felt embarrassed when I spoke up and people disagreed with me. When I had a good idea, I didn't share it. I felt like my opinions weren't valuable. Later, I would tell my boss and she would take credit for the idea.

"I also didn't speak up in social situations and people sometimes forgot that I was there. I was hurt and frustrated that people didn't remember me.

"I didn't say what I needed to say when I got angry. I never let the person know and so the behavior would continue and make me even angrier. I would bottle it up and eventually explode.

"While clearing out the fifth chakra, I realized my perceived payoff was that if I didn't speak up, I wouldn't get noticed and be wrong. I ended up getting ignored, taken advantage of and being invisible.

"Now I am speaking up in meetings and social situations, expressing my opinions, ideas and feelings. I feel empowered. I also feel more engaged, like I'm a part of something. My self-esteem is improving because my ideas are acknowledged and often used at work. They aren't dismissed like I previously assumed. I'm no longer afraid to speak my truth. I don't care if I'm wrong. I'm not embarrassed to speak my mind and I don't let anyone else take credit for my ideas," Suzanne concluded.

People do not vote because they do not trust politicians. Yet they have given their power away and now they feel that they do not have any voice or say. Women in abusive relationships do not speak up because they feel they have no say, and they do not count. As a society, we have lost our voice and we need to speak up.

Young children are the exception. They have the ability to speak the truth before they learn not to. Children two or three years old, by and large, are able to say things without being censored. We are taught to censor and stifle and swallow our words, and as we evolve into higher and higher levels of consciousness, we need to reclaim our voice.

Feeling Unsafe to Feeling Free
"I believe I was persecuted in the past for my beliefs," Henry relayed quietly. "As a result of being judged, I had a fear of communicating the truth. I take a while to communicate because I dwell on things and develop thoughts and concepts. If you ask me something, I am sometimes in a state of not hearing it fully. I came from a family where verbal communication was limited. When I was a young child, I was vivacious and ebullient. The spontaneity was removed over time by other people's beliefs and limitations. I became less than I could have been if I had been allowed to express myself.

"It feels like a multi-life lesson. My belief was it is safer to be quiet because the truth can cause you to suffer and even die. If you do not rile things up, you will not be hurt.

"After releasing the blocks in my fifth chakra, I am now speaking my truth and have more freedom. I now know that I need to be in truth for the sake of my spirit, soul and body. It makes me feel lighter and more joyous. I feel like I can be valued for who I am, not for who others want me to be. I am using my voice in song and positive actions. I feel much more connected to the Divine."

Our job is overcoming old programming that has kept us stifled, and knowing when it is appropriate to speak up and knowing when it is appropriate to set clear boundaries and knowing when it is appropriate to speak the truth, even though people are not going to like having what they don't want to look at pointed out.

In my family, I was known as the person who pointed out the pink elephant in the middle of the living room. Since I could see it, I wondered why are we not talking about this? And my stepfather played a big role in helping me find my voice for my own self-protection.

As a planet, we have to decide to overcome our own insecurities, our own doubts, our own fears, our own suppression and start to defend what is right, what is correct and in balance. The only way that injustices are going to change is if we speak up.

Again, if we are able to tune in to not only *what* needs to be said, but also *how* it can be said with the most impact possible, then that is a beginning because one of the major things that keep people from speaking the truth is they are afraid of the repercussions. Yet everybody knows truth when they hear it. Whether they really want to know it or not, they still recognize truth. When you get truth bumps or goose bumps or have that feeling inside, you know that it is the truth.

Your job is to figure out the best way to communicate that information rather than *not* saying it.

From Being Unseen to Making a Positive Impact

"My communication had been blocked all my life since childhood," Cindy told me. "I was not able to communicate my true feelings because it was a matter of survival. I was afraid to say my truth, so I learned to always acquiesce to others. Even if I knew that what they were saying wasn't exactly accurate, rather than cause waves, I would not disagree. I thought what they felt was more important that what I felt and said. I practiced remaining unseen and unheard.

"After releasing the blocks in my fifth chakra, I now realize that what I say or think has a positive impact. Seeing that has been a major insight."

Finally Speaking Up

Natalie didn't think she had many issues in the fifth chakra because she was always good at speaking her truth. Then her twenty-four-year old daughter got engaged and her ex-husband—who had left when the baby was an infant!—showed up to discuss the wedding and Natalie found herself starting to give in to him, just like she had done twenty-five years ago. After she cleared out the blockages in her fifth chakra she said, "Now I can stand up for myself knowing who I am, even in a situation like that. I realized that I have a powerful tool in this chakra and I am creative and I can express myself exactly the way I want to in a graceful, beautiful way."

Regains Her Voice

One of my students, Juanita, used to be a professional singer. "I haven't been singing professionally or any other way for years and years and years. My voice just seemed to dry up.

"Then while doing the exercises to open up and clear my throat chakra, I saw my body releasing iron restraints from my neck, hands and feet that were all connected by chains. I could actually feel my neck and throat freed up when the restraints came off. And my voice became unstuck and returned. Now I'm singing again after all these years. At the conclusion of my last performance, they were still on their feet cheering when I got back to my seat. Now I know how a rock star must feel!"

Speaking From Your Unlimited Divine Self

When you begin speaking from your unlimited Divine self, it will create transformation. It is going to free you up to have Divine communication available to you to share with the world. There are many people who know more than they are saying—you can see it in their eyes that they have wisdom. Yet, they do not share it.

Expressing Divine Inspiration

Jack told me, "In the past I had a hard time expressing my emotions to others. I held back in conversation. I wasn't able to give them the full story. It made me feel sad that I was not able to say what I needed.

"In doing these exercises, I saw that the perceived payoff was it allowed me to not fully participate so I wouldn't get hurt. As a result of this work, now I am much more expressive and saying what is going on with me. I feel good about myself. And I am allowing my Divine self to inspirationally speak its truth."

When you open to receive this wisdom and this truth, it can be guidance for you, as well as others. The information and knowledge that you receive from the Divine can benefit many people. It is not just for your own amusement and entertainment. It is an opportunity for you to help make this a better world by communicating it.

Stuttering Transforms to Easily Sharing

"I have had a lifetime of stuttering and not speaking up," Craig shared. "There have been times when my speech was very disjointed and that made communication difficult. I was less inclined to participate in more than a one-on-one conversation, and in groups I rarely spoke. I often felt on the edge of things—the wallflower—rather than a full participant. That self-limiting behavior made me feel less than in one more area and certainly not good about myself.

"After doing this work with Laurie, I now see this as a life lesson to learn that I am able to share my perceptions with others and that this is a gift. That I will be able to use this connection to Divine Source and to others is very exciting!

"It has been very helpful to learn about 'direct voice.' It has helped explain what I have done for a long time. I read something and in a day or so I have a conversation with someone and realize the information applies to them and now I allow the Divine wisdom to flow through me and share it.

"Recently at work, this very heartfelt woman had created a life challenge and I had the realization there were several lessons I could share with her. I found a quiet time to share each piece I was led to share with her. She was most grateful and it has benefited her greatly. I am so glad I listened and spoke up.

"I now feel connected and part of a community. I feel so good about myself knowing that I can make a difference in someone's life by stating the truth as I see it. I now realize I bring value to my community!"

There are so many ways you can contribute to others' lives by using your Divine communication. For instance, if you see a child being hit in a playground and you remain mute about that—even though you know that is wrong and you know that somebody needs to go over and say something to that parent who just lost control—if you don't do it, you are going to take that home with you. You are going to think about it over and over and over, "That poor child, I should have said something, I could have said something. Why didn't I say something?" You can beat yourself up about remaining silent *or* you can go over there and say something. Even if it is something to the parent like, "You must be having a really hard day. Do you want me to sit here with your child and you for a moment?" Sometimes that is the best thing to say.

Again tune in and ask: *What is the best way to say something in this particular situation that honors everyone involved?* You want to communicate in a way that honors the child and the parent, if it is a mother that has just lost it with her child. Odds are it is because the stress within her has gotten to the point that she can't take it anymore and she is taking it out on the child. The mother may need your compassion in that moment, rather than your fury. That does not mean that the child doesn't need protecting, so you can say: "You must be having a really hard day. Do you want me to sit here with you and your child while you take a breath?" That may be much more effective than telling her what a bad mother she is. Focus on how you can help the child and help the mom.

Sharing Divine Truth Appropriately
"I have had a lifetime of speaking the truth," Martha shared, "knowing things people did not think I should know and experiencing their negative responses to the way I communicated my information and point of view. When I shared what I knew in ways I now see were very inappropriate, people reacted negatively. I then allowed people's negative responses to

cause me to edit more than was good for me, to dampen or restrict my direct voice and my spiritual gifts so they were more comfortable. I allowed this to stop me from speaking my truth, and went to the other side of the spectrum, avoiding conflict, placing myself second and denying my gifts. It made me quiet and less expressive in certain areas of my life and less communicative with others.

"It was both a life lesson and a perceived payoff. My lesson is about achieving balance in my communication and the perceived payoff was denying my gifts, which would allow me to not do what I came here to do.

"How did it transform? I now feel like I can speak my truth in a way that works for me and others. The more I am true to myself and my gifts, the more Divine I am and the more I shine that out from me."

Finding the Appropriate Words

"In the past, I have never had the appropriate words at the appropriate time," shared Penny. "It was like I had a mental block to expressing knowledge and feelings. Not sharing my thoughts kept me on the sidelines. I missed out on lots of things. It made me feel very unconnected and not able to share what I know with others. My potential was definitely stymied. It felt like a life lesson.

"Doing this work has opened up my throat and freed the blocks. I saw and felt the bands being removed from around my throat in meditation. I am now talking to people I didn't before with surprising results—people listen to me and accept my healing work easily, which in the past always felt risky to speak about. I am proud of myself. What a great feeling!"

Communicating What You Want

Stating your desires *out loud* gives it even more power. Communicate clearly in positive terms:

> *I am now easily, effortlessly and enjoyably manifesting*
> *(whatever is your heart's desire).*

Saying anything out loud gives it more power. Tell yourself on a daily basis how much you love and appreciate yourself on all levels, and what a good job you are doing. Also tell that to the people in your life, especially the children. They need to hear the positive affirmations that you hold for them.

You can always put loving positive affirmations around the house for yourself and your children to communicate your love, such as little sticky notes on the bathroom mirror.

2. CRITICISM AND GOSSIP

It is in the fifth chakra that we verbalize our judgments in the form of criticism. When we judge ourselves or others, we not only close our hearts, we stop our Divine flow. Gossip and criticism are lethal because they disconnect you from the Divine and limit your ability to receive the limitlessness of the Divine.

Often people's tone of voice carries judgment, even if it is not clearly spoken. Our communications reveal our judgments. Instead of speaking from the Divine self, most of what is said in the world is spoken from our limited personality self, seeing what is wrong and criticizing rather than seeing what is good and praising ourselves and others.

Our judgments are taught to us. We are born with very free open Divine spirits in these little bodies. And by age two we have been told "no" so many times that it begins to shut down our connection with our Divinity. There are amazing statistics that show that a child has been told "no" hundreds of times in their first year of life.

Here is a cure for saying "no" to children: If a child is asking, "Can I have a piece of candy?" rather than telling them "no," you can say, "Maybe after dinner or after . . ." Instead of the first thing that comes out of your mouth being negative, you are telling them when that would be appropriate. Or if your child is asking, "Can I have a bike?" you can respond, "Maybe for your birthday." So the answer is coming out in a positive format rather than in a limiting negative one.

Our initial judgments about ourselves are judgments from our parents or teachers or Girl Scout or Boy Scout leaders. As children, by the time we are eight or nine, we have taken that on as the truth about us, which then becomes our judgments of ourselves. And the cycle just continues. Then we are taught to judge others because we were judged. There is such a low self-esteem epidemic in this country that people judge others in an attempt to feel good about themselves. We know that is the opposite way to go about it because in order to feel good about ourselves, we need to acknowledge the Divine within, and then we can see and honor the Divine in everyone else.

Transforming Judgments

How can you transform your own self-criticism or judgments? How can you transform your criticism of others? Follow these steps:

1. When you have criticism of yourself, the first step is to be aware of it.

2. Next ask yourself: *Is this really the truth? In that moment was I doing the best that I could?*

3. Then simply say: *I'll do better next time.* This is a great way to handle self-judgments instead of criticizing yourself.

   I tell my students, "Unless you can walk on water, you probably still have more you can learn. And if you still have more you can learn, it means that you're probably not going to do it perfectly, you're not going to master it all of the time. So as you're learning it, give yourself some slack." Just like when you were learning to walk, you stood up, you took a step, you fell down; you got back up, you took at step, you fell down; you got back up, you took two steps, you fell down, and eventually you figured it out. You did not judge yourself, for little kids do not judge themselves for falling down, they just get back up again. Have the same patience with yourself and belief in yourself that you will do better next time. Instead of going into that old critical pattern, tell yourself: *I'll do better next time.*

4. Then align with your Divinity so you can receive the Divine flow. Bring that Divine energy in and radiate it out.

When you have judgments of others, follow the same four steps above applying it to the other person or persons. First, became aware of your judgment, notice that they are doing the best they know how in that moment. Ask yourself what chakra lifetime they are working on. And with that understanding, tell yourself, "I'll do better next time." Then align once again with your Divinity so you can step back into the unlimited flow of the Divine.

What Holds These Blocks in Place

Life lessons, perceived payoffs and judgments about our intelligence and communication abilities hold these blockages in place.

Regardless of what chakra lifetime you are working on, when the energy in any of the *seven* layers of the *fifth* chakra get stuck and are not expressing the Divine, the result is some variation of the list below, depending on your level of growth:

1ˢᵗ layer (the survival aspect of communication) - not speaking up for yourself in a threatening situation, such as not yelling for help or not telling someone to stop threatening behavior; saying limiting things to others or to yourself about your body or your life, and verbalizing limiting statements to your body.

2ⁿᵈ layer (the emotional and sexual aspect of communication) – not expressing your emotions and your sexual desires: not expressing your emotional issues; or not expressing your sensual desires, either by repressing them in yourself or stopping yourself from expressing them to other people you were attracted to.

3ʳᵈ layer (the will, willpower and manifesting aspect of communication) – not communicating clear boundaries and not expressing what you need or want to manifest: not setting a limit clearly—verbally or non-verbally—

when someone is invading your space; berating yourself for not having enough will or willpower; making limiting statements about not being able to manifest what you want or need.

4ᵗʰ layer (the love and affinity aspect of communication) – not communicating your love for yourself or others: having loving feelings for another and not letting them know; withholding love from yourself by not expressing it to you; verbalizing unloving statements to yourself or others; telling yourself that you do not deserve love or that you are not loveable; or telling somebody else that you do not love them or somebody telling you that they do not love you.

5ᵗʰ layer (the communication aspect of communication) – *not* communicating on any level: When you lied to yourself; when others lied to you; when you put your foot in your mouth; when you wished you had said something that you didn't; when you thought you said the wrong thing; any constriction around easily and effortlessly speaking your truth.

6ᵗʰ layer (the psychic, perception, creativity and healing aspects of communication) - not communicating psychic messages; not expressing your perception of things; not using your creative communication, such as writing, dance, art, singing, acting or directing; or not communicating your healing abilities.

7ᵗʰ layer (the spiritual aspect of communication) - whenever you *would* not or felt you *could* not communicate with God or with Spirit, whether that is the Divine, Great Spirit, I'O, universal consciousness, universal love or whatever you think of as the Source.

Blockages in the fifth chakra can result in throat problems, such as thyroid cancer, goiters, even something as mild as laryngitis, ongoing sore throats, a cough if something you are not saying is trying to be coughed up or a dry mouth and being unable to speak. For example, I was performing a wedding ceremony and the groom immediately got a dry mouth and could not say his vows. Blocks in the fifth chakra can also result in ear problems, such as blocked hearing or deafness.

Letting the Blocks Fall Away

PERSONAL ASSESSMENT

The full potential of the *fifth* chakra is easily, effortlessly and enjoyably receiving information from the Divine and relaying that information in the best way possible so that it is clear and can be heard and understood the most effectively. Ask yourself:

1. How are you doing in general with your communication?

   a. Do you hesitate to speak your truth? Or on the other end of the spectrum, do you have truth turrets?

   b. Since communication is not just verbal, what non-verbal ways do you communicate?

   c. What creative ways do you communicate? Do you communicate through your writing, through dance and through artistic expressions?

   d. Do you use your Divine abilities to communicate through clairaudience (clear hearing) or through direct voice (saying something you did not know you knew until you said it)?

2. What areas of your life do you need to put some energy into so you can communicate more effectively?

   a. Could you improve your verbal or non-verbal communication with a significant other?

   b. How about your children? Is this an area where you could improve your communication skills?

   c. How are you communicating with your parents, if they are still around? Or even if they are not and they are on the other side, when was the last time you said "hello" to them?

    d. How is your communication at your work, at your job?

    e. How is your communication with your friends and family?

  3. How are you doing with communicating to yourself?

    a. Do you tend to live in denial, and not tell yourself the truth? Or do you clearly perceive what is in front of you and communicate your perception on all levels?

    b. How is your communication with your own Divine self?

Remember to say to yourself: "I will do better next time." And you *will*—you have learned and grown, and you *will* be more conscious and aware in that same situation, and you *will* choose differently the next time it occurs.

Identifying All the Ways You Have Kept Yourself From Being Divine in the Fifth Chakra:

This exercise will show you how your Divine nature is being blocked and what you would like to transform in your *fifth* energy center.

As you answer the following questions, make a list of everything you would like to release and transform:

- Have you ever been told, "Children should be seen and not heard?"
- Have you ever been told, "If you can't say something nice, don't say anything at all?"
- Have you ever been told, "You're making a mountain out of a mole hill?"
- Have you ever been told to shut up?

- Have you ever felt nobody was listening to you when you were talking?
- Have you ever tried to get somebody's attention to tell them something important, and they didn't care?
- Have you ever felt unheard?

- Have you ever had someone tell you they didn't love you?
- Have you ever told someone else you didn't love them?
- Have you ever withheld telling someone that you loved them?
- Have you ever said unloving things to yourself?
- Have you ever said unloving things to others?

- Have you ever said something that you wished you hadn't, and it went around and around and around in your head?
- Have you ever thought, "I wish I had said . . .?"
- Have you ever felt "If I had only said . . .?"
- Have you ever thought, "Why didn't I say . . ." and you played that over and over and over again in your mind?
- Have you ever felt "Why couldn't I say . . .?"
- Have you ever felt "How come I didn't say . . .?"
- Have you ever thought, "I should have said . . .?"

- Have you ever had to give an oral report when you were in elementary school and it was totally embarrassing?
- Have you ever felt you said the wrong thing?
- Have you ever felt that you were misunderstood?

- Have you ever felt someone lied to you?
- Have you ever lied to anyone for any reason?
- Have you ever lied to yourself?

- Have you ever felt somebody judged you for not being intelligent enough?
- Have you ever been told that you were dumb or stupid?
- Have you ever judged yourself for not being intelligent enough?

- Have you ever felt you had any learning disabilities?
- Have you ever hid your intellect?

- Have you ever said somebody else's truth, instead of your own?
- Have you ever not spoken your own truth?
- Have you ever felt your communication, or lack of it, caused trouble for you?

- Have you ever gotten a psychic message about someone and you stopped yourself from saying it?
- Have you ever stopped yourself from using your creative flow to communicate?
- Have you ever not communicated your healing abilities?

- Have you ever felt you *could* not communicate with the Divine?
- Have you ever felt you *would* not communicate with the Divine?

- Are you willing to transform all of the old energies that you have pushed into this area of your body that perhaps have caused you throat problems such as dry mouth, ongoing sore throats, coughing, laryngitis, goiters, thyroid cancer or ear problems such as blocked hearing or deafness?

- In the areas that you identified as being limited, what is your perceived payoff? What is the benefit your body personality is getting out of it?
- Are you willing to let it go?

- Has this been a recurring theme in your life? Is it a life lesson?
- What is the lesson you have the opportunity to learn here?

- Are you willing to completely transform this area of your life that is stopping you from communicating appropriately and effectively with ease and grace, and allow yourself to honor your own Divine nature?

Releasing the Blocks

Now that you are aware of how you have kept yourself limited, it is time to release everything on your list that you have stuffed in your throat chakra over the years, so that you can begin to transform the nature of your communication to manifest your Divine life.

1. Close your eyes and go into a relaxed state.

2. Create a big bubble out in front of you and put everything from your *fifth* chakra list that you no longer want into the bubble.

3. Release the bubble out to the sun and have it evaporate.

4. Now envision what you do want on the levels of communication. See and feel that clearly.

5. Create a powerful statement of transformation that allows you to experience what you want to be, feel and have easily, effortlessly and enjoyably. Repeat this statement to yourself often every day until this is your reality.

Returning to Your Divine Essence

As you have now learned, you can come back to the way that you were Divinely designed by bringing your attention to activating the Divine within every layer of your fifth chakra and moving out any blockages that stop you from *feeling* your connection with the Divine on all seven of those levels.

Begin by centering yourself. Draw energy up from the earth and the universal energy from the cosmos down to blend within so you can grow to your fullest level of consciousness.

Sit with your feet flat on the floor so you can feel that connection with the earth, your hands uncrossed on your lap, and imagine bringing that earth energy up through you, drawing it up through your feet, filling every cell in your body. See it, sense it, feel it or hear it.

Imagine it flooding every cell of your body, down the arms, out the hands. Then fill each chakra center and move it out to the edge of the skin, all the way up to the top of your head and fountain out the top. At the same time, feel your connection with the earth.

Turn your hands palms up on your lap and ask for the highest level of universal energy that you can easily accommodate to gently come down into the crown of your head. Then imagine it going into every chakra center, mixing with the earth energy, spreading out to the edges of the skin, especially the heart chakra, where your own special blend of earth and cosmic energies are created, so it is mixed really well. Next send it down your arms out the fingers, down the legs and out the feet, and any excess universal energy goes down into the center of the earth. Then experience your connection to the earth and to the universe.

Next use your intent to fill the fifth chakra back up with the Divine, which you can see as white, as golden energy, feel as warmth, hear as a tone, feel it as a particular vibration, or you can just know that you are filling up every one of those layers. Activate the Divine in every layer, *until you can feel those feelings in your body* establishing:

> *"I am easily receiving information from the Divine*
> *and communicating that information*
> *effectively and appropriately.*
> *I am One with the Divine.*
> *I feel that connection at all times.*
> *I emanate that Divinity out into the world*
> *through my feelings of love, joy, bliss,*
> *harmony, peacefulness and gratitude."*

I recommend that before beginning a busy day, remember to reconnect with these Divine feelings of peace and harmony within you. Simply go into this centered meditative state and connect with the earth energy and the universal energy and then bring your attention to your fifth chakra, and activate the Divine in every layer until you can feel it in your body. Now you are ready for your day!

Returning to Divine Feelings Throughout the Day

Just as you did with the first four chakras, anytime you want your body to automatically return to this Divine state, decide on which two fingers to place together for the fifth chakra. Then once you have gotten in that state where you are feeling the connection and the Oneness with the Divine in the fifth chakra, and it is flowing through every layer—you are feeling peacefulness, contentment, bliss, and love—when you are there and you are connected with the earth and you are connected with the universe and it is exactly where you want to be, then take those two fingers and put them together and say to yourself:

> *Every time I think Divine harmony in my fifth chakra*
> *and I place these two fingers together,*
> *my body will automatically go into this state.*

And then place those two fingers together.

Throughout the day if you start to lose that connection and feeling, you have a way to return to this state easily. Go within and get centered and say to your body:

> *When I count to three and place these two fingers together,*
> *I'm going to go into Divine harmony in my fifth chakra.*
> *One, two, three, Divine harmony.*

And put those two fingers together.

Don't forget to remember to write down the hand and finger you chose for the fifth chakra so you can commit it to memory.

You are now ready to move on to Chapter 7 and uncap your psychic, perception, creative and healing abilities.

Uncapping Your Psychic, Perception, Creativity & Healing Abilities

What if you knew that you were unlimited in your ability to have clear, accurate perception and you could act on that clarity to make wise choices and lead a happy life? What if you knew that you were unlimited in your ability to utilize your intuition, your psychic ability, your sixth sense, and to trust it implicitly to guide you to always be in the right place at the right time as well as take care of you in all situations? What if you knew that you were unlimited in your ability to utilize your creativity in any form that you choose, such as art, dance, music or writing? What if you knew that you were unlimited in your ability to use your inherent healing abilities to heal yourself and others? Imagine how that would transform your life! This chapter will show you how to access these Divine gifts.

The sixth chakra is your center for your psychic gifts (clairvoyance or inner seeing), perception of things (clear vision), creativity and healing abilities. All of these capacities are contained in one energy center. This is enormous! *Being able to use your intuition and the Divine guidance coming through your intuition to help you navigate through the world is priceless!*

Developing the Divine Characteristics Within

When the blocks that keep you from aligning with your truest self are released, here are the Divine qualities available to you in the *seven* layers of the *sixth* chakra:

1. You will use your psychic ability, perception of things, creativity and healing abilities to help you survive easily, effortlessly and enjoyably.

2. You will use your psychic, perception, creative and healing abilities to easily perceive your own and other people's emotions and sexual feelings. You will know intuitively when someone is sexually attracted to you, for example, or have loving feelings for you.

3. You will effortlessly manifest your psychic, perception, creative and healing abilities.

4. You will lovingly use, and love using, your psychic, perception, creative and healing abilities.

5. You will communicate your psychic, perception, creative and healing abilities effortlessly.

6. You will truly open and use your psychic talents, clear perception, creative gifts and healing abilities with ease and joy in *all* situations.

7. You will receive psychic messages, have clear perception of things, and use your creativity and your healing abilities from the Divine with grace, bringing them forth in this lifetime in a way that serves the Divine and leads you forward in the spiritual flow.

This chakra truly gives you the opportunity to express the Divine in a multitude of ways.

What Blocks Your Divinity

1. Dormant Psychic Abilities

In prehistoric times people had to rely on their sixth sense in order to survive. They had to know which direction to head for water and what berries were edible and what was poisonous. They had to know who their friends were and who their enemies were. And that is how they survived.

Then along comes modern technology and now we just go to the sink to find our water, which we have realized may not be the best for us, so we have to use filters or buy bottled purified water. We trust that the food at the grocery stores is edible and now we have genetically altered food, which is no longer healthy wholesome food and does not even have to be labeled as such. We believe the police and the politicians are going to protect us from the bad guys and then corruption disclosures reveal that they *were* the bad guys. We go to the doctor and we trust they are going to give us a magic penicillin pill that it is going to heal everything and now there are super bugs that are immune to the antibiotics.

Obviously, just trusting that somebody else is going to take care of all of those survival areas without us using our innate abilities to take responsibility for our own lives is not the wisest way to go. Look what has happened when we cut ourselves off from our sixth sense and relied solely on things outside of us!

The really good news is that if you have not been using your intuition, it has not gone away. It has just become dormant like a muscle that has atrophied because of lack of use. It only takes two basic things to open it up again.

First is the willingness or the desire to use it. It is one of your major senses. It is no different from your other five, except that it has probably become dormant somewhere along the line. Trust it. The more you trust your intuition and take action using it, the stronger it becomes.

Second is to act on it. A good example of using intuition to avert disaster is Joseph from the Bible. In the Old Testament Joseph, who was a prophet and had visions through his dreams, had premonition dreams in which he was shown that it was going to be necessary to gather the wheat and store it for the next year. He told the pharaoh who acted on those visions and ensured that the wheat was stored. Because Joseph used his intuition, his sixth sense, through his dreams to predict what was going to happen, he saved Egypt from starvation and was hailed as a hero. Joseph's psychic abilities literally saved the population of Egypt.

Act on Warning Signals

Oprah Winfrey had three women guests on her show who all had horrific experiences. She asked them, "Did you know before it got really dangerous that something was wrong?" All three said, "Yes." When your intuition alerts you with a warning signal, pay attention and take action to get out of there.

Trust Your Intuition

Intuition manifests as clairvoyance in the sixth chakra. Using and following your intuition strengthens this important ability. The most successful people on the planet, such as CEOs of major corporations, use their intuition and score very highly on ESP (extra sensory perception) tests. They are successful not because that is the only sense they use, but because it is one of them. We have left brains and right brains for a reason. Our left brain allows us to access our logical, rational, linear thinking. And we access our creative, intuitive, psychic and healing abilities through our right brain. We have both hemispheres of the brain to use them together in harmony and balance with one another.

When many people start on a metaphysical or spiritual path, they think they need a lobotomy on their left brains. That is not the way we were designed. We are meant to have logic, reason and rational thinking to use it in conjunction with our intuition and higher levels of consciousness, creativity and healing abilities.

It is not logical to get rid of the part of ourselves that scrutinizes things, yet it is also important to be open to the bigger picture. When the skeptic in you arises, you can say, "Oh, that's just my doubting Thomas that's coming up here and I'm going to ask it to step aside for a little bit longer. It was great that it stepped aside for a minute, and now I'm going to ask it to be two minutes or five minutes or whatever I need here." Just stay out of your skeptical mind a little bit longer. Repetition is what helps our body personalities make changes. It may be for only two minutes the first time. The next time it may be five, and then it may be eight, until you are using both sides of your brain and all of your senses in balance.

If you are not using your sixth sense along with the other five, you are not playing with a full deck of cards. You are not using all the information that you have access to, like deciding to put a blindfold on when you were born and not using that sense, even though you could. You are missing out on all this information that is readily available to you that would help you navigate in the world. If you cut your sixth sense off, you are cutting yourself off from a form of receiving input that could make your life much, much easier.

You have probably had an experience of using your intuition, whether it is the phone ringing and you knowing who it is *or* you thinking about somebody and you run into them that day *or* you have a dream about somebody you have not thought about for years and you hear from them the next day. You have had experiences for which there is no other explanation, other than your intuition.

Claiming Intuitive Gifts
Tammy was not aware of how intuitive or psychic she was. After her mother passed away, she started receiving internal messages that she felt were coming from her mom. Since Tammy was not aware that she had the ability to do that, she decided to test if these communications were indeed coming from her deceased mother by asking for a sign.

While sitting in a park she said, "Okay, if this is my deceased mother who is trying to communicate with me, I want a bird to land at my feet and walk around in a circle three times." She was amazed when a bird landed at her feet and walked around in a circle three times. She really could not believe this had just happened, so she asked for another sign. Now she said, "If this is my deceased mother talking to me, I want a dog to come jump in my lap." Sure enough, a dog came and jumped in her lap!

Tammy decided to claim her intuitive abilities by affirming, "I fully utilize my intuitive powers in a way that is confident, peaceful and accurate."

Psychic Powers of Animals

Science has established that large lizards like iguanas use their pineal gland as psychic radar. This small gland in the very center of the head looks a little like an upside down pine cone. Iguanas use this gland to send out energy to sense whether there is a bug above them that they cannot see, since their eyes are on the side of their head. They then use their intuition from this energy to tune into that bug, sight unseen with their physical eyes, and then their tongue comes out and grabs that bug and pulls it down into their mouth.

The interesting thing is that science has not yet made the leap to deciding that the pineal gland in humans is also our psychic radar. We all have a pineal gland, but science has not established its purpose. My ex-husband's medical books said that they thought the pineal gland might be the seat of the soul. What I find surprising is they do testing on rats to see if foods or medicines are going to be beneficial to people, but they have not yet made the connection that if the pineal gland is being used as a psychic radar device in animals, that it might also be its purpose in people.

My guess is the pineal gland is where our psychic radar and our sixth sense originate. Many people already experience their intuition in the very center of their head—which is the pineal gland.

Learning to Use My Full Psychic Abilities

When I was twenty-two, I was taking an advanced class to deepen my psychic abilities. In one particular session, I was surprised when my teacher instructed me to read the energy bodies of the other students in the class—something I was already teaching my beginning psychic students to do. Feeling a bit grouchy by this assignment, I nonetheless did it. As I was sitting there in an eyes-closed meditation internally looking at the energy body of a woman who was doing acupressure on another woman, I'm thinking, "What did I pay all this money for? Why am I told to do something that I'm teaching others to do?"

Suddenly I see her skeleton—I was shocked! It looked just like a moving x-ray, and then I see that her right hip looks like it had been pulled out of the socket and it did not grow back right. Now how I knew what that looked like compared to what a normal hip looked like, I did not know. Since I had dyslexia for so many years, I never studied anatomy and physiology or anything.

Then just when I got used to seeing the skeleton, it shifted just like a slide projector and I saw all of her main organs. Next I was able to see the lymph nodes underneath her right arm were swollen and those underneath her left arm looked normal. Again, how I knew it was normal and what was swollen, I do not know. Then it shifted again and I saw her circulation, which looked like it was slower in her extremities. Now again, how I knew this is anybody's guess. Finally it shifted a last time and I saw her nervous system and that looked fine to me.

I wondered if I could do it with anybody else. With my eyes still closed, I looked around the room to find another energy body, and I saw organs, and with somebody else I saw their skeleton. Then I heard this voice—neither loud nor soft, male nor female—that said, "This is what you're meant to do with your psychic abilities, and your specialty is going to be working with doctors when they are unable to diagnose their patients. You'll always get what is going on and what is healthy and what is disease, but it would be beneficial if you studied anatomy and physiology so you could speak to the physicians in their language."

When everybody came out of the meditation, I asked the woman who was doing acupressure about what I had seen. She confirmed that yes, she was a dancer and her leg had been pulled out of the socket and had not grown back correctly, and underneath one arm her lymph nodes felt swollen and hurt and tender and underneath the other arm felt fine. She also confirmed that she had cold hands and feet and poor circulation, and her nervous system was fine.

Just two weeks before that through a psychic experience I had gotten over my dyslexia. I was now being told that was because it was time for me to study anatomy and physiology.

Then that became my specialty fifteen years before Caroline Myss coined the phrase "medical intuition." I just called them body readings. All kinds of amazing things occurred.

For example, a man came to see me who was coughing up blood. He had been to the doctor and they wanted to do thousands of dollars worth of tests to find out why he was coughing up blood. Without any insurance or any savings, he could not afford the tests. When he came for a reading, I was not told what was wrong or anything about his work or his life.

The guidance flowing through me said that he was breathing some sort of dust and that it was irritating his lungs and that he was around this dust all the time and that when he was there, he needed to wear one of those gauze masks so he would not breath it in. When I told him this, he started laughing and said that he was a sculptor and he sculpted these tiny little wooden animals. He said that right before he started coughing up blood, he had been preparing for a show of his work and had been sculpting day and night to finish all the pieces. And he never wore a mask. After that he wore a gauze mask and he never had the problem again.

That is how it started, which got my attention. Not only would I be shown what was wrong, I also would be given the remedy. For instance, this woman came in for something, I don't remember what and my intuitive Source told her that she needed to take takakachiquita tea. As those words were coming out of my mouth part of me thought, "That sounds like a brand of banana! Does this stuff even exist?" It just sounded really out there. Yet she wrote it down and asked me later where she could get it. I was embarrassed because it just sounded made up to me. I said, "Well, you could try the health food store." She called me back later to tell me that the health food store had it and it was for exactly her problem.

In the beginning, I was just so amazed that these things came through that obviously I had no awareness of—it was definitely beyond me. Little by little, as I began to trust the information that flowed through me, I started to have people come to me whose lives were saved by this information.

For example, a retired brigadier general was dying and because he was a brigadier general they had flown in specialists from all over the country to try and figure out what was wrong with him and save his life. When they could not figure it out, his daughter who was a psychiatrist running a mental facility and taking my classes said, "You have to see my teacher. She can do a reading for you and find out what's the matter." Of course, he thought that was rubbish.

When he proceeded to get progressively worse, finally he agreed that he would do it, but he specified that I had to come and see him. My student said, "She's not going to travel down to see you. She doesn't make house calls. You're just like everybody else. You have to go up and see her."

Eventually he did come and see me. He was in a wheel chair and very grouchy. In readings some people are very positive and encouraging and give you way too much information. Then there is the other type that just sits there and says nothing. Of course, he was the say nothing type.

The Source through me told him all these things he knew he had. Next he was told he had this rare virus that he had gotten when he was in a jungle twenty years before while on active military duty, which had been dormant, then reactivated and now it was very active in his body. He was told to go to a naturopathic physician that I worked with. In the state of Washington naturopathic physicians are considered the same as regular physicians and can take insurance. To his credit, he went to the naturopathic physician who treated him for the virus and he had a full recovery. Needless to say, he became a true believer.

Another woman who was dying a very slow death came to see me. For eight years her doctors told her she was dying, but they could not figure out the cause. It just got progressively worse and worse until she was totally incapacitated and could not leave her apartment. Finally she was brought in, again in a wheel chair, for a body reading. The Source through me said that she was allergic to the formaldehyde in the pressboard in her apartment. It was like a toxic poison to her and was literally killing her. She was given specific directions to turn the thermostat up to eighty-three degrees, move out of her home for three days and when she came back in, the apartment would no longer be harmful to her and she would then be fine. This woman followed the instructions to the letter and that is exactly what happened—she completely regained her health!

Then I started doing readings on surgeons who wanted to know if they needed to have surgery or not. It was a very surreal experience. One of the persons I read back then was the doctor that saw the patients of a famous holistic cardiologist while he was on the road. She was so amazed with the results of the reading that she required her patients to get readings from me either over the phone or in person before she would treat them. They had to listen to the tape, write down exactly what the Source through me said their condition was and the treatment plan, which she then followed. With that kind of strong recommendation from a respected doctor, I was soon booked solid for over a year in advance. All of the doctors, every single one of them, said that the Source through me had a hundred percent accuracy rate.

I also worked with a chiropractor who I sent my clients to when spinal adjustments were needed. The Source through me would say exactly which vertebrae were out of alignment. They would next go to see her and she would do a full body x-ray of the entire spine. It always showed exactly the same vertebras that were out—every single time. Then she just stopped giving my referrals x-rays because why bother when the Divine Source had already identified the misalignments!

Because of my reputation, the people that called for an appointment were those that nobody had been able to diagnose what was going on and they were dying. I was always booked over a year in advance, so when people called me, maybe I was able to squeeze them in for a phone reading at six or seven o'clock in the morning. However, if I could only squeeze one person in, who was I going to choose? Which dying person was I going to choose? I didn't like that choice. So I just stopped altogether. I announced a year before that I would not be doing body readings the following year. I finished doing the rest of the year and then that was it.

I next returned to teaching full time, moving from doing it *for* people to teaching people how to do it for *themselves*. I wanted to empower others to make their own decisions whether they were going to live or die, as well as learn how to heal themselves. I still teach Medical Intuition as well as I'O and ARCH Healing classes to this day. I also teach students to open up their psychic gifts to be able to help others.

From Fear to Compassion, Self-love and Assurance
Caroline wrote to me after a teleseminar: "I have been plagued all my life with fear of persecution for knowing what I know. Fear of the consequences, real or imagined, of knowing unpleasant truths and trying to cope with them have been a constant in my life. I had some gifts as a child and young adult, which I put aside because the environment did not support them. This was a life lesson from many lives. The perceived payoff was the illusion of feeling safe. I realized this was keeping me from moving forward.

"After clearing out my sixth chakra, I now enjoy working with my Divine guidance and healing. I feel fully alive, connected to the Divine. I can feel myself transforming more each day. Knowing more creates more compassion, self-love and assurance. I am more in the flow of the universe doing what I was intended to do."

Honoring the Gift of Intuition
"I hadn't been open to receiving and accepting my gifts," Rachel told me after a seminar. "I knew that I was different as a young child and it always made me feel weird. My mom was always chastising me for my 'vivid imagination.' I was only praised for my linear thinking. My parents found

out that I was intelligent at a young age and pushed me to excel intellectually. They didn't encourage my creative thinking or pursuit of art or music. I ended up keeping my creative ideas to myself and living in my head.

"I had a difficult time accepting my spiritual gifts. I wanted to listen to my intuition, but at the same time I would think things to death and didn't always go with my gut. I got angry and upset when my gut was right and my linear thinking was wrong. Then I would beat myself up for not following my intuition. And I would always ask others for confirmation of what I was thinking of doing instead of listening to my higher self.

"The perceived payoff was if I didn't accept my gifts I'd be normal like the rest of the kids and the rest of my family. Instead, I didn't shine the way I needed to. I also liked the praise I received from my parents, teachers and friends for being the smart kid in class.

"I now accept that I'm gifted with sight. I now take the time to listen to my intuition and I'm following my gut. I feel good knowing that I have a very special gift and purpose in life."

Fear Transformed to Understanding
Joyce sent me this email during one of my teleseminars: "I always assumed that my hesitance in allowing my insights to be known stems from lifetimes of fear when I was killed for what I saw.

"After clearing my sixth chakra, I now have a much greater understanding of the things I perceive and why. Instead of my psychic gifts being associated with fear, I now see the great benefit to me and others. I now see this as a great healing and teaching tool. What a transformation!"

Removing the Shield to Seeing Clearly
Dawn reported, "I had such resistance to recognizing, acknowledging and using my psychic and spiritual gifts. As a small child, I placed a film over my sixth chakra because I was scared by the extent to which I could see. So I haven't used my intuition in all the areas of my life that I could. If I had

been more open and used my intuition, my life would have been much less stressful and more in the Divine flow.

"Having the shield made me feel like I wasn't psychic at all. The result was I felt less than worthy or on a lower level than the other people in the spiritual classes I was taking. I never really felt like I had the skills or gifts to be equal to the others.

"I feel like it's a life lesson to learn to embrace and fully use my gifts. The perceived payoff was that I didn't have to be afraid of my gifts if I wasn't aware of them.

"After I removed the shield I began having a series of really vivid dreams, where I could see people and situations very clearly. The more I acknowledge myself and my gifts, the more I am living in the Divine flow, and the more I can help others."

2. LACK OF CLEAR PERCEPTION

The sixth chakra also allows us to have clarity in our perception of things. We sometimes are very good at putting clouds over our eyes and being in denial and not wanting to see the truth. As Jesus said, "The truth will set you free." Using the Divine to see the truth absolutely sets us free. What an incredible gift to see an expanded vision of the world rather than a narrow limiting view. From the perspective of that larger vision, we are able to see that people are by and large doing the best they can, instead of seeing them as bad and wrong from a limited point of view. This energy center gives everyone an opportunity to have clearer vision.

What blocks your perception of being able to see things clearly? Fear. Fear that you or others cannot handle it. Probably a more accurate statement is you just do not want to deal with it. For example, if you are in a relationship with someone and intuitively know that they are cheating on you and you don't want to deal with it. You're afraid to confront it and really look at it. Or afraid that you're going to lose that person or you've already lost them.

How do you transform that?

First, realize that you may be doing that. Awareness is always the first step.

Then, literally decide to create a bubble out in front of your head and ask that any energy that is blocking your clear perception go into the bubble. Envision that you are blowing into the bubble and the bubble is like a magnet sucking in all of the energy that stops you from seeing the truth. See the bubble dissolving this limiting energy into neutralized energy and send it down to the center of the earth.

Next, imagine standing in your sixth chakra and giving yourself permission to see what is really going on.

How can you shift from seeing things from the view of the personality self to the unlimited perception of the Divine self that includes the whole?

First, begin by pulling yourself back to expand your perspective. Start with looking at your family from that expanded point of view. Instead of looking at how everybody else's actions in the family affect you, imagine being an outsider and looking down at your family interaction or lack of it and pretend that it is a different family. What do you see? What are all the components? What is the bigger picture of the interaction that is happening there?

Next, pull yourself back further and look at what is happening in your job, your career. What is the dynamic with everybody? How is everybody being affected by everybody else's actions?

Then, do the same with your community, with your state, your country and the world.

Seeing from the Divine Perspective
Know that everyone perceives things through their own eyes. Did you know that every single person sees a different rainbow, even when they think they are looking at the same rainbow? Because the light reflecting off the water

droplets is at a different angle—even if you are standing just a fraction of an inch away from somebody—you are still seeing a different rainbow. Yet we all think it is the same. Therefore, we are all seeing a slightly different perception of the world, literally. We may all be one, but we are viewing different facets of it.

For instance, you could look at a cup and swear it does not have a handle because you are only looking at one side of it. Another person looking on the other side of it can say, "Well obviously it does have a handle" because they are seeing the side that has the handle. Who is right? Both people. We see it from the perception of our own subjective point of view.

When we see it from the Divine perspective, we realize that everyone sees the rainbow at a slightly different angle and we acknowledge that. Seeing things from the Divine perspective is the only way we can really solve problems that will create harmony and peace.

3. Stifled Creativity

This wonderful chakra also carries our creative abilities. People like Beethoven, Bach and Leonardo DaVinci were incredible expressions of the Divine through their creative art of music and painting. When we look at Michelangelo's "David," we can feel the presence of the Divine that came through him, as he was chipping away what was not David.

What blocks our creativity? When I was five, I was coloring Santa Claus purple because I loved Santa Claus and my favorite color was purple. So what other color would I possibly be coloring Santa Claus? The teacher came over and scolded me, "Santa Claus isn't supposed to be purple!" Now fortunately I had enough self-esteem at five to think she was out of her mind. However, you can see that that kind of message from an authority figure can really dampen a child's ability to express him or her self in any creative form. Whether they get the message that their drawing does not look like the cow it is supposed to be, it just looks like scribble or they are told that they are not singing correctly, it affects the child's self-esteem and their ability to create.

When I was in junior high I was singing a song that I really enjoyed and my mother yelled at me, "Can't you sing on key?" It took me many years to start singing in public again, and when I did, I realized that whatever was going on with my mother in that moment she did not mean to stop me from ever singing again. She had very sensitive hearing and could hear if the notes were on key or not, and it was bothering her that I was not on key. Now I sing in my classes a lot. When it gets too serious, I sing some silly related song to lighten things up and we all laugh. It now is even funnier when it is not on key.

Maybe you got messages in your youth that stopped you from expressing yourself creatively in many ways. But as an adult you can decide to open up your creativity. You do not have to stay in that limiting stuck spot anymore. Let the Divine flow through you. The more you enjoy it and the more joyfully you express yourself, the more the Divine is able to come through—even if it is off key.

You can envision that flow of Divine energy coming through you, coming in through your crown, into your sixth chakra and having that ripple out through all the layers of your sixth chakra and going out in the world. If you are about to paint a masterpiece, you can envision this Divine energy going all the way though your fifth chakra, then into your heart, opening up your heart, coming down your arms and out your hands. Or into your fingers and onto the keyboard of the computer if you are about to write. If you are about to sing, you can see it going into your fifth chakra and radiating out.

Creativity Now Flowing
One of my seminar students, Brad, told me, "I was not expressing my creativity. I wasn't doing all the creative things I could. I would not jump on creative activities. The perceived payoff was not getting too out there.

"Now I am doing creative projects. I feel more flowing and creative. I feel good about myself. I now know my Divine self is creation creating all the time!"

4. THWARTED HEALING ABILITIES

This chakra also contains the opportunity to bring in healing energies through the Divine. When Jesus brought the dead back to life, he was using Divine healing abilities. Remember, Jesus said, "You will do all that I have done and even greater things."

I believe that part of what Jesus did was see the Divine in people. He saw their wholeness and saw them as perfect, and then brought that Divine frequency through him into them to activate their wholeness. This is what true healers do.

We would not have been given that gift of healing if we were not meant to use it. Start by using it on yourself. Many healers forget to use it on themselves. They are very good at being led to use it on others, but you cannot be a great healer for others if you are not healing yourself too. You do not have to be able to walk on water, just work on healing yourself as well as other people. It is always a balance.

What blocks our healing abilities? Certainly childhood programming fears of "Who are you to think that you could have that kind of ability to transform somebody on a cellular level?" The truth is we are simply a vessel of the Divine and the Divine, of course, can heal anything any time. If we are not using those healing abilities, which I believe we all have the ability to tap into, it is like deciding not to use the water that comes out of the hose because it is coming out of the hose instead of out of the nice clean faucet in the kitchen sink. The same water that comes out of your garden hose comes out of your kitchen faucet, unless you have a water filter. You are criticizing the vessel rather than realizing that no matter what the vessel looks like, it is all Divine anyway—even though we may not always perceive it that way, the Divine can still flow through.

Believing in the Power of Her Gifts

Cynthia, a teleseminar student, described her situation this way: "I didn't want to believe in the power of the gifts that I have been given or that they were 'real.' My cycle was to take classes, not believe what was being taught was true and not use the information. I limited myself by staying closed and not being that open lotus flower that I am seeing now. I didn't get to be of service and feel the benefit of self-worth and confidence that comes from knowing you can truly make a difference.

"When you said to me, 'Do you want to look back with that large of a regret?' my immediate answer was *no*! It was daunting to step outside myself and say, 'Hey, you can do these things and you're good at it—you're a star!' I realized that for so long I'd heard the critical voices of my childhood whispering, '*Who do you think you are?*'

"This was a big time life lesson. I've got the gifts—from being artistic to being a wonderful healer, to being able to pay attention to things no one around me seems to see—yet I wasn't using them so I could stay small and conform to the limited behavior I was taught.

"As I took the time to listen to the classes repeatedly, did the clearing and ran the energy myself, my life transformed. I'm now doing lots of healings and I've started creating my own color therapy work. I am much more peaceful and others can see my clarity and aliveness. I am developing inner confidence to say what I see. I like that! And I am now more of my Divine unlimited self. I can do lots of cool stuff and I'm enjoying inviting others to come play with me."

Transforming Blocked Healing Abilities
If you have blocked your healing abilities, here is how to transform it:

a. Open up your palm chakras. There is a secondary chakra system in every joint in the body and also in the palms of your hands and the arches of your feet. Envision them literally opening up and a stream of Divine energy flowing through you. You may see it as either a white or a golden or whitish gold flow of energy. See it coming down through your entire body and down into the center of the earth, and also coming down your arms and out your hands, especially out your palm chakras.

b. Now try using this stream of healing energy on yourself first. Some people like to rub their hands together. I do not think that is necessary, but for some it brings their awareness to that area of the body so they can more easily open it up. If that is helpful, you can do that. Then try putting your hands together and start gradually pulling them apart until you can *feel* that energy between the palms of your hands, and then pull a little bit further out and further out as you separate your hands. You can also do this with somebody else, feeling that energy connection between the two of you.

c. Then use your intent to ask for the perfect healing energy that is beneficial to you on all levels to come through you. That is the basics for all forms of hands-on healing, regardless of what particular vibration or frequency people are tuning into. It is opening up the floodgates and letting the Divine energy pour through.

d. You can put your hands back on yourself and feel that energy. You may experience it as warmth or tingling or pulsing. If the body is taking it in really rapidly, it also can manifest as coolness because it creates almost like a vacuum sucking it in so quickly. Do not think the coolness is an indication that nothing is happening.

From the time I received how the ancient kahuna healed bones and other ailments instantly, which I teach in my ARCH and I'O classes, both my students and I have had many, many wonderful experiences of opening up and using our healing abilities.

Bird's Broken Wing Healed
When my youngest twins were in kindergarten they played in the playground after school almost everyday, as did lots of other kids. The other moms and myself would sit outside and chitchat while the kids were playing.

One day I saw a bird, a magpie, about twenty feet from me that could not fly. It kept trying to leap up and it would fall back down, leap up and fall back down. I suspected it had a broken wing. I asked permission from its soul for permission to send it healing energy and I heard a "yes."

Now this was a time when I was trying to not be too conspicuous in this group of parents that I had recently met. I had not yet told them what I did. There is a time and a place for everything and I did not think that was really the time or the place. I wanted to be incognito as I was sending the bird healing energy.

Seated on a rock wall, I asked that the Divine send the ARCH energies down to my hand, out through the palm of my hand and to the bird. I was resting my hand on the rock wall and aiming the palm of my hand at the bird. As soon as the energy hit the bird, it turned around and started hopping toward me, following this beam of ARCH energy. The bird got to my feet and then it hopped onto one of my children's backpacks next to me. Then it hopped up into a crevice in the rock wall. Finally the bird hopped up onto the rock wall and into my hand.

At this point it was very hard to be inconspicuous because all these little children had noticed that the bird had just hopped up into my hand. They all started running over exclaiming, "Oh, that bird just hopped right up into your hand. Why would that bird hop into your hand? What is it doing?"

I believe that when children ask you a question, that their being, soul, spirit wants that knowledge or that wisdom or that understanding that you have and it is our privilege to answer them. I replied, "The bird was injured, probably had a broken wing, and I asked the higher part of it if it would like some healing energy and it said 'yes' and so I started sending it healing energy out of my hand. And it followed that energy all the way up and it hopped into my hand where it's soaking that up. When it's coming out of one hand, it's coming out of the other hand too. Do you want to feel it?

As I put my other hand out and let them all touch me, they said, "Oh, that's tingly. Oh, that feels funny. Oh, that's hot. Oh, Mommy, Mommy, come see what she is doing!" And I am thinking, "Oh no, don't say Mommy, Mommy!"

The bird sat in my hands for five minutes and then flew away. That was how long it needed to allow itself to have its wing healed.

Eyesight Enhanced

Diane reported, "I had an extraordinary healing on my eyesight with ARCH. My eyesight was getting so bad with floaters, little black specks that float around in your line of sight. It made reading almost impossible. I also had a terrible time seeing at night, which made driving difficult.

"In an ARCH workshop with Laurie, I volunteered to receive a treatment. At first we discussed the perceived payoff for my vision problems, which had to do with judgment and not being able to *see* in silent observation. Laurie brought the ARCH energy down to me. I saw colors that were not of this world, and a feeling came to me that took my breath away. A tear rolled gently down each check, and I felt total love, peace and bliss. When I opened my eyes, one of the other students was sitting in front of me, and I saw in her so much beauty. My life changed then and I was able to see so much love and light in this world.

"My floaters are gone, though once in a while they will show up just to let me know I'm being a bit judgmental; but as soon as I realize this, I readjust my eyes and they disappear. My night vision is great. My next visit to my eye doctor revealed that I had a twenty percent improvement in my vision. Thanks to Laurie and ARCH I now have clear vision—in more ways than one."

Uterine Fibroids Healed

My apprentice Kristi had this experience: "A client come in to see me who had uterine fibroids and serious bleeding. It was very extreme. Doctors could not find a way to control it so they recommend surgery. She did not want to have surgery, yet she had tried just about everything else, including other holistic remedies. Her surgery was already scheduled when she found my brochure, yet she knew she wanted to give this a try. Otherwise she would have to succumb to surgery.

"Before the I'O healing treatment, I spoke with her about the perceived payoff that the body personality gets from creating dis-ease and she immediately saw what it was. I also told her that my job was to bring in the highest level of healing energy that her body could handle, and her job was to receive and allow that healing to take place. I told her it wasn't up to me, but I knew that it could heal instantly if she was ready and would allow it.

"A few weeks after the treatment I received this email from her: 'Thank you for helping me heal. Just as you said, sometimes all it takes is one session and that is all it took. Since that time I've been feeling great and have had no symptoms at all. It is truly amazing what can happen if you just let yourself go to the higher power. Thank you again for showing me the way.'

"I feel incredibly blessed to be able to share these healing gifts with people and very grateful to have learned them from Laurie."

Brain Tumor Disappears
A student of mine, Sam, told me that his four-year old nephew had a brain tumor the size of an orange and they were about to do surgery on it. He did an ARCH treatment on it and it disappeared completely. Everyone was puzzled except Sam.

Breast Cancer Disappears
Peggy, another student, had a mass in her breast that was cancer about the size of a plum. We used the ARCH energy on it and it disappeared.

Broken Arm Heals
When one of my twins was four she broke her arm. She and I both worked on it using ARCH. When they x-rayed it again, it was totally healed. She wanted to know if she could still wear her dinosaur sling to school anyway, even though her arm was healed. The perceived payoff was attention, since as a twin the attention gets divided. What made her special was wearing a sling with pictures of dinosaurs.

Back Surgery Averted

My ARCH practitioner's daughter was severely injured in a major skiing accident. The x-rays showed that she needed back surgery. As soon as Grace was brought home, Douglas began doing ARCH treatments on her. He continued this for the first twenty-four hours and not only did her pain go away, she healed completely without surgery.

Creating a Peaceful Transition for a Loved One

When I was teaching the beginning ARCH weekend class recently, my student Andrea's father had a massive heart attack and they thought he was going to make his transition Saturday night. She came to me on Sunday morning and told me about it. I said, "It looks to me like you have made peace with him passing, but you have a sister that hasn't. It looks like she has a lot of angst."

Andrea asked, "Will you send him some energy?" I replied, "Only if his higher self says *yes*." She asked if she could send him energy. I said, "Yes, but again you have to ask his higher self for permission first."

Andrea stayed on Sunday to complete the class and then flew home to New York and went directly to the hospital. Her father was all hooked up on a respirator and life support. "The doctors told me that he had no brain activity and that he was gone and they were very sorry," Andrea related. "Since I was the oldest, I had the responsibility for unplugging him. The doctors advised me to take him off life support and let him go because he was basically already gone. I said, 'Go ahead and unplug him; take him off the respirator and life support. I just can't watch, so I'll go to the bathroom and then come back.'

"They then unplugged him. When I came back from the bathroom, I was astounded to see my father had his eyes open. He looked at me and said, 'Who was that angel in white with blonde hair that thinks she's a human? She came to me and told me that your sister needs to make peace with me before I go, otherwise she's going to have a hard time if I leave without her making peace.' He was awake for thirty-five hours and talked to me the entire time. I got my sister in there, they made peace and then he passed."

What an incredible energy center the sixth is! Not honoring it and not using it is really stifling your life and your enjoyment of it. This is an incredible area to open up and play in and be excited and inspired by what you can bring through you. Instead of thinking of it as you do not have these gifts, realize that it is the Divine that is the pure gift. All you have to do is turn that hose on, regardless of what the hose looks like, and magic happens!

What Holds These Blocks in Place

Life lessons, perceived payoffs and judgments about your psychic gifts (clairvoyance), perception of things, creativity and healing abilities hold these blockages in place.

Regardless of what chakra lifetime you are working on, when the energy in any of the *seven* layers of the sixth chakra gets stuck and not expressing the Divine, the result is some variation of the list below, depending on your level of growth:

1ˢᵗ layer (the survival aspect of your psychic, perception, creativity and healing abilities) - not using your intuition, perception, creativity or healing abilities to get you out of a challenging survival situation; or when you blocked these abilities or stopped yourself from using them to make your survival easier.

2ⁿᵈ layer (the emotional and sexual aspect of your psychic, perception, creativity and healing abilities) – not "seeing" someone's anger, emotions or fear; or when you were in denial of your own emotions that affected your intuition; or when you let your fear stop you from using your psychic, perception, creativity and healing abilities; or when you blocked your perception of yours or other people's sexual energy.

3ʳᵈ layer (the will, willpower and manifesting aspect of your psychic, perception, creativity and healing abilities) – blocking your psychic, perception, creative and healing abilities and willing yourself not to use them; putting blindfolds on to really stop yourself from using these gifts.

4th layer (the love and affinity aspect of your psychic, perception, creativity and healing abilities) - hating your psychic gifts, perception of things, creativity and healing abilities. For example, hating your psychic abilities because you do not know what to do with them.

5th layer (the communication aspect of your psychic, perception, creativity and healing abilities) - not passing on a psychic message from Spirit; or not communicating your perception of things; or not communicating your creativity or your healing ability.

6th layer (the psychic, perception, creativity and healing aspects of your psychic talents, perception of things, creativity and healing abilities) - not using or blocking your psychic ability, your perception of things, your creativity and your healing gifts.

7th layer (the spiritual aspect of your psychic, perception, creativity and healing abilities) - not allowing yourself to open up and be guided by Spirit with your psychic, perception, creativity and healing abilities.

Blockages in the sixth chakra can result in eyestrain, eyesight problems and headaches, including migraines. There is a huge correlation between head colds and unshed tears. If we are not crying our tears and we get a cold, the body behaves the same way as if we were crying, with watery eyes and runny nose.

Letting the Blocks Fall Away

Personal Assessment

You were all very psychic and creative as children—and still are if you will let yourself. Ask yourself:

    1. Are you using the gifts of your sixth chakra?

a. How are you most likely to receive your ESP, your extra sensory information? Are you most likely to see it? To hear it? To feel it? Or to know it? Which one of those ways is the strongest for you right now, as it may change or expand?

b. How are you using your clear perception of things?

c. How are you using your creativity? What forms have your creativity taken?

d. How are you using your healing abilities for yourself and others?

2. *What can you do to strengthen your ability to receive information in this chakra?*

a. How can you strengthen your ESP and your clairvoyance or clear seeing?

b. How can you enhance your clear perception of things?

c. How can you enhance your creativity? What ways can you use your creativity that you are not already doing?

d. How can you make your healing abilities stronger and more effective, both for yourself and using it with others?

Identifying All the Ways You Have Kept Yourself From Being Divine in the Sixth Chakra:

This exercise will show you how your Divine nature is being blocked and what you would like to transform in your *sixth* energy center.

As you answer the following questions, make a list of everything you would like to release and transform:

- Have you ever felt somebody judged you for not seeing something?
- Have you ever been told, "Oh I can't believe you didn't see that coming?"
- Have you ever been told, "I can't believe you didn't see right through them?"
- Have you ever been told, "I can't believe that you didn't know that they were conning you?"
- Have you ever felt anybody judged you for having blindfolds on and for being in denial?

- Have you ever judged somebody for not seeing something?
- Have you ever judged yourself for being in denial?
- Have you ever judged yourself for not seeing the truth?
- Have you ever judged yourself for not seeing who someone was and being taken advantage of by them?

- Have you ever felt somebody tried to hide the truth from you, and you let them?
- Have you ever tried to hide the truth from yourself?
- Have you ever felt your perception of things or the world invalidated?

- Have you ever felt somebody judged your intuition or psychic abilities, thinking that it was dumb, or stupid, or scary, or "woo-woo?"
- Have you ever felt you didn't trust your own psychic abilities, and you discounted them, and later you found out you should have paid attention?
- Have you ever felt your psychic ability scared you?

- Have you ever felt somebody judged your creativity, such as "Santa Claus isn't supposed to be purple" or "What's that supposed to be? It doesn't look like anything?"
- Have you ever felt somebody judged your expression of creativity, such as "Can't you sing on key? That's not music?"
- Have you ever felt your creativity judged, such as "You wrote this?"

- Have you ever felt somebody judged your creativity—artistically, musically or your writing, dancing or inventing abilities?
- Have you ever judged your own creativity?

- Have you ever felt somebody judged your healing abilities?
- Have you ever judged your own healing abilities, such as "I can't really do this" or "I don't feel anything" or "I don't think this is working for me" or "I didn't see my Divine self" or "I didn't hear Divine Source talking to me" or "I didn't feel the Divine energy?"

- Have you ever numbed your creativity with the use of drugs, cigarettes, alcohol, food or busyness?

- Are you willing to transform all of the old energies that you have pushed into this area of your body that perhaps have caused you eyestrain or eyesight problems or headaches, including migraines?

- In the areas that you identified as being limited, what is your perceived payoff? What is the benefit your body personality is getting out of it?
- Are you willing to let it go?

- Has this been a recurring theme in your life? Is it a life lesson?
- What is the lesson you have the opportunity to learn here?

- Are you willing to completely transform this area of your life that is stopping you from using your psychic, perception, creative and healing abilities, and allow yourself to honor your own Divine nature?

Releasing the Blocks

Now that you are aware of how you have kept yourself limited, it is time to release everything on your list that you have placed in your sixth chakra over the years, so that you can use your psychic, perception, creative and healing abilities to transform your life.

1. Close your eyes and go into a relaxed state.

2. Create a big bubble out in front of you and put everything from your *sixth* chakra list that you no longer want into the bubble.

3. Release the bubble out to the sun and have it evaporate.

4. Now envision what you do want on the levels of your psychic, perception, creative and healing abilities. See and feel that clearly.

5. Create a powerful statement of transformation that allows you to experience what you want to be, feel and have easily, effortlessly and enjoyably. Repeat this statement to yourself often every day until this is your reality.

Returning to Your Divine Essence

Once again, you can come back to the way that you were Divinely designed by bringing your attention to activating the Divine within every layer of your sixth chakra and moving out any blockages that stop you from *feeling* your connection with the Divine on all seven of those levels.

Begin by centering yourself. Draw energy up from the earth and the universal energy from the cosmos down to blend within so you can grow to your fullest level of consciousness.

Sit with your feet flat on the floor so you can feel that connection with the earth, your hands uncrossed on your lap, and imagine bringing that earth energy up through you, drawing it up through your feet, filling every cell in your body. See it, sense it, feel it or hear it.

Imagine it flooding every cell of your body, down the arms, out the hands. Then fill each chakra center and move it out to the edge of the skin, all the way up to the top of your head and fountain out the top. At the same time, feel your connection with the earth.

Turn your hands palms up on your lap and ask for the highest level of universal energy that you can easily accommodate to gently come down into the crown of your head. Then imagine it going into every chakra center, mixing with the earth energy, spreading out to the edges of the skin, especially the heart chakra. Next send it down your arms out the fingers, down the legs and out the feet, and any excess universal energy goes down into the center of the earth. Then experience your connection to the earth and to the universe.

Next use your intent to fill the sixth chakra back up with the Divine, which you can see as white or golden energy, feel as warmth, hear as a tone, feel as a particular vibration, or just know that you are filling up every one of those layers. Activate the Divine in every layer, *until you can feel those feelings in your body* establishing:

> *"I am easily receiving psychic messages,*
> *clearly perceiving and*
> *using my creativity and healing abilities.*
> *I am One with the Divine.*
> *I **feel** that connection at all times.*
> *I emanate that Divinity out into the world*
> *through my feelings of love, joy, bliss,*
> *harmony, peacefulness and gratitude."*

I recommend that before beginning a busy day, reconnect with these Divine feelings of peace and harmony within you. Simply go into this centered meditative state and connect with the earth energy and the universal energy and then bring your attention to your sixth chakra, and activate the Divine in every layer until you can feel it in your body. Now you are ready for your day!

Returning to Divine Feelings Throughout the Day

Just as you did with the first five chakras, anytime you want your body to automatically return to this Divine state, decide on which two fingers to place together for the sixth chakra. Then once you have gotten in that state where you are feeling the connection and the Oneness with the Divine in the sixth chakra, and it is flowing through every layer—you are feeling peacefulness, contentment, bliss, and love—when you are there and you are connected with the earth and you are connected with the universe and it is exactly where you want to be, then take those two fingers and put them together and say to yourself:

> *Every time I think Divine harmony in my sixth chakra*
> *and I place these two fingers together,*
> *my body will automatically go into this state.*

And then place those two fingers together.

Throughout the day if you start to lose that connection and feeling, you have a way to return to this state easily. Go within and get centered and say to your body:

> *When I count to three and place these two fingers together,*
> *I'm going to go into that Divine peace in my sixth chakra.*
> *One, two, three, Divine peace.*

And put those two fingers together.

Don't forget to remember to write down the hand and finger you chose for the sixth chakra so you can commit it to memory.

You are now ready to move on to Chapter 8 and deepen your spiritual connection.

Deepening Your Spiritual Connection

You have now reached the most significant chakra of all—the Gateway to Source. Located at the crown or top of your head, this is the gateway for the Divine to come down into you. Once it is open, the Source can come through the seventh chakra, down into the sixth, the fifth, the fourth, the third, the second and the first. That's why it's called the Gateway to the Divine.

When we are born, the crown chakra is wide open because we have just come from Source, and we remember and we know that we are a Divine Spirit of Light. It is not a coincidence that our skull is actually still open when we come into the body—known as the baby's soft spot on the top of the head. Whether you want to think of it as symbolic or as energetic, the Spirit has the opportunity to descend all the way down into the human body.

Little children are bright sparks of light because that is what they know, that is where they have been, and that is who they know they are. That is why a two-year old can say to a newborn, "Tell me about God, I'm starting to forget." Up until that time, they still remember.

When one of my children, Kendra, was about two, she said to her four-year old sister Katelyn, "Oh, I was just flying around the room without my body on." And Katelyn replied, "Oh yeah, I used to do that all the time. Isn't that fun?"

That limitless being unimpeded by the body is alive and well in the early part of life when the crown chakra is wide open to the Divine. Because of this, it is also very easy to get information from children about their past lives.

Past Life Awareness

When Katelyn was eighteen months old, I was expecting my first set of twins. I wanted to give her some awareness in advance about having a baby around, so I gave her a baby doll that was supposed to look like a newborn with half-closed eyes that were not all the way open yet. "What do you want to name your dolly, honey?" I asked her. She already had two dolls that she named "Janet" and "Allison." When I asked her what she wanted to name this dolly, she said, "Nehoho."

I repeated in disbelief, "Nehoho?"

"Nehoho!" she replied quite indignantly, like why was I questioning what she wanted to name her baby.

"Okay," I said, "Nehoho it is."

It sounded kind of Asian to me and I realized that if you looked at the doll as Asian rather than as a newborn, the narrowness of the eyes could definitely be seen as an Asian child. This was confirmed when I finally had a chance to ask someone who was Chinese. "My daughter just named her baby doll Nehoho," I told him.

"Oh, that means 'you good' in Chinese," he replied.

"Could you name somebody that?" I asked.

"Certainly," he said.

We would go into a Chinese restaurant and she would want me to read her the menu in Chinese. Of course, I'm reading "potstickers, fried rice," which is not what she was looking for. She pointed to the Chinese characters wanting me to read those to her, and said, "How am I supposed to know what I want if you won't tell me what it says?"

I read, "Won ton soup. . ."

"No, Mommy!" she exclaimed, losing patience with me.

Then as I got more and more pregnant, we knew it was twins and she wanted to name them Chinese names that were so Chinese, I couldn't make my mouth correctly repeat it back to her, and she was very frustrated with me.

One day we went to the zoo and she spotted a Chinese family. "Mommy, did you notice that Chinese family over there?"

"Yes," I replied, "what are they talking about?"

"Oh, they're talking about the kangaroos." I found that interesting as we were not by the kangaroos; we were in front of the monkey exhibit.

Then when she was two, she was watching a PBS Special for two hours. Most people know that a two-year old does not do anything for two hours, let alone sit and watch a PBS Special. Most two-year olds do not sit for two hours even with Sesame Street—fifteen minutes maybe. The program was about little Chinese boys who were doing Tai Chi. She said, "Mommy, mommy, they're just like me! They're just like me!"

Then I said this terrible thing. "No, they're not, honey. They're Chinese and you're American and they're little boys and you're a little girl and they have black hair and you have blond hair and they have dark eyes and you have blue eyes. And they're seven to nine and you're two."

She started to cry and said plaintively, "You're right, they're not like me anymore."

"Honey, did you have a past life when you were in China?" I asked.

She rolled her eyes at me and she said, "No Mommy, my last future life is in China!"

I quickly tried to digest this information and finally asked, "Well, when you were in China . . ."

"Awww, I'm in China now!" she interrupted.

"What part of you is in China now?" I asked.

"My being! My being's in China now!" she quickly retorted.

"Honey, I know Mommy's slow, but I'm really doing the best I can," I said.

Then she began to tell me that her father's name was Arondososhi, her mother's name was Mockosui, that she grows rice and she dies in a flood in the Yangsee River. There is no way that this child knew anything about the Yangsee River or was around anybody who spoke Chinese or anything about China, or had any discussion with me or anybody else about last future lifetimes, let alone simultaneous time. It boggles the brain.

When she was almost four, she went to Montessori School. Then a two-year old Chinese girl started at the school and Katelyn translated for her to the teachers. She would tell the teachers that the Chinese girl wants a drink of water or that her crayon broke or that she needs to go to the bathroom. Katelyn did this so much that one of her teachers said to me, "How did your daughter learn Chinese?"

Then when she was four and a half she said, "Mommy, I'm beginning to forget how to speak Chinese."

Later when she was nineteen and in college, she called me up clearly distraught, "Mom, I died."

"Are you okay?" I asked.

"Mom, I died," her voice shaking with emotion.

"Honey, are you okay?" I'm trying to think is she talking about a near-death experience? Or what? I'm frantically trying to figure out what to do, what's wrong.

"Mom, I died!"

"Honey, how, when, where? Are you okay? Do you need me to come and get you?"

"No! In my life in China, I died," she replied.

"Oh," I said trying to take in what she was saying. I did not really understand. How at age two did she know that she would die in a flood in the Yangsee River and then it does not happen until later? I do not know.

Past Life Choices Reflected Now

Kyla, one of my older twins, was born this very intentional loving little spirit. From the time she could reject food, she refused to eat any meat. She would not eat the ground up chicken or turkey that you feed babies at eighteen months. If you're not a parent, you probably wouldn't know that ground up chicken looks a whole lot like ground up rice. It is very hard to tell one brownish ground up substance from another, but she knew. She would just push it away. She would eat the ground up banana, the grains and the vegetables. She was a self-chosen vegetarian from the moment she was born. And she was very clear about that.

When Kyla was three, my sister asked her why she was a vegetarian and she made a sign with her hand that we later found out was a Buddhist mudra (hand movement) for compassion. Then at age five Kyla was sitting on the floor when she remembered, "I was a Buddhist monk. We sang over and over again, 'We are from the kingdom of the monks.'" She didn't know the word "chant" at the time.

Past Life Behavior Resolved

Just as Kyla was very passive and loving, her fraternal twin, Kendra, was very assertive. Kendra wanted onions and spicy meatballs and things that had garlic, mostly Italian food, which young children don't usually like because of the strong flavors. She also was very aggressive with Kyla, including biting her. I tried all kinds of things to stop that behavior. But every time she got mad, she would beat one fist into the other hand and say defiantly, "Okay, Joey." She called everybody Joey—Mommy, Daddy, Kyla, everybody was Joey. She would react with, "Okay, Joey" and this huge aggression would come out of this tiny little child.

Finally when she was two, she bit Kyla so hard it drew blood. Exasperated I exclaimed, "Kendra! Where were you before you were here?"

"The Bronx," she retorted with an unmistakable Bronx accent and attitude.

"The Bronx?" I asked, not believing my ears.

The older one, Katelyn, who was four at the time said, "Isn't that a football team?" thinking of the Broncos. The four-year old did not know that the Bronx is a place, and the two-year old also didn't know the Bronx is a place. We were living in Bonny lake, Washington at the time.

Taking all of this in, I asked, "Kendra, does that mean that you were Joey from the Bronx?"

"Yeah. Yeah!" she said.

Every time Kendra would start to act out, I would say, "It's okay, Kendra, you don't have to be Joey anymore. Mommy's here and I'm going to take care of you." Clearly, she was still fighting for her survival. Then Kyla would do that too. When Kendra would start getting aggressive revving up to bite her, Kyla would say, "It's okay, Kendra, you don't have to be Joey. Mommy's going to take care of you." So Kendra stopped! All her aggressive behavior stopped, and she was fine. She still wanted spicy meatballs and was a carnivore, definitely a carnivore.

Past Life Wisdom

Later when Kyla was sixteen, she was really upset with me for making her clean her room before she left the house. Kyra, one of my four-year old twins said to the sixteen-year old, "Listen! Before this lifetime, we all agreed that Mommy was going to be the Mom. If you weren't going to like it, you just should have chosen someone else!" The sixteen-year old responded with, "Awwh!" And went and did her chore.

Kyra has amazing strategies for coping, particularly with her twin sister. Last year Kiana said to Kyra in a sarcastic put-down way, "Oh, you're just Captain Terrific, aren't you?" And Kyra replied, "Oh, I'm a Captain. I love that! Okay, I think I'm going to sail our ship to the beach today. Come with me." She totally diffused her sister's negativity. She was ten. Most children that age do not have the ability or the consciousness to diffuse things. That was her evolved soul coming out.

When I asked Kiana at an early age who she was before she was here, she wisely replied, "The Light! I was the Light!" revealing her awareness of coming from the Divine before being born into a body.

How did my children have this knowing? Not only do we bring our unfinished lessons with us from past lives, we also bring our awareness. Just as our intuition is in our second, fifth and sixth chakras, it is also in our seventh. Our intuition manifests through clairsentience in our second, through clairaudience in our fifth, through clairvoyance in our sixth and through clear knowing in our seventh.

Developing the Divine Characteristics Within

Remember, this chakra is the Gateway to your Divine Source and your spiritual and religious center with its many gifts. When the blocks that keep you from aligning with Source are released, here are the Divine qualities available to you in the *seven* layers of the *seventh* chakra:

1. You will be truly living your spiritual path and living in the Divine flow in all aspects of your life.

2. You will feel trust in God/Goddess. You will feel connected to the Divine through all of your acts, including lovemaking. You will feel that sensuality is part of living in a human body, and consensual lovemaking between two people can be a Divine state of heightening your connection to the Divine. You may use Tantric sex to get closer to God or Goddess, if that is your path.

3. You will co-create with God/Goddess and live in the Divine manifested flow creating true abundance in your spiritual life on all levels.

4. You will have a true love of God/Goddess or the Divine, and a true love of your spiritual or religious path as well as honoring others' paths. And you will love the Divine within you and within others.

5. You will bring in your own Divine messages and communication from Source, and be able to truly hear and receive them and know what is right for you. And you will honor those messages, allowing you to live in the Divine flow.

6. You will use your ESP—seeing, hearing, feeling or knowing—to open up to the Divine and clearly experience your connection to Source. Your perception will be of love and a loving God/Goddess and you will truly love the Divine in yourself and others and really *see* that in everyone, including yourself. You will fully use your creativity and healing abilities in the Divine flow.

7. You will open up to receiving the Source and allowing it to flow through you unimpeded. You will truly acknowledge that you *are* the Divine and surrender to the Divine flow coming through all aspects of you, feeling the bliss of Oneness.

What Blocks Your Divinity

What blocks you from being able to access the Gateway to Source and the incredible feeling of bliss that accompanies your direct connection to the Divine?

Very simply, the messages you took on from authority figures—primarily your parents—that *you were not good enough.* What has held you back from experiencing your natural state of blissful Oneness with the Divine are those mistaken beliefs and ideas given to you by others that you took on as your own. The good news is it's not the truth.

Realize it is *not* the truth of who you are. Release it to the dirt where it belongs and energetically and consciously compost all of those things that have served their purpose and are no longer needed.

The truth is you are the Divine—all of the time, regardless of whether you are allowing yourself to experience it or not in this moment. This is the truth of your being, as the ancient Hawaiians and so many other cultures knew.

The purpose of this chapter and this book is to give you the awareness and the tools to clear whatever programming has kept you from this truth so that you can experience your natural state of Divinity and enter into ecstatic Oneness with the Divine.

Resistance Dissolves into Openness

"I had a lot of resistance to being One with Source," Randy shared during a class. "I wasn't sure I could be One and in this world, balanced at the same time. I pondered how I could be both not of this planet and of the planet.

"Not being open and One with Spirit and my Divine self fed my feelings of *Is this it? Why am I here?* I always knew I was supposed to be so much more. I always felt like something was missing. I felt very much on the outskirts, like there was no place I belonged, or people that really fit with me. When I started taking spiritual classes and found those I resonated with, I would still hold myself apart as not quite capable or worthy. I thought I didn't deserve to be enlightened.

"This has been a life lesson of recognizing and acknowledging myself. Giving myself credit for who I am, where I've been and how far I've come.

"Accepting myself as worthy, being good enough, and deserving to experience myself as Divine has been transformational. Now I feel lighter and ready to integrate all the changes into my life on all levels. I am open to what was unimaginable before—Oneness with the Divine."

From Self-Doubt to Passion

"Although I tried many spiritual paths and wasted a lot of time, I couldn't find a spiritual path that seemed right for me," said Jill. "I felt like my way was blocked. I was left with a lot of self-doubt. I realized it was a life lesson in finding my true self.

"Once I cleared my spiritual center and connected with my Divine self, suddenly I had no doubts and I could see my right spiritual path before me. How do I feel about myself? Woo hoo! Now my passion is my spiritual life."

Coming Back to Myself

"I was raised in my family's church and had some old religious fears and conditioning that I needed to clear," Polly explained. My religious upbringing taught me that women are inferior, that I should feel guilty because Jesus died for 'your sins and you better repent.' I was taught that the Bible and its stories are to be taken literally, and that you don't question the all-knowing

God. Religion for me was always fear-based and was never a comfort. I was scared that I could die at any second and go to hell. I also felt that it was the role of the man to lead and spread the word of God. This early training was hurtful, made me angry and question everything that I'd ever been taught. I knew at a young age that this wasn't the path I wanted to take.

"Yet I was afraid to question religion and to explore other options. I felt like an outsider at church and at home because I didn't believe the teachings of the church. I felt like I was backwards or wrong for not believing. I felt like women were not as important as men, that they were the weaker sex and should look to men for religious counsel and leadership.

"This was definitely a life lesson—to follow what's in my heart and to believe in the natural balance of the Divine feminine and Divine masculine. I know that men and women are equal and that when the feminine is not valued, a man has no intimacy or respect for his wife. I don't believe in hell. I also don't believe that someone died for my sins and that I need to spend the rest of my life repenting.

"I've let go of those old ideas and I'm embracing the path I have chosen and my soul resonates with. I feel at peace. I don't feel any guilt about religion. I don't feel that I need to turn to a man for religious counsel. I can meditate and get my answers and assistance from my higher Divine self and the Source.

"I feel like I have come back to myself. I'm back in touch with the beliefs that my soul has always held. I've connected to my spiritual essence of beauty and grace."

An Expression of God

"I grew up feeling I may get in trouble for my beliefs, particularly my religious beliefs, so I wouldn't share them," said Ava. "I was very secretive about my religion. It made me feel very closed and not good about myself. The perceived payoff was I was safe from bias.

"After clearing all that out, I feel so much better. I feel good about my religion. I feel good about myself. And when I meet people, I am now open to sharing my religious beliefs. I realized my Divine self is an expression of God and uses religion to serve God and mankind and as a way to express itself."

Many Paths

At the end of a seminar, Virginia shared these wise words: "I was not brought up in a particular religion so I have been free to choose my own spiritual path. There are many paths to the same place; each one of us is heading that way in our own way and in our own time. I have felt this way for as long as I can remember. I walk the Divine path. I endeavor to walk more and more in this path until I am on the path always."

Life Transformation

Nicole, a student of many of my classes, related: "I have been a 'closet' spiritual person—even to myself. I grew up Catholic, which shaped my values and experiences. There is still something I like about cathedrals and the energy that has built up after years of prayer. I still love to come to the chapel to feel the energy. When I moved into the more evolved part of Spirit, I yearned to have conversations about the ideas I was learning, but my silence kept me from finding a community. This was one more way I felt separate and I would wonder alone or just read books.

"When I first started taking classes from Laurie, she said 'it was a privilege and responsibility' to share the knowledge. I hadn't wanted to accept the responsibility and couldn't imagine it being a privilege.

"Then as I went through the ARCH and I'O classes, everything began to change. I was so happy to be there. I felt so at home. I finally understood that 'it was a privilege and a responsibility.' Accepting myself as a light worker and knowing that was the work I was here to do transformed my life. I became a minister and my congregation loves what I share with them. The people I am drawn to the most have a sense of Spirit and connectedness about them. My partnerships have a sense of Oneness and connection to God.

"I feel really good about being me. There are times when I am in a store or on the freeway and I realize that each one of us is a part of *All* and that we are One and that is at once so amazing and so simply perfect!"

Oneness with the Divine

Here is Esther's experience of going into Oneness with the Divine:

"The belief that I needed an intermediary to connect with the Divine kept me going to rituals, instead of experiencing the Divine flow in the here and now, everywhere. Believing that the energy was greater there, not within limited my life. I allowed other people to put constraints on me and I really put constraints on myself.

"This was a life lesson from past lives that was still reverberating in the present. The perceived payoff that 'there was someone who is an intermediary' kept me giving that person or spiritual being some of my power, instead of using my power to make my own direct connection with the Divine.

"I now know I do not have to go for a pilgrimage to experience a sacred place. *This* can be a sacred spot for it is in the universe.

"I now know that the Divine loves me. I am worthy. I am a child of Mother/ Father God. I am a co-creator with the Divine. As I clear the chakras, I become more of my real authentic self. I can feel my Divine connection and I become a clearer channel of Source love and truth. I am becoming One with the Divine. I am One."

What Holds These Blocks in Place

Life lessons, perceived payoffs, spiritual beliefs and judgments about our self-worth and ability to connect with the Divine hold these blockages in place.

No matter what chakra lifetime you are working on, when the energy in any of the *seven* layers of the seventh chakra get stuck and are not expressing the Divine, the result is some variation of the list below, depending on your level of growth:

1st layer (the survival aspect of your spirituality and religious energy) – belief in original sin, belief that you are a sinner just because you were born or needing to die for your sins or a belief that you are going to hell because of your sins; belief that your life was going to be problematic and challenged spiritually or religiously because of something you did or did not do.

2nd layer (the emotional and sexual aspect of spirituality and religions) – fear of God; or guilt because of your spiritual path or lack of it; or guilt from being a sexual sinner.

3rd layer (the will, willpower and manifesting aspects of your spiritual or religious energies) – forcing your religious or spiritual beliefs on others or allowing others to force you to believe their spiritual or religious beliefs; or anything that has you *resisting* the Divine flow and going against the natural state of being One with God/Goddess; or believing you are a victim of God/Goddess.

4th layer (the love and affinity aspect of your spirituality or religion) – hating God or religion; hating others for their spiritual or religious beliefs; or others hating you for your spiritual or religious beliefs.

5th layer (the communication aspect of your spiritual or religious endeavors) – all of the negative messages you were given about a punitive, punishing God; all the negative messages that you received about your true spiritual path; all the times when the preacher was yelling at you about what you should or should not believe regarding your religion or spiritual truth; any hypocrisy you heard about what the church did and what it said.

6th layer (the psychic, perception, creativity and healing aspects of your spiritual or religious path) - a belief that ESP or psychic abilities are evil; a belief in possession; or all negative perceptions of God/Goddess; all negative forms of creative energy that honor the anti-Christ; any healing rituals that stop your flow, and any beliefs that your true connection to Source is limited.

7th layer (the spiritual aspect of the spiritual and religious path) - Satanic worship or worship of Satan or the devil, or a belief in the devil; or cutting yourself off completely from your Divine Creator and the connection to the Divine flow.

Blockages in the seventh chakra can result in headaches on the top of the head, pain on the top of the head, not feeling like you can connect and feeling pressure on the top of the head.

Letting the Blocks Fall Away

PERSONAL ASSESSMENT

The seventh chakra represents your spiritual path, your connection to Spirit. Ask yourself:

1. How are you doing along your spiritual path?

2. What can you do to enhance your spiritual evolvement?

    a. Is there anything in particular that you need to clear? Is there anything that you have been holding onto that stops you from living in the true Divine flow of your own spiritual path?

    b. Is there any programming left over from childhood, such as if you were raised in a particular religion that you do not subscribe to any longer?

    c. Were you raised in a particular religion that you felt was limiting?

    d. Were you raised an agnostic and taught that there was nothing outside of you?

    e. Were you taught that when you died, you died—that was it, your soul did not continue on?

Identifying All the Ways You Have Kept Yourself From Being Divine in the Seventh Chakra:

This exercise will show you how your Divine nature is being blocked and what you would like to transform in your *seventh* energy center.

As you answer the following questions, make a list of everything you would like to release and transform:

- Have you ever felt you were not good enough?
- Have you ever been told you were not good enough?
- Have you ever been told you were a sinner just because you were born?
- Have you ever felt you were going to hell because of something you did or did not do?
- Have you ever been told your life was going to be problematic spiritually or religiously because of something you did or did not do?

- Have you ever felt afraid of God?
- Have you ever felt guilt about being a sexual sinner?
- Have you ever felt guilty because of your spiritual or religious path?
- Have you ever felt guilty because of your lack of a spiritual or religious path?

- Have you ever felt other people were forcing you to believe their spiritual or religious belief?
- Have you ever tried to force others to believe your way of connecting with the Divine Source?
- Have you ever resisted the Divine flow?

- Have you ever gone against the natural state of being One with God/Goddess?
- Have you ever felt what you *should* or should *not* believe spiritually or religiously was forced upon you?
- Have you ever felt you were a victim of God/Goddess?

- Have you ever hated God?
- Have you ever hated religion?
- Have you ever hated others for their spiritual or religious beliefs?
- Have you ever felt others hated you for your spiritual or religious beliefs?

- Have you ever been given negative messages about a punishing God?
- Have you ever been given negative messages about your true spiritual path?
- Have you ever felt a preacher was yelling at you about what you should or should not believe concerning your religion or spiritual truth?
- Have you ever heard any hypocrisy about what the church did and what it said?

- Have you ever felt you were taken over by negative energies?
- Have you ever felt you had been burned at the stake?
- Have you ever felt negativity clouded your perception of things and your spiritual truth now?
- Have you ever had negative perceptions of God or Goddess?
- Have you ever experienced healing rituals that stopped your Divine flow?
- Have you ever been told your connection to Source is limited?

- Have you ever been told to believe in the devil?
- Have you ever had a belief in the devil?
- Have you ever cut yourself off completely from the Divine?
- Have you ever felt cut off from the Divine flow?

- Are you willing to transform all of the old energies that you have pushed into this area of your body that perhaps have caused you headaches, pain or pressure on the top of your head?

- In the areas that you identified as being limited, what is your perceived payoff? What is the benefit your body personality is getting out of it?
- Are you willing to let it go?

- Has this been a recurring theme in your life? Is it a life lesson?
- What is the lesson you have the opportunity to learn here?

- Are you willing to completely transform this area of your life that is stopping you from connecting with Source and Oneness, and allow yourself to honor your own Divine nature?

Releasing the Blocks

Now that you are aware of how you have kept yourself limited, it is time to release everything on your list that has been stuck in your crown chakra over the years, so that you can have clarity about your spiritual path, live in the Divine spiritual flow, and truly be and do all that you came here to do and to be spiritually.

1. Close your eyes and go into a relaxed state.

2. Create a big bubble out in front of you and put everything from your *seventh* chakra list that you no longer want into the bubble.

3. Release the bubble out to the sun and have it evaporate.

4. Now envision what you do want on the levels of spirituality. See and feel that clearly.

5. Create a powerful statement of transformation that allows you to experience what you want to be, feel and have easily, effortlessly

and enjoyably. Repeat this statement to yourself often every day until this is your reality.

Returning to Your Divine Essence

As you now know, you can come back to the way you were Divinely designed by bringing your attention to activating the Divine within every layer of your seventh chakra and moving out any blockages that stop you from *feeling* your connection with the Divine on all seven of those levels.

As before, begin by centering yourself. Draw energy up from the earth and the universal energy from the cosmos down to blend within so you can grow to your fullest level of consciousness.

Sit with your feet flat on the floor so you can feel that connection with the earth, your hands uncrossed on your lap, and imagine bringing that earth energy up through you, drawing it up through your feet, filling every cell in your body. See it, sense it, feel it or hear it.

Imagine it flooding every cell of your body, down the arms, out the hands. Then fill each chakra center and move it out to the edge of the skin, all the way up to the top of your head and fountain out the top. At the same time, feel your connection with the earth.

Turn your hands palms up on your lap and ask for the highest level of universal energy that you can easily accommodate to gently come down into the crown of your head. Then imagine it going into every chakra center, mixing with the earth energy, spreading out to the edges of the skin, especially the heart chakra, where your own special blend of earth and cosmic energies are created, so it is mixed really well. Next send it down your arms out the fingers, down the legs and out the feet, and any excess universal energy goes down into the center of the earth. Then experience your connection to the earth and to the universe.

Next use your intent to fill the seventh chakra back up with the Divine, which you can see as white or golden energy, feel as warmth, hear as a tone, feel as a particular vibration, or just know that you are filling up every one of those layers. Activate the Divine in every layer, *until you can feel those feelings in your body* establishing:

> *"I am easily connecting with the Divine*
> *and allowing the Divine to flow through me.*
> *I am One with the Divine.*
> *I **feel** that connection at all times.*
> *I emanate that Divinity out into the world*
> *through my feelings of love, joy, bliss,*
> *harmony, peacefulness and gratitude."*

I recommend that before beginning a busy day, once again reconnect with these Divine feelings of bliss within you. Simply go into this centered meditative state and connect with the earth energy and the universal energy and then bring your attention to your seventh chakra, and activate the Divine in every layer until you can feel it in your body. Now you are ready for your day!

Returning to Divine Feelings Throughout the Day

Just as you did with the first six chakras, anytime you want your body to automatically return to this Divine state, decide on which two fingers to place together for the seventh chakra. Then once you have gotten in that state where you are feeling the connection and the Oneness with the Divine in the seventh chakra, and it is flowing through every layer—you are feeling peacefulness, contentment, bliss and love—when you are there and you are connected with the earth and you are connected with the universe and it is exactly where you want to be, then take those two fingers and put them together and say to yourself:

> *Every time I think Divine bliss in my seventh chakra*
> *and I place these two fingers together,*
> *my body will automatically go into this state.*

And then place those two fingers together.

Throughout the day if you start to lose that connection and feeling, you have a way to return to this state easily. Go within and get centered and say to your body:

> *When I count to three and place these two fingers together,*
> *I'm going to go into Divine bliss in my seventh chakra.*
> *One, two, three, Divine bliss.*

And put those two fingers together.

Don't forget to remember to write down the hand and finger you chose for the seventh chakra so you can commit it to memory.

Awakening Your Divine Potential

Now it is time to listen to the first audio meditation I have created for you to deepen your cleansing and to fully receive the Divine energy into all layers of all seven of your chakras. Know that I am not putting in anything that is not already within you, I am *awakening* what is already there. Using the Divine matrix, I will facilitate you moving to a new level of consciousness where you can walk your path in the Divine flow. To download this free audio recording, please email audio@TransformYourLifeNow.net for instructions.

Note: Be aware that this audio meditation contains very powerful energy and should ***not*** be listened to while you are driving a car or operating machinery. Choose a quiet place to sit and relax so you can receive optimum benefit from these transforming energies. Your job is to ask the Divine within you to integrate these energies easily, effortlessly and enjoyably into your chakras and the areas of your life that need transforming.

I strongly recommend that you listen to this first meditation daily for the next thirty days, filling yourself with the unlimited energy of the Divine to truly transform your life *now*!

As you allow the qualities of the Divine to develop and strengthen within you, you will begin to awaken to your birthright—your unlimited Divine potential.

After you have done the exercises in the first meditation, you are now ready to move on to Chapter 9 and reclaim your freedom and your power to manifest the life of your dreams.

Reclaiming Your Freedom and Your Power to Manifest the Life of Your Dreams

You now have the opportunity to remove the cords that bind you and that keep you from truly transforming your life on all levels. If you have ever felt stuck in the past or unable to get out of an unfortunate situation and do not know why, this chapter will be most liberating for you. It will allow you to reclaim your freedom and your power to manifest the life of your dreams.

In this chapter you will learn what you can do on a regular basis to change your life in ways that you cannot even imagine. If you have energy cords from other people stuck in you, *they* are running your life or at the very least blocking your new life and not allowing you to step into true transformation. To build the tallest pyramid, you have to build the strongest foundation.

If you are carrying around these blockages and barriers that stop your energy from going out into the world to create what you want, now is the time to remove them once and for all. Just like a heart cannot beat at full capacity if its arteries are blocked, chakras cannot operate at full capacity if there are blockages.

In this chapter we will focus on removing the energy projections that are sent from one person to another in the form of an energetic umbilical cord. Often these cords are sent subconsciously, yet they are *always* manipulative.

The ancient Hawaiians knew about them and they called them aka cords. Some people believe that it is okay to cut them off. I will show you why it is not okay *ever* to do that and what you can do if you have already cut some cords.

I first discovered cords in 1978 when I was doing professional readings. I happened to read this woman who had been in Guyana and was the person who called to report the problems within the Jim Jones complex. It was her phone call that initiated Senator Ryan going to Guyana to investigate the mass suicide and killings that occurred afterwards.

While I was reading her, I saw that half or more of her crown chakra was missing. It was just gone. Since the crown chakra is our spiritual connection, I wondered what had happened. How could anybody be missing so much of their crown chakra?

When I asked her higher self what had occurred, I was told that Jim Jones had corded her. Many cult leaders intentionally cord their followers in their crown chakras to usurp their connection with the Divine, enabling the leader to become the Source or the God of that person's life, making them like a puppet on a string.

We spent numerous sessions disentangling her energy from Jim Jones' cord that she unconsciously ripped out of her crown chakra. When she ripped out the cord, half of her crown chakra was ripped out with it and left in Guyana. She escaped with her life but not with all of her spiritual energy. After we disentangled her energy from Jim Jones, we had to rebuild—literally—and heal her crown chakra. This was the first time I had ever seen something that ruthless be done energetically to someone.

Cording Appropriately

That prompted me to ask the Divine Source, "What are these cords?" This is what I received:

When a baby is conceived, the mother and ideally the father take some of their energy in the form of an energy umbilical cord and plug it into the baby's *first* chakra to give it energy to help it survive. The baby reciprocates and sends a first chakra cord out into its mother and ideally the father to take in that survival energy. That is how bonding occurs.

If the child is adopted, the cording usually happens when they get to their adoptive parents. Hopefully, the cording is all the way down to the core of the chakra, which is ideal. When it does not go all the way down to the core, there is not enough of a strong bond between the parents and child, adopted or not.

Weaning the Dependent Child

Whether these cords are to the child from the adopted parents or the birth mother and ideally the birth father, those cords stay in there until about the time the child reaches adolescence. This is the time a weaning process must take place for the child to grow up to be a self-sufficient, functioning adult capable of taking responsibility for their own survival needs and wants. It is like weaning a child off of mother's milk.

This is why adolescence can be so stressful for parents and child. One moment they want to be the child and want you to take care of them, and the next moment they tell you that they are a grownup and want the car keys. If you are a parent or grandparent you know that it is difficult to determine when the child wants to be corded and dependent upon you and when they suddenly want to be *un*corded trying to be the adult. That can happen instantaneously and it can be a bit crazy making for parents of teenagers.

My oldest daughter started taking my first chakra cord out of her at age ten. But she has always been very precocious. Her twin sisters, the older ones, started thinking about taking theirs out when they were eighteen. There is a big range between when parents need to continue to keep those cords plugged into their more dependent children, and the time to remove them when the child decides that they have had enough.

A classic example of this is when my friend's daughter was seventeen and had a big fight with her mother. "I'm done, I'm finished," declared Jennifer. "I don't need parents anymore, I'm out of here. I'm moving out." When she left, she ripped out her first chakra cord to her mother and sent it back and pulled her own energy back from her mom. Then that night at two o'clock in the morning, Jennifer freaked out and came back to the house. She went into her mother's room pleading, "Mom, I'm really scared. Can you come spend the night in my room? Will you sleep on my bed and I'll sleep on the floor?" Obviously the daughter was still in the confusing cycle of *I want to be the grown up* or *I'm scared to be the grown up. I want to be corded* or *I don't want to be corded.* This is the kind of bewildering drama that parents experience going through during this weaning period with their children.

The only time I think cording in the first chakra is desirable or appropriate is between parent and child under the age of eighteen or nineteen. If a child has developmental disabilities or has to be dependent on the parent for longer than that, it can stay in place for as long as it is needed.

Yet children really cannot fully grow up and be self-sufficient and responsible for their lives until they get *un*corded in the first chakra.

Cords that Bind

Even though that is the only time it is appropriate does not mean that is the only time and place when people cord each other. People cord each other *all the time* before they know not to do that. Every time a manipulative or controlling thought is sent out to another, they have probably just been corded. If there is anybody you give your power away to, you may have allowed him or her to cord you. Nobody can cord you unless you let them. The question is: *Why did you let them?* Why did you give your power away? It's time to stop that limiting pattern.

The cords look like energy projections, always circular. The average size of a cord is about the diameter of a pencil. Although I have seen one as large as a tree trunk when somebody gave their third chakra energy over to their partner, and they had none for themselves. They were living in total victim mentality.

1st Chakra Inappropriate Cording

People cord each other in the *first* chakra, the survival center, to get the other person to take care of them, almost as if they were their parent.

For instance, in the 1950s it was very common for men to call their wives "Mom" and to expect her to take care of them almost as if they were a child rather than the spouse. It was also very common during that time for men to cord their wives in the first chakra and wives ended up with many, many major back problems as a result. When someone allows himself or herself to be corded, the cord replaces their life force energy in that area. This creates a weakness on a physical body level and they are more prone to dis-ease in that region. Yet this pattern was socially sanctioned, at least in this country and perhaps other places around the world.

When my father was about to change addresses, as the Hawaiians would say, and cross over to the other side, he tried to cord me in the first chakra to anchor him here so he would be able to stay. He was an agnostic and was scared of dying because he wasn't sure there was anything on the other side. He was very frustrated that I wouldn't let him; yet I knew that wasn't going to help him in his next adventure and it probably would have just prolonged his suffering.

2ND Chakra Inappropriate Cording

People cord each other in the *second* chakra, the emotional and sexual center, to get you to feel about them the way they want you to feel about them and not necessarily how you feel. Or to get you to be sexual with them the way they want you to be sexual with them, and not necessarily how you feel.

This is what singles bars are about. People go to a singles bar and they drink and they start leaving their bodies. They are really looking for a mutual cording experience in their second chakras. Then they get drunk and they put flashing neon signs on their second chakra that say: *"Choose me! Choose me! Choose me!"* They choose somebody, they go home and sleep together—hopefully with a condom these days—and when the alcohol wears off, they wonder, "Oh my God, what did I do?"

Now that cord is still there! They may get up and leave, sneak out in the middle of the night or maybe even leave in the morning, but that cord does not leave—it is still stuck in there.

Another important aspect of cords is *cords never go away unless you consciously or unconsciously remove them!*

Cords left in a woman's second chakra can become fibroid tumors.

3RD CHAKRA INAPPROPRIATE CORDING

People cord another in the *third* chakra, the will and willpower center, to control, manipulate and impose their will on them. This is where power struggles happen, when someone is trying to will another to do it their way.

When I was doing professional readings, I read a couple who virtually had each other's energy in their third chakras because they were each trying to use their *will* to control the other. It was a big mess and we had to untangle all of that and put the energies back where they belonged.

This is also where stomach pain can happen and where ulcers can get their start. Science has now discovered that many ulcers are caused by bacteria known as H. Pylori. Many, many people have these bacteria, but not everybody with H. Pylori turns into ulcers. Something changes energetically that allows that to manifest. One of the ways is through cording.

4TH CHAKRA INAPPROPRIATE CORDING

People cord others in the *fourth* chakra, the heart or the love and affinity center, to get that person to love them the way they want to be loved, rather than how the other person actually loves them. Before knowing not to, most people in an intimate, loving romantic relationship cord each other in the heart chakra. What they are really doing is looking for bonding in a love way that they hopefully felt from their parents in a survival way when they were young. The problem is that it is still manipulative. It is still trying to get somebody to love you in the way you want to be loved, not in their intrinsic natural way.

I am sure you have all had experiences of knowing people that decided that their relationship was over and they were going to go about their own ways and still be friends, and have a harmonious separation or divorce. All is fine and well until it gets right down to it and then they are fighting about the $1.99 spatula. What is actually happening is they are trying to unconsciously remove those cords that they placed into each other. Those cords have to be removed before they can go on and start a new life.

Many people, especially women, have broken off cords in their heart chakra from broken off relationships, when they unconsciously broke off the cord trying to move on. It is very common for breast cancer to be created in the place where there is a broken off cord because the life force energy of the woman is not there; it is foreign energy instead, which takes on a life of its own. You will learn how to remove broken off cords later in this chapter.

Really good elementary school teachers, before they know not to, have heart chakras that look like spaghetti factories, with all the little children putting their energies out saying, "Love me, love me, love me!" Of course, that makes the elementary teacher's heart chakra and her body be drained by that energy because it is sucking the love right out of her. First-rate elementary school teachers are going to love those little children anyway.

We all need to keep our heart chakras clear—and all of our chakras clear.

5TH CHAKRA INAPPROPRIATE CORDING

People cord you in the *fifth* chakra, the communication center, to get you to say what they want to hear or to get you to *not* say what they don't want to hear.

The boss who is a pain in the neck might really be a pain in your neck. Chiropractors make hundreds of thousands of dollars from cords. What happens is the majority of cords come in from the back, not the front. Most people are not direct about cording others—they are sneaky about it. They think that it will be less likely to be discovered if they send this manipulative cord to somebody's back.

All cords are headed for a chakra. Why? Each chakra has a particular energy focus, or a particular intent, and that cord is trying to get that particular energy from that person. If somebody does not let them in, then they can be off to the side, but they are always headed for a chakra. Nobody ever gets corded in their elbow or their ankle because there is no specific juice or energy there that anybody would want.

People who allow themselves to be corded from the back oftentimes have it go right in the center of that chakra, right in the center of the back, which pushes the vertebrae off to the side and out of alignment.

Then you go to a chiropractor and the chiropractor forces the vertebrae back into alignment and by the time you get in the car, it is out again. Why is that? If you have a cord in that area, it is really hard for your energy to hold your vertebrae in place because the life force energy is not in that spot—instead it is foreign energy from somebody else who has sent it to you. It is not the chiropractor's fault.

If you have a pattern of your back going out or your neck going out immediately after you leave the chiropractor, I would definitely check the area for cords.

6TH CHAKRA INAPPROPRIATE CORDING

People cord you in the *sixth* chakra, the psychic, perception, creativity and healing abilities center, to find out what you know about them. The more psychic you are, the more predisposed you are to have people try to cord you here. You need to know how to block others from doing that. In this chapter you will learn how to fill yourself all the way up with energy so nobody can cord you.

Another reason why people cord you in the sixth chakra is for you to see it their way, so they can get you to perceive things the way they perceive it, rather than the way you perceive it. Or they are trying to get you not to see what they don't want you to see.

In addition, if a person is threatened by your creativity, they might cord you in the sixth chakra to try and block your creativity or try to take it for their own use. Actors or actresses who are in a competitive relationship with each other may cord one another in the sixth chakra.

7TH CHAKRA INAPPROPRIATE CORDING

People cord you in the seventh chakra, the spiritual center at the crown, to get you to be like a puppet on a string, and manipulate you and your way of being. Also, people cord you in this chakra to literally usurp your connection to the Divine so they can become the voice of God for you.

Many cult leaders intentionally cord their followers in the crown chakra to get them to be their puppets. Do you ever wonder why people would drink Kool Aid that they knew contained poison, as Jim Jones' followers did? Or have themselves castrated, as Heaven's Gate followers did, and then commit suicide? Because they were not in their own right mind—they were being controlled energetically by the cult leader.

The crown chakra is the only chakra I believe people can carry over cords from past lifetimes because there is a spiritual connection. If you have cords in your crown chakra from past lives—especially cults that you might have been in then—or cults you might have been in this lifetime, it is extremely important to remove them.

Another arena where cording occurs is in an institution, such as the military, that makes control over somebody's life imperative. Sometimes high-ranking military officers cord their subordinates to have control over them.

Also, people can be in a relationship where they have given their entire well being over to somebody else and allowed themselves to be corded in the crown chakra.

Left Abusive Relationship

After learning my Cord-Removing Process and taking my Medical Intuition Course, one of my students was doing an intuition reading with a client and told her about all the cords she had in her chakras. Jayne then talked her through removing them.

The next day her client called her up and said she left her husband that had been physically abusing her for forty-nine years. *Forty-nine years!* She said before she couldn't ever leave ~ until she removed the cords. That is the power of getting those cords out of you.

Cords in Summary

The *only* appropriate cord is between parent and dependent child, ideally under the age of eighteen or nineteen and only in the first chakra. Or if they have a disability, it can be longer than that, but again *only* in the first chakra or the survival center.

Other than that, they are manipulating you. They are stopping you from putting your energy out into the world to get whatever you want and need on survival levels, on emotional and sexual levels, on will and willpower levels, on love and affinity levels, on communication levels, on psychic, perception, creativity and healing ability levels, and on your spiritual path levels.

Let me be really clear about cords:

1. Cords are always manipulative. If a cord is not between a parent and dependent child in the 1ˢᵗ chakra, they are not okay.

2. Cords are aimed for a chakra center. If somebody does not let them in a chakra center, they can be off to the side of a chakra center because they are looking for the energy that that particular chakra has.

3. No one can cord you unless you let them—consciously or unconsciously.

4. Cords never go away by themselves, unless you consciously or unconsciously remove them.

5. If you cut them or break them off, they take on a life of their own.

6. You cannot remove a cord for someone else. That person let it in and they have to pull it out. However, you can talk them through removing it.

7. Cords can cause major as well as minor physical body problems.

8. You do not have to know the person who corded you.

For example, lets say a beautiful young woman is standing in line at the supermarket, she is spaced out waiting to pay for her food and the checker thinks she is a hot ticket. He sends an energy umbilical cord out of his second chakra and plugs it into her second chakra, and she is unaware of it because she is not in her body. Then she goes out to get in her car and suddenly feels aroused and cannot figure out why. She might never know who that was, but that doesn't mean the cord isn't there. She needs to get it out of her.

Broken Cords

I first saw broken off cords when I was reading the woman who started the fallout in the Guyana massacre with Jim Jones. She got out with her life, but not with her full crown chakra.

Broken off cords look kind of metallic in nature, hard dense energy that becomes their own entity. They are not that person's who sent them anymore, they are not your energy any longer; they are like a foreign object or a foreign substance in your body. The more I began to look at these, the more I realized that they could create havoc with the body. The longer they are in there, the more they can create disease on all levels.

I have seen them in the *first* chakra create vesicular cancer. I have seen them in the *second* chakra creating fibroids. I have seen them in the *third* chakra creating ulcers. I have seen them in the *fourth* chakra creating masses, especially in women's breasts that form into breast cancer. I believe the *number one cause of breast cancer is broken off cords.* Broken off cords in the fourth chakra can also cause hardening of the arteries. I have seen them in the *fifth* chakra as goiters or thyroid cancer. And I have seen them in the *sixth* chakra as brain tumors.

The size of broken off cords can vary. They can be as tiny as a grain of sand and they can be as large as an orange. That was the largest one I ever saw and it was, unfortunately, in a little boy's head that had grown into a brain tumor. We got the broken off cord out and he was healed—it was a miracle!

Some broken cords have been in there close to your entire life, and some might be newer. Whether they are new or old or whomever they are from does not matter. You have to get them out. Just like you do not have to know the source of the wooden splinter that is in your finger to know that it needs to come out.

Identifying the Cords to be Removed

This exercise will show you how your Divine nature is being blocked from manifesting the life you want. Make a list of all those people who you let— and the operative word is *let*—cord you. *Who are the people that you have allowed, and are currently allowing, to manipulate you throughout your life?* The following questions will help you identify the cords that need to be removed. Ask yourself:

- Have you ever felt someone was trying to get you to take care of them?

- Have you ever felt another was trying to get you to feel about them the way they wanted you to feel, rather than how you actually felt?
- Have you ever felt someone was trying to get you to be sexual with them the way they wanted you to be, rather than what you wanted?

- Have you ever felt somebody was trying to control or manipulate you?
- Have you ever felt another person was trying to impose their will on you?
- Have you ever felt someone was trying to get you to do it their way?

- Have you ever felt another was trying to get you to love them the way they want to be loved, rather than how you actually felt?

- Have you ever felt someone was trying to get you to say what they wanted to hear?
- Have you ever felt another person was trying to get you to *not* say what they didn't want to hear?

- Have you ever felt someone was trying to get you to reveal what you psychically knew about them?
- Have you ever felt somebody was trying to get you to see it their way, rather than how you saw it?
- Have you ever felt another was trying to get you *not* to see what they didn't want you to see?
- Have you ever felt someone was threatened by your creativity and they were trying to block your creativity or trying to take it for their own use?

- Have you ever felt that another person was trying to get you to be like a puppet on a string?
- Have you ever felt that someone was trying to dominate you and your way of being?

- Have you ever felt that somebody was trying to usurp your connection to the Divine so they could become the voice of God for you?
- Have you ever felt that you have given your entire well being and control over your life to another?

- Are you willing to release all of the cords that have been placed in your chakras, that perhaps have caused you physical problems such as vesicular cancer, fibroid tumors, stomach pain, ulcers, breast cancer, hardening of the arteries, goiters, thyroid cancer or brain tumors?

- Has this been a recurring theme in your life?

- What is the lesson you have the opportunity to learn here?

- Are you willing to completely release all the cords that are stopping you from manifesting the life of your dreams, and reclaim your power?

Before the end of this chapter, I am going to guide you through how to remove the cords from anyone who has corded you inappropriately. In addition, there could be many other cords from other people that you do not even know their names or that it happened or when or where or why. That does not mean the cord is not there. You need to pull it out anyway, regardless of who it is from. The good news is I am going to show you how to get rid of all of them so you can stop feeding them with your life force energy. Remember, all cords are energy drains. You want to remove all cords to reclaim your freedom and your power.

How to Prevent Others from Cording You or Re-cording You

The way not to be corded is to be filled up all the way with your own energy. If every morning before you left the house, you filled yourself all the way up with your being, your soul, your spirit, then there is no room in there for anybody else's energy.

Did you ever get up in the morning and trip over your shoes that are lying on the floor where you left them the night before, spill your tea all over yourself and put your sweater on inside out? Are you in your body when that is happening? No, you did not come all the way down from the causal plane during your sleep state, and you are not all the way into your body. Instead just sit down and take a couple of deep breaths with your intention to have your being, your soul, your spirit come all the way down into your body and fill yourself up with your own energy. Later in this chapter, I will guide you through a process of filling yourself up with energy so no one can cord you. If you are all the way filled up with you, nobody can cord you anywhere except for your young dependant children._

In addition, if you feel that there is somebody that is continuously cording you and you cannot seem to keep them out with just filling yourself up, after you have removed the cord you can always create an elastic mesh energy bandage to put over that area that was corded. It is like a screen door, but made out of golden elastic energy fibers with the outside like Teflon. As you put this in place, state your intention:

Only positive energy can get in through this elastic mesh bandage
and any other energy will be sloughed off.
Any energy of mine that is ready to flow out can easily and effortlessly
flow out through this.

You can only leave these energy bandages up for a couple weeks until you strengthen that area and then dissolve the energy bandage into neutralized energy, and send it down to the energy-recycling center at the center of the planet.

Cording Others

If *you* have tried consciously or unconsciously to manipulate another and corded them to get what you want, you also want to take that energy back because it is out there with them instead of in you helping you live your life in the best way possible. It is strewn around the planet trying, for example, to get your mother to buy you a Besty-Wetsy dolly or to get your father to buy you that ten-speed bike that you do not want any more. Your energy is still out there trying to make those things happen even though there is no need anymore. Wouldn't it be helpful to have that energy back? Also, you could still have somebody corded who is now on the other side and you need to have your energy back and they need to be able to move on.

As we get higher and higher up into our expanded levels of consciousness, we need to be impeccable in our integrity with our energy systems and not cord another, unless it is your dependent child and then only in the first chakra.

I first discovered not to cord another inappropriately in my early twenties when I went to this great place to dance. The women could dance with the men or with each other, the men could dance with the women or with each other, or we could dance by ourselves. I was drinking Perrier at the time, so I didn't even have the excuse of drinking.

I was waiting in line for the women's bathroom, which was ten times as long as the men's bathroom line. It was so long it went out into the dance area. As I was standing there waiting my turn, I was admiring—now remember I was in my early twenties—this man's back side. Suddenly he turned around and followed the energy over to me. I realized he was really drunk as he staggered over to me.

"Wanna dance?" he asked, as he precariously swayed back and forth.

Oh my God, I realized, *I have inadvertently corded him!* There I was admiring him and I sent this cord out of my second chakra right into his back side. He felt that cord and it made him spin around and start following it back to me.

When I realized what I had done, I immediately pulled my cord back in by breathing it back into myself.

"No, thanks," I replied, "I'm standing in line waiting for the bathroom."

He looked at me really confused, and then staggered off. I learned to never do that again and vowed on the spot not to cord anyone inappropriately ever again.

When you notice yourself doing something like that, make a commitment that you will never do it again.

Difference Between Desire and Cording

What is the difference between having a desire and cording someone? It is the intent. We have to be clear with our intent, rather than manipulative. Make sure there is not any manipulation involved in what you are sending out. That is the difference.

If you feel like you have to have power over others, it is time now to let go of that. If you have corded those you love, you need to take those cords back so you no longer are controlling or manipulating them. That does not mean you are disconnecting from them—they already know you love them—you are just taking back the controlling or manipulative aspects.

Identifying the Cords You Placed in Others

This exercise will show you the energy blockages that keep you from creating the life you want and identify the cords you have placed in others that need to be breathed back into you. Make a list of all those people you have corded. Include all those that you have tried to control or manipulate throughout your life. The following questions will help you remember the cords you have placed in others. Ask yourself:

- Have you ever tried to get someone to take care of you?
- Have you ever tried to get somebody to help you find a home?
- Have you ever tried to get another person let you live with him or her?
- Have you ever tried to get someone to ground you?

- Have you ever tried to get another to feel about you the way you wanted them to feel about you?
- Have you ever tried to get somebody to be sexual with you the way you wanted them to be sexual with you?

- Have you ever tried to impose your will on another person?
- Have you ever tried to control another?
- Have you ever tried to manipulate someone by engaging in a power struggle?

- Have you ever tried to get somebody to love you the way you wanted to be loved?

- Have you ever tried to get someone to say what you wanted them to say?
- Have you ever tried to get another to *not* say what you didn't want them to say?

- Have you ever tried to get somebody to tell you what they know about you?
- Have you ever tried to get another person to see things your way?
- Have you ever tried to take another's creativity?
- Have you ever tried to block someone's creativity?

- Have you ever tried to get somebody to be like a puppet on your string?
- Have you ever tried to manipulate someone's religious or spiritual beliefs?
- Have you ever tried to manipulate another's way of being?

- Are you willing to remove all of the cords that you have inappropriately put into others?

- What is your perceived payoff in cording others inappropriately? What is the benefit your body personality is getting out of it?

- Are you willing to let it go?

- Has this been a recurring theme in your life? Is it a life lesson?

- What is the lesson you have the opportunity to learn here?

- Are you willing to completely transform this limiting pattern that is stopping you from using your life force energy to create the life you want?

Increasing Your Awareness

None of this is to make you feel guilty. It is simply to make you aware and conscious of not sending your energy out in any way, shape or form that has a manipulative intent behind it. Forgive yourself. Do not beat yourself up for anything you have done in the past when you were not aware of the consequences of your actions. Now you know never to do it again.

One of my students has an annual cord removing party. They listen to my CD guiding them through removing the cords and sending them back to the people that sent them, and next breathing back the cords that they sent out to others. Then they party all night long with no drugs or alcohol because they are so filled with the energy that they have reclaimed.

Now that you are aware of the cords that need to be removed, that's what we are going to do next. I am going to guide you through the chakras and facilitate you pulling that energy back into yourself, so you are free and empowered to create the life you want.

Here is an overview of how we are going to remove the cords: By now, you know never, ever cut cords. Instead, flood that area with healing energy, grab hold of the cord at the base, turn it, twist it and jiggle it so it is loosened. Pull it all the way out past the edge of your aura and let it go, so it can return back to the one who sent it. Then fill that hole back up with healing energy.

Yes, you do need to remove them one at a time. Think of what happens if you try to pull a handful of weeds out of the ground all at once. You break the roots off that then become stronger. The same thing happens if you try to pull out more than one cord at a time.

Then we will breathe back the cords you have inappropriately placed into others and reclaim your energy and your manifesting power.

Reclaiming Your Freedom and Your Power

Now it is time to listen to the second audio meditation to free you from any limiting cords that have been placed into you by another or any cords you have placed in another that have created blockages, including broken cords, so you can reclaim your freedom and your power to transform your life now. To download this free audio recording, please email us at audio@ TransformYourLifeNow.net for instructions.

Note: Be aware that this audio meditation contains very powerful energy and should **not** be listened to while you are driving a car or operating heavy equipment. Choose a quiet place to sit where you will not be disturbed, so you can receive maximum benefit from these transforming exercises. Once again, ask the Divine within you to assist you in removing all cords unless they are with your dependent children, including broken cords, easily and effortlessly, so that you can manifest the life you desire.

Continue listening to this second meditation so you can continue to pull out all the rest of the cords within you, except for any cords from your dependent children under the age of eighteen or nineteen. If you have waited until the age that you are now to weed your garden, there would be a lot of weeds. But once you weed the whole garden, if there is a new weed the next day, it will be a tiny little sprout and you can just pluck it out, it will be no big deal.

I strongly encourage you to remove and keep removed all the cords that stop you from creating the life that you truly want. Make it a permanent habit of keeping your energy systems clean and clear by re-listening to this second meditation whenever you feel that you have allowed yourself to be corded, so that you stay in the freedom and empowerment of the Divine.

Deepening Your Connection with Your Loved One

To have a stronger connection with those you love, invite them to link with your heart chakra. You are inviting them to make that connection with you without the manipulation of a cord.

Think of someone you want to have a stronger love connection with. It does not have to be a sexual relationship. It can be a parent, a child, a grandparent, an auntie or an uncle. It can be your brother or a sister. It can be a soul mate or your significant other or your partner.

Bring your attention to your heart chakra in the center of your chest at your heart chakra. Think of the person you want to invite to have a heart connection with you. Then think to their being or soul or spirit that you are inviting them to have the opportunity to link with you at the heart chakra. You cannot make them do it. If you are singing, "You made me love you, I didn't want to do it," that is a cord. We are not doing that.

If you have not met your soul mate yet, you may want to invite their being or soul or spirit to be sitting across from you, and again you cannot make them do it. If it is a soul mate, you can create a rainbow-colored ring of heart energy, about two-foot in diameter, that comes out of the very core of your heart center and goes out about two feet. Then invite your soul mate to reciprocate and send a rainbow-colored ring of heart energy out of the core of their heart center, and have the two rings link like links on a chain.

If it is not your soul mate, send a rose-colored loving ring out in front of you from the core of your heart chakra about two feet in diameter. If you get a different color, that is the one that you want to use. Invite—you cannot make them do it—invite that other person to link with you, like links on a chain. Since these links are energy, you can be on the other side of the planet and have that heart link still be there. These links are flexible and freeing because you are making that connection without the manipulation of a cord. Invite them to link with you now and if they are going to do it, they will. If they are not ready, they are not going to. And that's fine.

Since you have been interacting with their being, soul, spirit—their light body—send them back to their physical body, having the link remain, and ask them to easily and effortlessly integrate this heart link into their body personality. If it is a soul mate you have not yet met, you can ask them to use this link to lead them to you, and you to them in physical body form.

I believe these energy rings linked at the heart chakra are the origin of wedding rings.

Later, if the relationship ever ends, I encourage you to unlink those heart links and breathe your link back in and have the other person also breathe their link back in. Then you have reclaimed your energy.

After you have done the exercises on the second meditation and reclaimed your freedom and your power, you are now ready to move on to Chapter 10 and live in the Divine flow.

Part II:
Realizing Your Destiny

Living in the Divine Flow

What would your life be like living from the unlimited Divine and excelling on all levels? What does living in the Divine Flow look like to you? What form would that take on a daily basis?

Since you probably have not given yourself permission to even contemplate those questions, here is an opportunity to begin expanding your thinking into claiming your natural birthright.

Write down the answers to the following questions:

1. How would a spiritual master live in the Divine flow in the survival aspects of their life?

2. How would they live in the Divine flow in the emotional and sexual aspects of their life?

3. How would they live in the Divine flow in the will, willpower and manifesting aspects of their life?

4. How would they live in the Divine flow in the love and affinity aspects of their life?

5. How would they live in the Divine flow in the communication aspects of their life?

6. How would they live the Divine flow in the psychic, perception, creativity and healing aspects of their life?

7. How would they live in Oneness with the Divine?

Living in the Divine Flow in All Aspects of Your Life

Once you have done that, then go within and imagine yourself living in the Divine flow in all of those same areas, for imagining leads to manifestation. Allow yourself to really *feel* it in every chakra of your body.

1ˢᵗ Chakra - Imagine living in the Divine flow in your survival aspect easily, effortlessly and enjoyably creating perfect health, creating the perfect form of income and abundance and the best way to put your gifts out into the world to receive monetary acknowledgment for your service. Imagine having the best living accommodations for you, eating the healthiest diet for you. Imagine gliding rather than plowing through your life, thriving rather than just surviving.

2ⁿᵈ Chakra – Imagine having emotional balance and living in the Divine flow, being happy and peaceful and joyful and blissful—regardless of what is going on outside of you. Imagine drawing to you healthy, appropriate, nurturing, supportive, sensual experiences to feel your sensuality as just another emanation of the Divine flow, either with a healthy, supportive, nurturing, balanced partner *or* to experience your sensuality in a way that is honoring who you are as a sensual being.

Imagine living in the Divine flow, using your clairsentience or clear feeling to tune into what is going on in the world and responding in a harmonious way that keeps you in the spiritual flow.

3ʳᵈ Chakra – Imagine living in the Divine flow using your will and willpower or manifesting abilities in healthy ways that co-create with the Divine and draw to you the abundance that you need on every level, knowing that there is plenty for everyone and allowing those Divine creative manifesting energies to flow through you so you easily and effortlessly create whatever is for your highest good.

4ᵗʰ Chakra - Imagine living in the Divine flow in the love and affinity aspects of your life, truly loving yourself first and foremost—yet not from an egocentric way—loving who you are and acknowledging the Divine within you and living in that truth, so you can clearly love others and acknowledge the Divine in them. Imagine honoring the true Divine essence within you so you may truly see that in totality in somebody else, and give them the opportunity to radiate that out as well.

Imagine living your life in a way that you are looking for and seeing all the positive qualities within yourself and others, which amplifies and strengthens those qualities within you. Imagine *only* seeing the Divine within yourself and others, for this is the best way to *be* the Divine yourself and to experience the Divine within others.

5ᵗʰ Chakra – Imagine speaking your highest truth and living in the Divine flow in the communication aspect of your life. Imagine truly speaking truth in a way that whoever you are communicating with, including yourself, can hear it easily and effectively.

Imagine opening up your clairaudience or clear hearing as well as your direct voice and being able to clearly speak spiritual truth as well as easily hear Divine truth.

6ᵗʰ Chakra – Imagine using your psychic ability and your clairvoyance or clear vision in oneness with the Divine flow. Imagine using your intuitive abilities to know exactly how to respond to any given situation and how to share that information with others, if it is called for.

Imagine enjoying one of the great benefits of living in the Divine flow of having the Divine perspective, and being privileged to see the world through the perception of Source, and to see that it is all Divine all the time, and to know that everything, regardless of how it appears at the moment, is really in Divine order.

Imagine living in the Divine flow and seeing from the Divine perspective and clearly *knowing* what opportunities to take full advantage of, whether it is a job, a relationship or new spiritual truths that are opening up to you. Imagine always looking at everything from the higher perspective, rather than taking things personally.

Imagine living in the Divine flow of your creativity as great composers and artists like Beethoven, Bach, Leonardo DaVinci, Renoir and Rembrandt did. Imagine allowing inspiration to come through you, just like many writers of uplifting songs, books and movies do today. Imagine allowing that Divine creativity to flow through you and magic happening.

Imagine the true healing that comes from the Divine flowing through you, making you the most powerful healer that you can possibly be for yourself and others. Imagine seeing the perfection of Source on all levels—physical, emotional, mental and spiritual—as you bring this healing energy through these different aspects. Imagine this Divine healing energy coming down into the person being healed, so that the perfect resonance and frequency from Source gives them the opportunity for wholeness, health and well being on all levels.

7th **Chakra** - Then imagine living in the Divine flow in your spiritual center in Oneness with the Divine, knowing that you are the emanation of the Divine, knowing that you are made of the Source and knowing that is within you. Imagine knowing that you are truly Divine, knowing all things are possible. Imagine not limiting yourself on any level. Imagine opening up the crown chakra and allowing the Source to flow through you, and stepping into complete alignment and Oneness with the Divine, knowing *that* is who you really are.

Imagine yourself using this great gift of living in the Divine flow.

The more you return to this exercise, the more you will begin to live in the Divine flow in every area of your life.

Living in the Divine Flow

Here are some examples from my own life of living in the Divine flow.

THRIVING IN THE 1ST CHAKRA

When I decided to move to Maui, I found a house to buy and everything was in place. I sold my house in Oahu and I had the movers coming and it was all set up; all the dominos were in place. I sent the inspectors to inspect the new house and they found out that the people who had owned it previously had taken the support wall out and the roof was collapsing. I was very happy to know that, but because everything was in place to move, I needed to find a house quickly.

I had my realtor in Oahu contact a realtor in Maui and I flew over to find where I was going to move. And I had four hours to find my new house, so I put myself in the Divine flow of knowing that I would be led absolutely, perfectly to that house, that it would be very clear and I would know it instantly. I totally trusted that I was going to find it in four hours.

The realtor in Maui picked me up at the airport and told me that she had found four houses in the price range and the description that I had given her. She drove me to the first one and we got to the house and I said, "That's not it!"

"You haven't gone in it yet," she quickly responded.

"Why would I go in when it isn't it?" I replied.

"You don't want to see it?" she asked in disbelief.

"No," I said, "why would I see it if it's not it?" I confirmed.

Then we drove to the second house on the list and as we reached the street where it was located, I said, "It's not it."

"But you don't even know which house it is," she said, clearly perplexed by my response.

"Yes, but this isn't the street that it's on," I replied.

"Okay," she said with hesitation, not believing her ears.

Then we drove to the third house and as we entered the community and the area, I said, "It isn't it."

"We're not even on the street," she replied in disbelief.

"Yes, but it isn't it."

"There's only one more house," she replied wearily.

"Okay, why don't we drive there?" I responded.

As she was driving up the hill, I knew that this was it. We turned into another street and I wasn't even sure that this was the street that the house was on, but I knew. And I said, "This is it!"

"You don't even know which house it is," she said with amazement.

"Yes, but this is it," I affirmed.

We park the car and we go into the house. I walk through the living room to the back lanai and I say, "This is it."

"But you haven't even seen the house yet," astonishment dripping from her voice. "You haven't seen the bedrooms or the bathrooms, you haven't seen the rest of the house."

"This is it!" I confirmed.

She was very uncomfortable with all of this. I told her how much I was going to pay and the date I wanted it to close, which was the date when my other house was going to close.

"Oh, that will never happen," she immediately responded.

Of course, that was the date that the sale closed and that was exactly how much I paid. This is an example of living in the Divine flow.

Magnetizing a Sensuous Relationship from the 2ⁿᵈ Chakra

I decided I was ready for a sensuous relationship. While sitting on my lanai, I put out to the universe what I wanted in a relationship. Then I felt this presence that was so clear to me that I actually stood up. It was this man's being, soul, spirit. I felt him embracing me and I knew he was tall. I knew he had long, dark hair. I could feel him kissing the side of my neck and I felt his body size and shape and I knew he was younger than me.

"Okay," I said, "you need to appear in body now." I knew that I had called in his spirit.

Shortly after that while in a museum in Hana, I learned that one of the Hawaiian princesses had sent out a white owl to find her life partner and to bring him back to her. I went out to the same park where she had sent out the owl and I called in a white owl so I could send it out as a messenger to find the man whose spirit had come to me on my lanai.

What came instead was a dragonfly and it flew all around my head and then his mate came and they mated. "I guess it's the dragonfly for me," I thought. Then I asked the dragonfly to go find the one from my lanai.

Not too long after that I met Derek who was exactly the body, size and shape of the spirit I had seen and kissed me on the side of my neck just like he had. Then one day when he was cooking for me outside, a dragonfly came and flew all around his head and I started laughing. "That's my lucky symbol," he said. "Something always good is happening when a dragonfly shows up."

We had a wonderful relationship for many, many months. I knew that I had called him in and he would show up once I called in his spirit and made that connection. And I knew he was going to appear exactly when he was meant to, and he did.

Manifesting Affordable Cars from the 3ʳᵈ Chakra

Because I know I can manifest cars, I do it easily and effortlessly. When my older girls were teenagers and were starting to drive, I wanted to get them a car. I manifested an older car that only had 36,000 miles on it. They were asking $4,000 for it, yet I knew they would take half. When I told them I would give them $2,000, they were happy to take it.

When my older girls' father wanted a truck, we got him a brand new truck for $200 over the dealer price. I have done that many times. When somebody stole my car from my driveway when we lived in Oahu, I could have flipped out about it, but I had insurance and why do that. When the car was found, it was totaled. The insurance company paid me $2,500 more for the car than I had paid for it.

It all started when I was thirty and I was in a car accident that totaled my car. I decided my insurance company would pay me what I paid for the car five years and 90,000 miles before, which was $3,200. This was a long time ago when you could buy a brand new Honda Civic for $3,200! The insurance company *did* give me $3,200, but I forgot I had a $200 deductible, so I received $3,000 for a car that was five years old with 90,000 miles on it.

I live in the Divine flow of manifesting great deals on cars. All of my friends and family members take me with them to get their car.

ATTRACTING A LOVING RELATIONSHIP FROM THE 4ᵀᴴ CHAKRA

When I was twenty-eight, I told my mother that I was getting married the next May. She asked, "Who are you marrying, honey?"

"I don't know," I replied, "I haven't met him yet."

"Okay," she said, "can you make it the end of May because I'm teaching at the State university of New York at Albany and the school doesn't get out until the end of May."

"I'm sure that can be arranged," I assured her.

Then just a couple of weeks later, I met this man. Four weeks after that I had a dream that he was on this big clipper ship with a wedding ring on. I woke up and asked the universe, "What does that mean? Tell me what that means right now. I want it to be very clear. I do not want it to be symbolic."

I went back to sleep and I had a causal plane experience of his being, soul, spirit and my being, soul, spirit talking about getting married, so I knew we were getting married.

Then when he did ask me to marry him, I said, "When were you thinking of?"

"How about May," he said.

"Can we make it the end of May because my mother's classes don't get out until the end of May," I replied.

"Sure, that's fine," he responded.

When he chose his wedding ring, it had a big clipper ship engraved on it. I realized I had dyslexia in my dream—I just reversed things—instead of him being *on* a clipper ship wearing a wedding ring, in reality he had a wedding ring with a clipper ship on it because he had sailed half way around the world in a thirty-two-foot sailboat.

This is a good example of living in the Divine flow. I had already received information that I would be getting married in May before I met him. Once we met, I was shown in a dream that he was wearing a wedding ring and the clipper ship. Then I was given the awareness on the causal plane that we were getting married. In actuality, I got married at the end of May and the wedding ring that he chose had a clipper ship on it. This man became the father of my grown children.

COMMUNICATING MY TRUTH FROM THE 5TH CHAKRA

When I was in my early twenties, Jerry Brown was running for a second term as Governor of California. He was giving a talk in Ukiah, California where I happened to be at the moment. I decided I wanted to talk to him, so I walked up on the platform where he was going to speak. I just sat there and waited for him to arrive. When he came, he gave his talk and then turned around to leave and I said, "Hello Governor Brown, I'm Laurie" and gave him my words of wisdom.

This is an example of living in the Divine flow of faith. On the one hand, who am I to walk up on the platform where Governor Brown is going to give a talk and take a seat. No security guards removed me; nobody said, "You have to leave." Why? Because I knew that I was guided to go up there and to talk to him, which I did.

He was able to hear me because I was doing it in the Divine flow. If I thought, "Oh I know I'm going to get in trouble for being up here," you bet the security guards would have come and hauled me off the platform. But I wasn't. I was led to be up there, and I allowed myself to be guided and to speak the words that were coming through me.

USING PSYCHIC ABILITIES FROM THE 6TH CHAKRA

I had a relationship with a man Steven many years ago who was incredibly psychic. He would read my mind all the time without me saying anything. One day I was sharing with a friend, "Even if I just think of Steven, he will call me." And then I immediately said, "Cancel, cancel, cancel" to the universe because I didn't have any reason for him to call me right then. Shortly thereafter, Steven called and asked me, "Were you trying to cancel lunch for tomorrow?" That is an example of being in the Divine flow in the 6th chakra.

EXPERIENCING DIVINE UNION FROM THE 7TH CHAKRA

All my experiences of union with the Divine and ultimately Oneness non-duality as well as my ongoing state of Oneness with everyone and everything are examples of living in the Divine flow.

Choosing to Live in the Divine Flow

After Sara's house was destroyed by fire and she lost everything she owned except her family, she consciously chose to use the spiritual tools she had learned to live in the Divine flow. Then magical events began to unfold and she found all her families' needs met with grace and love. This is such a classic case of having this horrific thing happen and *still* living in the Divine flow. Most people would just crumble when their house completely burned to the ground and stop themselves—for a while at least—from moving forward in life. Instead Sara took it as a sign of an opportunity to learn the lesson of not being attached to physical things and the real importance of family and friends and turned everything around to be completely in the Divine flow in the midst of an extremely challenging time. This is such an inspiration for all of us, especially in the face of adversity, to be able to maintain that Divine connection. And to shepherd her whole family through that experience to the point where her son said, "The fire did us a favor, Mom. It brought us so much closer together!"

Despair Turns into Bliss

Here is report from one of my teleseminar participants, Trudy, once she cleared her chakras and cords to live in the Divine flow:

"Before doing this work with you, my life was pretty awful, feeling hopeless and despair. I felt totally disconnected from Source. That's when the serious thoughts of leaving the planet kicked in.

"After clearing all the chakras and removing the cords, I began experiencing joy in my life, trusting my feelings and honoring my choices to just say, 'No, thank you.' Life got so much lighter and easier. I liked me a lot and I had so much less judgment of others too! People in my life actually got nicer and easier to work with. I've been able to clearly articulate the truth so people are able to hear it. And I'm back to thinking of someone that I need to speak with and having them call me within a few minutes. I've been watching the 'psychic' activity and it covers the gamut from having things tell me which drawer they are in, going to the window when deer 'happen' to be in the yard, to connecting with a woman who has the perfect retreat site for me that I have been looking for in the woods about thirty minutes from here. And I'm hearing messages from Source again and loving my life! How cool is that!

"Here's how I envision my life unfolding living in the Divine spiritual flow: I awake joyfully in the morning knowing that life will unfold easily, effortlessly and enjoyably. I thrive in and honor the sensuality of my being. I use my feelings to guide me to make choices that will support my life's work of creating healing environments with toning and sound. I am totally supported in exploring and sharing this work with others. I have clarity of communication that allows me to express my talents in ways that are easily understood. I use my perception of things to clearly see and hear what wants to be expressed next. I easily evolve and continually co-create my life with Source.

"Life is Good! And it just keeps getting better! I am blissed out by the beauty of life.

"Perhaps the simplest way to describe what has happened is that life just got so much easier. There is an ease of being around people who used to absolutely drive me crazy.

"Expressing my thanks doesn't begin to cover what an amazing blessing you and this process have been in my life. Thank you!"

Everything Now Unfolds with Ease and Grace

After taking the I'O Mastery seminar, Claire told me that her whole life shifted to living in the Divine flow. All the problems that she used to experience at work simply disappeared as everything unfolded with ease and grace. As a massage therapist at a heavily booked spa, Claire now magically was given her favorite massage room whenever she needed it, whereas previously she was assigned less desirable rooms. The noise from the other rooms that had been a problem ceased to exist. The perfect dates that Claire wanted to work just fell into place, giving her more time to play and enjoy her life. Her massage clients could feel the wonderful energy flowing through her and wanted to know what she was doing differently that felt so good. She found all the areas of her life unfolding with an easy flow that she had not known before. Claire now lives and works in the blissful state of the Divine flow.

Daily Checklist to Ensure Living in the Divine Flow

1. Go into a meditative state.

2. Envision the Divine filling up the *first* chakra and experience it flowing out through all the layers to the edges of the skin and to the aura and beyond.

Then do the same with the *second* chakra. Then the *third, fourth, fifth, sixth* all the way up to the *seventh* at the crown.

3. Next feel yourself experiencing abundance on all levels: abundantly *thriving, emotional and sensual* abundance, *manifesting* abundance, abundantly *loving yourself and others*, an abundance of *communicating clearly and effectively*; an abundance of *psychic, perception, creativity,*

and healing abilities, and of course the abundance of *living your Divine spiritual path.*

4. Create the intent that you are living your highest in all of those areas—even before you get out of bed in the morning.

Once you are in the Divine flow, what you can manifest is limitless because the Divine is the creative force of nature and when you are filled with that, then there is nothing stopping you from having whatever it is around you and within you that is your intent to manifest. The irony is that when you are able to do that, you are not attached to any of it—because you are living in the Divine, that place of limitlessness and Oneness with Source. That is why we are here. What is more important? Nothing.

Now you are ready to move on to Chapter 11 and stay in the Divine flow all the time.

Staying in the Divine Flow

"How do I stay connected to my Divinity?" you may be wondering. "If I'm not in the Divine flow, what do I do?" This chapter will help you stay on course and reset your compass if you find yourself going in the opposite direction from what you truly want.

As your body personality goes through this journey into amazing transformation, there are times when it decides to rebel and put the brakes on and suddenly—or sometimes not so suddenly—attempts to sabotage your forward progress. You may ask yourself, "Why is this happening? What is going on? Why am I doing this instead of allowing myself to move forward?"

Body personalities have their own agenda. They do not like to make change. That is why it is so hard for some people to lose weight or so hard for others to gain weight. Body personalities resist change and want to keep the status quo, even though it may be totally dysfunctional, at least they know what to expect. And here we are transforming your life!

Realize this might be a wonderful sign of your growth when the body personality attempts to slow things down. When you are on the fast track to enlightenment, the ego has to step aside and eventually fall away for you to get to your ultimate destination. Of course, your body personality is attached to the ego—it basically *is* your ego—so the ego comes up with all of the reasons why you should not be making these changes for fear of its own demise.

It can come up with very creative ways to get you to give up expanding your consciousness and go back to your old ways of being. For example, my friend Bob, an incredible healer, decided that he was ready to hang out his shingle, and he rented a space to do his healing work. The first of the month came when he had signed on to have the grand opening of his new practice and suddenly his back went out. Then he decided he could not do his healing work. He began to go into a downward spiral of even eating junk food, which he had not eaten for years. Even having a beer now and then, which he had not done for a great length of time. And he began to hang out with his former friends that were into partying. He began to get very grouchy and say things that were very unlike him to his friends.

As Bob was explaining all of this to me, I asked him how many ARCH and I'O treatments, which he had mastered, had he done on himself? He told me that he had only done one or two rounds of ARCH.

"Here you are this masterful healer and you're not working on healing your own back?" I questioned. "What is the perceived payoff? What is the lesson here?" Even though it was obvious to me, he had not connected the dots that his back went out just before he was opening up his healing practice. "If this were me," I said, "and I was about to open a big center and suddenly my back went out and I didn't do healing work on myself and I started eating junk food and not exercising and drinking a beer or two now and then and hanging out with my old friends that are not on my path and getting sucked up into the energy of where they are, what would you be saying to me? What do you think the connection would be?" And then he got it.

Clearly his body personality and his ego were in massive resistance to stepping into who he really is. The good thing about this is obviously he was ready for a major breakthrough; otherwise his body personality would not have rebelled in such an acute manner.

If you get to a place where your body personality is not only whining, it is shouting at you, it is time to step back and to applaud yourself, knowing you must really be transforming things! You must really be stepping into your true self-empowerment. Be ready to take a giant leap. Get prepared to take those next steps and to let the ego, or at least some of it, dissolve and stop controlling your life.

Correcting Your Course

What do you do if you find yourself off course? The first thing is to become aware of it and realize what is going on. Next, treat the body personality, essentially the ego, as you would a young child—with love and gentleness while setting very clear boundaries. Then focus on what you want and look closely at what you are currently doing. *Are the things you are doing helping you get what you truly want?* If not, find ways to stop doing them.

For example, eating junk food does not give you the clarity within your body you need to bring the highest levels of consciousness through you. Remember you can pour crystal clear spring mountain water into a dirty glass and you are going to get dirty water. If eating junk food is polluting your clear energy, it is simple—stop eating junk food. If the alcohol or the recreational drug is not allowing you to reach those higher levels of consciousness and are numbing you out instead, become aware of that and stop doing that. If hanging out with your old friends is pulling you back down, realize you can still love them, but you do not have to be with them.

It is very hard for a butterfly to socialize with a caterpillar. There is nothing wrong with the caterpillar. We have all been caterpillars throughout hundreds of lifetimes and they are doing exactly what they are meant to be doing. You cannot be angry at a caterpillar for not being a butterfly. They all have a Divine purpose, but clipping your wings to go back down to the level where a caterpillar functions of just seeing the grass or the dirt before them and whatever is happening on either side rather than being the butterfly that is able to fly around and see the whole expanse of opportunities is not for anybody's highest good, including the caterpillar.

Realize that as you are transforming into the butterfly and finding your wings so you can soar, there will be times when you do not quite know what is up ahead and it might feel safer to go back down to the old ways. But where's the adventure in that? You already know how the old lifestyle goes.

You are reading this book because now is your time to transform, to step into who you truly are. You know that you are here for bigger things. The tools in this book can help you get there. Will there be days when you trip and fall? Perhaps. When most people first learned to walk, they stood up and took a step and fell down; they stood up and took a step and fell down. There are others, like my oldest daughter, who learned to stand, walk and run all in a split second. The moment she found that balancing point to stand upright, she was off and she could walk and run in that same instant. For some, that is the way it will be. For others, you may take a step forward and fall down. Then you pick yourself up, dust yourself off and start all over again. And you lovingly, gently, love and nurture your body and your spirit, knowing that the important thing is the forward motion, not how quickly you get there.

As a wise person once said, "Happiness is not a destination, it is a journey." It is the same with enlightenment. The journey is living your life in the most conscious way—at least as conscious a way as you can while you're getting there.

Remember, if you do something that seems like backsliding to you, say to yourself, "I'll do better tomorrow. I'll do better next time." Because you will!

Staying Connected to Your Divinity

As you find your wings and start playing in the higher realms of consciousness, there will be those that come with you, and others that it's not their time to move forward yet. The great thing about the butterfly is that it's going to easily soar around and find the other butterflies. And I know you can do that too.

The school systems have found it is advantageous to place non-average students who have special needs with average students, yet it is not advantageous to place gifted students with average students because the gifted ones naturally gravitate to the level of the environment in which they are surrounded.

For instance, one of my daughters had dyslexia and when she was put in classes for special needs children, she sunk to the bottom and when she was placed in regular classes, she was in the middle of the class. I also had two gifted children and when they were put in classes for average students, they were at the higher end of the regular classes, but when they were placed in gifted programs, they excelled in incredibly amazing ways and reached their higher potential.

If you want to stay where you are, hang out with your old friends. If you want to transform into higher awareness, soar around and find like-minded others that are where you are now. It does not mean you stop loving the friends that you have known all your life, it means that you have new friends that you are able to join with at your new level and expand in even greater ways. As we know, when two or more are gathered in the name of the Divine, it allows our power to grow and expand exponentially, enabling us to create wondrous things together.

Focusing on Where You Want to Go

As soon as the butterfly emerges from the cocoon and begins to fly, they are no longer operating on a caterpillar level and the things they did and the ones they hung out with as a caterpillar no longer feel truly harmonious to them. Yet as they take flight, a whole new world opens in front of them and a whole *new* group of friends that are at this new level emerges that allows them to begin a new exciting even more wondrous adventure than before. The key to staying in the Divine flow is to *keep your focus on where you want to go*, rather than looking back to where you have been in the past.

When your ego's resistance to your forward movement, such as opening a new healing practice, draws you back into old habits and back to the old way like an old comfortable worn-out shoe, this is how to return to living in the Divine flow:

1. The first step is to notice yourself doing it.

2. The next step is to write a list of what you want. What are your dreams? What are your goals? What do you want to accomplish in this lifetime?

3. Then make another list of what you are currently doing, such as eating junk food, not exercising, hanging out with old friends whose goals in life are not compatible with yours.

4. Ask yourself: *Are the things I am currently doing helping me to achieve my goals? Am I moving forward or am I slipping backwards?*

When you backslide, you are giving away your power to create the freedom and the future that you want! It seems really subtle at the time, but what is happening is major. You are using your free will to do what? To self-sabotage! When you misuse your power to self-sabotage, you are discounting and negating who you really are and why you are really here. That is a choice. But is that the choice you want to make? Or instead do you want to put your energy and your powerful manifesting abilities into doing what you really came here to do? You could be choosing to live an empowered, free life, choosing the best life for you, aligned with your Divine Self and moving forward into a glorious future.

Resetting Your Compass

If you find yourself misusing your power and moving backward, do not judge yourself. Be grateful you are aware that you have begun the process of climbing up the mountain of enlightenment and you are making amazing strides. When you decide to climb back down to a lower level because you think it is easier, then catch yourself doing that, and applaud yourself for being aware of what you are doing. Then reset your compass, reset your direction—just like an airplane pilot makes hundreds of adjustments every minute, since the plane is on automatic pilot, to reach its desired destination. The good thing is you don't have to be on automatic pilot. You can decide to become consciously aware instead of being on automatic, and set your intention of where you want to be and what you want to do with your life and your spiritual journey.

Since the way we have been raised is to stay with the status quo and to fit within the rules of society or our family, do not be surprised if you are drawn back to the old way. Instead you can choose to be your own unique person and expression of the Divine that you truly came here to be and contribute the wonderful gifts that you came here to contribute, which are so needed at this time.

Remember, it is all Divine all the time, so do not beat yourself up if you find yourself headed in the wrong direction. Realize it's an opportunity to learn and grow from that experience. Then make a stronger commitment and intention to set your course forward again.

Bless those moments of awareness that you are off course that have come into your consciousness. It is all an opportunity for growth. It just means you are expanding your awareness and your perspective. Next time you will recognize those signs sooner, if there ever is a next time. If your body personality does start to rebel again, know you will catch it quicker and redirect yourself even more rapidly.

Whatever the choices are, they are never bad or wrong, as it is always a chance for growth. However, there are missed opportunities when people aren't quite ready to let themselves have that experience or they allow their fears to stop them from pursuing that opportunity.

As we go further along our path toward higher levels of consciousness, we become more and more aware of the chances that are being presented to us that we can take advantage of—like a sling shot—to propel us forward at a more rapid rate.

Taking the Bullet Train

Since you are reading this book, you have signed on for the bullet train in this lifetime. As I mentioned earlier, before coming into this lifetime we design our life script or life path and we choose our main lesson. In addition, we also choose the main players who are going to take this journey with us. Some of those players, like our parents, might be on the same train with us in the very beginning—perhaps the first eighteen years—and then they may get off our train or we may choose to continue another part of the journey at perhaps a more rapid rate on the bullet train.

Although it may not seem like it at times, you do chose your journey and your main players. I used to say that if you had chosen Robert Redford for a mate and he was not available, then you would go to Paul Newman, but then I had younger students and changed it to if Brad Pit was not available, you went to Tom Cruise, and if he was taken, then you went to George Clooney, but he will never really be available.

You make these contracts with others before coming into this lifetime, but we all have free will so they can decide to take another path and so can you. Realize that not all the people that you have written into your script as part of your train ride are going to be there for the duration. Many of them are not meant to be on the bullet train that you are on.

You may have started on the slow choo-choo train and got bored. Then you tried the drama and trauma route for excitement and entertainment, but that got old. Even though that's a very hard way to learn your lessons, it didn't stop you from trying that path in the beginning. It motivated you to become more consciously aware of how you are learning your lessons. That is why many chose challenging childhoods.

At some point as you changed trains, you got on the bullet train. How do you know you are on the bullet train? Because you have learned lifetimes worth of lessons and gone through lifetimes worth of experiences in this one lifetime. Whereas most people just have one lifetime in one incarnation, you have had multiples. And you are not done yet. That is the bullet train.

You may have changed careers, you may have changed significant others, you may have changed groups of friends, you may have changed locations, and you may have changed your spiritual awareness. Maybe you started out in a traditional religion and then you religion-shopped or spirituality-shopped until you came to the realization that although you might enjoy the rituals of certain religious traditions, it is not about any set formula that everyone has to follow. It is about what *your* truth is that's going to propel you forward on your spiritual path. And finally you awaken to the awareness that it is all Divine all the time.

Not everybody has signed on for the bullet train and your friends can still be your friends, even if they are still on the other train following the old route—going past the same sites, the same things that you have already seen and now are ready to grow beyond. That does not mean you do not love them. Yet you probably will find yourself spending less time with them.

It is not about judging yourself or them. You are all exactly where you are meant to be. However, there are opportunities to get on a different train that will take you up the mountain of enlightenment in a more expedient, efficient, effective way, easily, effortlessly and enjoyable. Since you are the conscious being, soul, spirit that you are, hopefully your intent is to get on *that* train rather than to get off and buy a ticket for the old choo-choo again.

If you do find yourself choosing to ride once more on that slow train and realize, "Oh my goodness, been here, done that," and then wonder, "Have I missed the bullet train? Can I still make the bullet train?"

You can. You can just jump off and buy another ticket with your intent to get back on the bullet train. *In every single moment of every single day, you have a choice.* Ask yourself:

What is it I want to do?
How do I want to respond?
Where do I want to put my energies?

In the next moment, you can make a different choice. Are you moving toward being One with the Divine, knowing that you *are* the Divine? Or are you moving in the opposite direction? Are you making choices thinking it is easier to be a victim? When you get tired of that, you can get back on the bullet train.

For example, Yvonne was once again experiencing victim issues that she had grown beyond. It was very clear to me that her being, soul, spirit was really stepping into higher and higher levels of consciousness and that her ego got scared and started doing things to sabotage her forward movement. Once she was aware that she had stepped back into her old victim mode, especially in relationships, she chose to step forward into who she really is.

Returning to Who You Really Are

Whenever you are feeling off course, how do get back on course and believe in yourself once again? By believing in the truest, highest part of you, which is the Divine. Or by believing in the Divine itself.

Or you can decide to surrender to being who you really are. Here is the really cool thing: I am not asking you to be something you are not. I am asking you to be who you really are—without all the crud you have armored around yourself. I am just asking you to be your real Self, your real Divine Self.

If you put a glass chimney over a candle flame and you never dusted the chimney, how much light would get out? When you are birthed from the Divine you are this bright light, and then all this crud gets placed on top of you just like dust on the glass chimney. Is your light inside any less? No. But how much light can get out? Not as much. All you will simply be doing is dusting off.

Decide to let go of the stuff that is not your true intrinsic nature and not who you really are. By the way, that is not your crud to start with. You got it from the authority figures in your life when you were growing up. You got it from your parents, your teachers, the girl scout or boy scout leaders, and your coaches. Now it is time to give it back.

Do the following exercise with the intent that you are getting rid of anything that no longer serves you. You do not want to hang onto stuff that is not serving you anymore.

Letting Go of Everything That is Not You for Your Highest Good

Imagine an energy vortex right underneath where you are sitting that goes from your bottom through your chair, through the floor, through the crust of the earth, through the mantle of the earth, all the way down to the energy-recycling center at the core of the planet. That vortex is going to easily and effortlessly vacuum out of you anything that is not yours.

I am going to count from one to three and I want you to have the intent that whatever is not yours and is not for your highest good energetically is going to get flushed down this vortex.

One, it is just stuff you do not need.

Two, it has served its purpose; you don't need that rubbish around you anymore. We are dusting the glass chimney so your light can shine through.

Three, just let it go! See anything that is not you, any of that energy that you took on from someplace or someone else that you do not need anymore going down that vortex. Just flush it down the vortex. Let it go, let it go, let it go! It is all going to get cleansed down to the energy-recycling center. Just let it go. It is not yours anyway. It's not yours. Know that this vortex is going to continue to work for a while.

Returning to the Divine Flow

Use this checklist to return to that empowered enlightened place of Oneness. Whatever the situation you are in, ask yourself:

1. How would I respond if I were living in the Divine flow?

2. How would I act in this situation if I were living in the Divine flow?

3. What can I do right now to return to the Divine flow?

Now you are ready to move on to Chapter 12 and live in Oneness.

Living in Oneness

Have you ever wondered what it would be like to live the words of John Lennon's song, "Imagine there's no countries…nothing to kill or die for…a brotherhood of man…Imagine all the people living life in peace…I hope someday you'll join us and the world will live as one"? That is the way living in Oneness is for me.

Since I was given the great blessing of being taken into the state of Oneness non-duality, it is my privilege and responsibility to pass it on to others. My service in the world is to provide that opportunity to as many as I possibly can who are ready to move into Oneness.

Once I had the understanding of the chakra lifetimes, I realized that I had been taken into the 7th layer of the seventh chakra. It is my honor to now invite *you* into that top level of the seventh chakra that allows you to go back into Oneness. To assist people to come back to the way they were Divinely designed, I began to teach my I'O seminars, in which I initiate people into the Divine energy of Oneness that I have been privileged to receive. In these live seminars, I do this through energy initiations, transmissions and blessings.

The Blessing

I was given permission to do these blessings in a most unusual way. Back when this level of my spiritual awakening started happening to me, I was awakened in the middle of the night with a vision of an eye—just one eye. Then my vision expanded until I could see the whole face, and I saw it was Jesus' face before me as I felt all this incredible unconditional love. Then he disappeared and I saw the woman that I knew to be Anna, grandmother of Jesus, mother of Mother Mary, come toward me. She was dressed all in white, wearing one of those Catholic short, white veils called a wimple. She said to me, "You have the authority to bless."

"Don't we all have the authority to bless?" I replied. "I mean we say 'bless you' when somebody sneezes. We all have the authority to bless."

She laughed and said, "Yes, but you have the *authority* to bless."

"I'm really honored," I said, "I'm very touched, but you look Catholic to me and I'm not Catholic. I believe all religions have truth."

She just laughed and said, "You have an authority to bless, and this is the way you do it." And she taught me how to do a blessing.

She pulled me toward her. "You put one of your hands on the side of the face like this and the other hand on the other side," she instructed. As she placed her forehead on mine she continued, "Put your forehead on their forehead and think to them, 'You are God, you are God, you are God.'"

"Really," I said, "I don't use the G word very often. Can I just think 'You're the Source, you're the Source, you're the Source?' because it's the same thing, right?"

"Yes," she replied, "but not to you." She went on to explain, "If you would think, 'You are the Source, you are the Source, you are the Source,' you could do that easily without even thinking about it."

It was true. I could put my hands on somebody and just be thinking, "You are the Source, you are the Source, you are the Source," but not really paying attention.

She continued, "But if you have to think, 'You are God, you are God, you are God' to them, then you are going to pay attention to what you are saying.

She was absolutely right. After that experience, I would never even consider doing it any other way.

The next day my nanny arrived completely distraught having had a fight with her boyfriend, and it was clear she was going to be totally dysfunctional all day. "Come here!" I said, and did this blessing thing on her. She immediately became peaceful. "Thank you," she said, "I feel much better." And I thought, "Hmmm, this has possibilities."

That night one of my eighteen-month old twins was awake and my husband tried to get her to go to sleep and she just would not go to sleep. "Let me try," I said. I went into her room and I did this blessing thing on her. When I was done, she said, "Night, night, Mommy." I thought, "This really does have possibilities."

Then the next day one of my sixteen-year old twins was having a fit about something and yelling. I said to her, "Oh, just stop for a moment," and I did this blessing thing on her. She started to cry and said, "I love you, Mom." Hearing 'I love you, Mom' from this teenager was music to my ears. "Oh my goodness!" I thought. "This is a keeper."

When I am giving blessings to people and thinking to them, "You are God, you are God, you are God," this creates a powerful transformation. This is why.

How Thoughts Affect Us

In my seminars I do a demonstration that shows how positive and negative thoughts affect us and others. Using kinesiology or muscle testing on a volunteer in front of the class, I ask the rest of the class to think either positive thoughts or negative thoughts on a signal from me.

"You can think positive things about our volunteer Kirk if you want, but not negative things. We're going to see if the strength in his arm is affected by what we are thinking. And he's not going to know whether we're thinking positive thoughts or negative thoughts first. When I make this symbol, we're going to think negative things—not about Kirk. Negative things like poverty and war, but nothing negative about him. And when I make *this* symbol, we're going to think all kinds of wonderful things—peace, love, harmony, joy and bliss. We're going to think positive things about Kirk. And we're going to see if his strength is affected by what we're thinking."

The results were clear. It was obvious when we were thinking negative thoughts because his arm went weak and when we were thinking positive thoughts, his arm remained strong. Notice that we were not thinking the negative things *about* Kirk. But just the same, he got weaker as we were thinking downer thoughts. Then when we were thinking positive things, he got really strong. He was even stronger than the first time when we did the pre-test to find his normal level of strength.

How to Bring Out the Divine in Others

What does that tell you that you could be doing for the people in your life when you are having challenges with them? Should you think of the bad stuff? "You lazy, good for nothing. . ." If you want them to be a lazy good for nothing, the best way to do that is to think they are a lazy good for nothing because then they are going to be an even better lazy, good for nothing if you are affirming that for them. If you want them to be angelic, heavenly, exhibiting Divine qualities, you want to think, "You are God, you are God, you are God." If you want them to be healed, you want to think, "You are God, you are God, you are God."

That is the reason why I do that, and why you want to do that too. Just as Anna taught me, having it be a charged thing will make you pay attention even more. It is meant to be a little bit jarring to make us have to focus on what our intention is for that person we are healing or healing our relationship with—including healing ourselves, when we do it for ourselves.

Divine Empowerment Blessings to Awaken the Divine in You

When I give blessings of Divine empowerment in most of my live events, I tell the participants, "When I give you a blessing, I am not putting anything *in* you. All I am doing is awakening what is already there to empower that God realization in you. You are just going to be a better, more expanded, enlightened version of you.

"I'm going to put my hands on the side of your face and put my forehead gently on your forehead and I'm going to awaken more of the Divine in you. It can make people feel a little wobbly, so we provide chairs in case you need to sit down. It is normal for people to go into spontaneous states of joy and bliss. Returning to our natural state of Divinity is always a wondrous transforming experience."

You can see for yourself what the Divine Empowerment Blessings do by watching everyone melting into Divine bliss. Go to: http://www.youtube.com and search: Laurie Grant.

Hearing Loss Restored

After I did a blessing on Richard who wears a hearing aid in each ear except when he's sleeping, he was awakened the next morning to the sound of birds loudly chirping outside his window. First he was annoyed that he was awakened until he realized he didn't have his hearing aids on and he could hear. The blessing filled him with Divine energy that cleared whatever limitation needed to be cleared, so he could hear again.

Divine Awakened

When I was a panel member at a conference, a woman came up to talk to me afterward and I gave her a blessing without telling her what to expect. She just melted into the energy. Then she said, "I feel like the Divine has been awakened in me."

Initiations

In my live seminars I give initiations, which are different than Divine Empowerment Blessings or Transmissions. This is a way I transfer even higher levels of energy and consciousness into the participants and I also initiate each of their chakras to the vibration of the healing modality the student is learning. The intention of the initiation is to raise their enlightenment levels and to empower and infuse the student with healing energy to use in the treatment of themselves or others. When I am giving an initiation, I ask for the highest level of a particular aspect of the Divine energy, for instance I'O 1, to come through me at the highest level that I can easily accommodate for the purpose of initiating my students to the highest level of I'O 1 that they can easily absorb. The energy then comes through me and by me putting my hands on the student, it travels into them.

Author and psychiatrist Dr. David Hawkins reports that when you are within the aura of someone who has gone into non-duality that your body becomes sensitized to the energy. Then, when you are ready, it is even easier to go into that state yourself. My experience is when I initiate someone into Oneness non-duality, they go into bliss!

Expanding to Oneness Non-duality or Self-Realization

Do not be surprised if you find yourself experiencing orgasms of bliss, as one of my students did, when you feel yourself returning to the Divine state of Oneness. After attending an I'O seminar, Gretchen called to tell me that each time she does the Oneness exercises, she has an orgasm. "It's so much fun," she giggled.

In the I'O seminars designed to awaken the spiritual God/Goddess Self within, you have the opportunity to go into the highest state of Oneness non-duality that you can easily accommodate.

"In your I'O Mastery seminar," Harrison shared, "I experienced Oneness non-duality in a working functioning body. I am still in the same space as when I left the seminar. All I have to do is close my eyes and say, 'I am living in the Divine presence' and it pulls it up to full power.

"What struck me the most was how natural and easy it was. You are still the same person, only enlightened. Of it and not in it, much like I feel right now. Everything seems different. I was sitting there at the end of class looking at everyone and they were all masses of light sitting on chairs that were not there, only they were. It is not that big of a change, only a small change in perception. The world did not change, only how I see it. Everything is perfect. I am so big I feel like I fill the universe. It feels so good and right and natural, like that is the way it is supposed to be. Very cool!"

Although my ARCH seminars and other classes are now available on DVD through my website, the advanced seminars such as I'O (Infinite Oneness Enlightenment) and Cosmic Source Healing are of such a high-energy frequency that they have not been able to be duplicated onto a DVD. These are the seminars that I will continue to do live so as many people as possible can be initiated into their Divinity and experience Oneness.

After attending an I'O seminar Nancy wrote, "I had my first experience of going into Oneness. I am so grateful."

Here is another seminar participant's experience of her initiation: "The minute you started breathing the breath of Cosmic Mother out, I had a vision: I saw your face and upper torso. Your skin was very white and totally transparent. I could see the universe through your skin, dark blue with stars and planets, and your long blond hair flowing like it was flowing in water. I saw this breath coming out of you toward all of us. I inhaled deeply and noticed that every pore of my body inhaled too. It was so beautiful and peaceful I wish it could have taken forever. Thank you for that gift of healing, love and energy. It transported me into Oneness and I feel sooo good."

If you want to experience this initiation for yourself, I invite you to come to a *live* seminar. To find out when my next live seminar is scheduled, please go to my website:www.TransformYourLifeNow.net.

I also find that the energy transmissions in my teleseminars can be tangibly felt by the participants, no matter where they are in the world.

"Since this was my first teleseminar," said Adrienne, "I was curious to see if the energy would be as powerful as being with Laurie in person. Even with me not attending *live*, it was wonderful—just like being in class with her."

Oneness with Everything

Here is an exercise that will allow you to adjust your focus, like a camera lens, to expand beyond your individual perspective and experience Oneness with everything and then bring yourself back. I suggest that you practice this at least once every day, better yet two times a day, to expand your perspective beyond your individual reality.

1. Get centered and start envisioning the web, the net, the quantum hologram, the Divine matrix that connects us all together as One. First, see all the strands that go vertically from Divine Source that come through everything, including you. Then, envision all the strands that go out horizontally through you forming that matrix.

2. Next, using your breath, enlarge your awareness of this matrix of Oneness and fill the room that you are in, then the house or the building that you are in, then the block, then the town or city that you are in, then the state that you are in. Then widening that out more and more to one side of the planet and then all around the other side of the planet. Some days you will want to be with the dolphins or whales, perhaps other days with the birds. Then allow your perspective to expand to being one with our solar system, then be one with our galaxy and extend yourself out to be one with the universe. Hang out there for as long as you want.

3. When you are ready, begin to narrow your focus, like turning a camera lens down, to being back one with the galaxy, one with the solar system, one with the planet, one with this side of the planet, one with

your state, one with your city, one with your block, one with your house, back to yourself.

The more you practice this, the more it will become automatic so when you go into the state of Oneness, you can easily bring your focus back whenever you want. Then your body personality will be reassured that you have a way to bring it back, and you will not be stuck in Oneness and live in bliss for the rest of your life. Oh my goodness, imagine living in all that bliss all the time!

Living in Oneness

Here is a checklist to help you live as you were always intended—in Oneness:

1. Acknowledge your Oneness with the Divine Source.

2. Look for and love the Divine essence in everyone and everything.

3. Treat everyone and everything (especially yourself) with Divine love.

4. Live life in the love, joy, bliss and abundance of the Divine flow.

Blessed Oneness Cords

A few years ago I woke up thinking, "How can I remind people that we are all One?" As bestselling author Wayne Dyer says, "It's a round planet and there is no choosing sides." Yet it is so much more than that: We are truly One with everything—with each other, the Creator, and with all life everywhere.

As a daily reminder, I thought we could tie a string around our finger. Then I realized that might look silly. "Oh!" I said aloud as the whole plan unfolded before me, "we can tie a string around our wrist like the Kabbalahists do! I can come up with a Oneness knot on Oneness Cords. I can make them up ahead of time, so we can have them available at all of our seminars and classes. And I can bless them."

Now about 18,000 students all over the world are wearing Blessed Oneness Cords. If you would like to receive a Oneness Cord, just send us a self-addressed stamped envelope to: Oneness Cord, Laurie Grant, P.O. Box 843, Wailuku, HI 96793 and we will send you a cord that I have personally blessed, along with how to perform the Oneness Commitment Ceremony. We will also include Divine Messages of Oneness.

When you receive your cord, I suggest that you tie it securely around your wrist with a square knot. If you were not a girl scout or a boy scout or a campfire girl or campfire boy, a square knot is tying right over left and then tying left over right—it just has to be opposite so it will not come off. Mine is on all the time—even when I shower. Note: Some massage therapists wear them on their ankles.

When you put it on, make a commitment to remember Oneness. Every time you look at it, you are reminded of Oneness. Rather than make it out of something that will never ever come off—like a tattoo—I made them out of a thin cord so at some point it will fall off. Why? If you wear anything all the time, after a while you don't notice it anymore. When your cord falls off, that is the universe saying to you, "Time for you to remember Oneness again." Then you can send us another self-addressed stamped envelope and we will send you a replacement. In this way you can continuously remember to make your recommitment to Oneness.

We also celebrate January 1st as Oneness Day by doing Oneness meditations, singing Oneness carols such as "Imagine" and engaging in random acts of kindness.

Meeting with the Divine Mother

My own commitment to my highest purpose was deepened and expanded when the Cosmic Mother, known as Uli to the Hawaiian kahunas, appeared to me at a sacred heiau (Hawaiian temple) and asked, "Do you remember what you were told?" At this point I was 57, I had been told a lot of things and I didn't know what she was referring to, so I tried listing a number of things.

"That I had made a commitment to come back when the time was right," I offered, "to remind people that we are all One."

"Yes," she said, "but that's not what we're asking you. "Do you remember what you were told in your near-death experience?

Immediately the experience she was referring to came flooding back into my mind. In 1987 I was taken up out of my body until I was One with the Divine, feeling unconditional love and total bliss. In this glorious state, I asked if I could send some of this energy to my children who were having a difficult time. As soon as I asked that, I heard this voice that was neither loud nor soft, male nor female say to me, "They are *all* your children. They are *all* your children. Go back and remind them of who they are."

As soon as that was said, I was sucked back down into my body. I knew what "go back and remind them of who they are" meant. I'd already been teaching people that they were their Divine essence, so that was very clear to me—I was to continue teaching them that they are Divine. Yet the rest of the message, "They are *all* your children," did not make sense to me.

Uli's voice brought me back to the present as she asked, "Are you willing to carry everyone in your heart as their spiritual mother?"

Tears flooded my eyes as the meaning suddenly became clear. "Yes, of course, I replied.

"Would you be willing to commit to loving everyone as a mother loves her child?" she asked again.

Touched to my very core, I managed to reply, "If that's my sacred responsibility, then of course I will."

At that moment, her energy came into me, merging with me, and it was an overwhelming feeling of incredible Divine love and bliss. I felt love for everyone, everything, and every life form in the universe. I was there for a long time. When I was finally leaving, I could still hear her talking to me inside.

From that time on, I start each morning and each night sending the healing energies of the Cosmic Mother to every living being, every life form in the universe on body, mind, spirit and emotional levels if it is for their highest good. This energy helps awaken the world to Divine Oneness.

Receiving a New Spiritual Name

I was sitting on a bench overlooking the ocean one evening when I next heard Uli's thoughts. She told me that it was time to use the name that represents the energy of the Divine Mother and the full expression of the Divine that was always there waiting to emerge. She said, "Your true name is URI," which is the Polynesian spelling and ancient form of the Hawaiian name for the Divine Mother or Cosmic Mother or Uli. "You've always been called URI," she said.

"No, I'm pretty sure I've been called Laurie," I replied.

"You've always been called URI," she confirmed.

"Nope. I think I would know. I'm sure I've been called Laurie," I said with certainty.

"You've always been URI," she stated again.

My left brain was thinking, "What is she talking about?" Then I saw "La URI e" spelled out before my eyes.

"It's the center of your given name of Laurie."

Yep! She was right. Then I realized that URI was all in caps because the deeper meaning of the sound of those three letters is "You are I!" It was a statement of Oneness.

"I wish you to use this name to show your commitment to restoring the balance of the nurturing, compassionate and unconditional love essence of the Divine Mother and the Divine Feminine.

"When the Divine Feminine in the ancient Ku-Hina tradition was abandoned, the balance that always assured harmony and peace diminished. You made a commitment to come back to earth to help restore that balance and peace. For how else can you restore the ancient lineage of Ku-Hina where all *knew* they were Divine without reawakening the Divine Feminine and honoring both the Divine Feminine and Divine Masculine in perfect balance.

"This name will remind you that you are an expression of the Divine Mother and carry the qualities that will bring balance to this ancient lineage, and can be a model to bring it back to the world."

Then she came into me and merged with me so completely, filling every cell of my body with such intensity, that I could not even move. It was like we were one being.

Then on Mothers Day, I received a phone call from Papa, ever tuned in, wishing me a Happy Mothers Day to the "mother of the world."

Expression of the Divine Mother

After that, my way of being in the world made a noticeable shift. I became more generous, more loving, more compassionate and more flexible. For example, when my office manager booked tickets for me to go to Ojai on the wrong date, I responded very differently than I would have before.

"You're going to fire me," she said, her voice filled with trepidation. In the past I would not have fired her, but I certainly would have let her know that I was not pleased.

"I guess there's a reason for that," I said instead, "and we'll figure out what it is."

"Don't you want me to pay the extra money?" she asked. "It will cost $150 to switch the tickets!"

"No, no," I replied. "There's a reason."

"Well, don't you want me to book the hotel for another night?" she asked not quite believing her ears.

"No, no, we'll know what we're supposed to do with that extra day," I assured her.

We ended up going to Yogananda's Lake Shrine in Los Angeles. Once there, I was guided to go into the windmill sanctuary. While in meditation Yogananda's spirit came to me indicating that people had forgotten the Cosmic or Divine Mother and that *it was time to re-awaken people to her once again.* So much energy began pouring through me that my assistant who was sitting next to me could not feel her body and wondered what was happening. When I came out of meditation, I noticed that only pictures of male saints and deities were hung at the front of the room, even though Yogananda revered the Divine Mother above all.

It is hoped that this book will remind people to embody the Divine Feminine qualities that have been missing for so long, such as love and compassion. Whether you are a man or a woman, this is so needed at this time for your own growth as well as the restoration of balance on the planet.

Transforming Our World

As more and more of us step into our Divinity and Oneness, we have the power to transform our world. How can we do that? First, by seeing the Divine in ourselves and in the other and then, by speaking our highest Divine truth that can transform people's lives from scarcity, struggle and strife into the unlimited peace, joy and abundance of the Divine.

Remembering that we are all Divine all the time—even when it is presented in a very different package that can fool us into thinking that the Divine is not there in front of us—we can create positive change.

Your Greatest Gift

Now that you know that we are Divine *all the time*, what is the greatest gift you can provide for yourself and others? *See the Divine perfection in everyone in your life and everyone you meet.* That very act allows you to see through the eyes of Mother/Father God, which strengthens and expands your own Divine qualities.

How do I know that seeing the Divine perfection in another is what creates deep healing and transformation on every level? I was privileged to witness it first hand.

Shortly before going into Oneness non-duality, I was sitting in bed one night when I saw Jesus appear in front of me. I had only seen him once before when Anna taught me how to bless.

He appeared at the foot of my bed and again I immediately felt all this unconditional love. It felt like he was opening me up as he came into my heart. Then he filled my entire body with his love. It was like he was within me. I discovered I could have a dialogue with him by thinking a thought and I would telepathically receive the answer. He was with me for three and a half days and for three and a half days I didn't want to sleep.

I was completely and totally focused on learning everything I could from him since I didn't know how long he was going to be with me. Finally on the beginning of the third day he communicated to me, "Just be still and know." Since I was not raised Christian nor did I study Christianity, I was hearing this for the first time. Then I had the great privilege and honor of just "being" in his wondrous loving presence.

Seeing Through the Eyes of the Divine

Before he silenced my questions, I thought to him, "How did you heal?" He said telepathically, "I will show you." Immediately I had the experience of looking out of his eyes and being shown how he healed and feeling it in my body. This is what I witnessed down to the cellular level in my entire body: He saw the perfection of the Divine in the other as he radiated his love to them and honored that Divine in them with every part and cell of his being.

I believe that the true masters do exactly that. They see just the Divine in everyone and they acknowledge that and they embrace that and they almost weep with joy at the privilege of getting to see that in everyone and everything. That's what is healing for people. That is how Jesus did his healing miracles. *The greatest gift we can give anyone is to hold that vision of their Divinity for them.*

The greeting "namaste" from the Hindu tradition in India captures that gift:

> *The God in me greets the God in you.*
> *The Spirit in me meets the same Spirit in you.*

One Hawaiian definition of the word "aloha" means:

> *I am in the presence of the Divine.*

Seeing the Divine in Others

What if you saw the Divine in everyone? What if you looked at them and instead of seeing their drama and trauma, you saw their Divinity? How would that change your life? It would definitely make your life better—more loving, more flexible and happier. You would love everybody. I love everybody without hesitation.

A simple way to start seeing the Divine in another is to think to them, "I honor the Divine in you" and watch what happens. I was walking down the street in New York City and I saw what appeared to be a homeless man and I thought to him, "I honor the Divine in you." He immediately stopped in his tracks. He held out his arms and he raised his head up to the sky and he said, "Ahhhhh." He just stood there and this incredibly peaceful, exquisite smile came across his face.

Here is what I teach my students: Go through your day without saying anything, just honor the Divine in everyone. Trust me, if you want good service in a restaurant, all you have to do is honor the Divine in that waiter or waitress. You want good service from the cashier at the supermarket, even if they are having a bad day? Honor the Divine in him or her, it will change the experience for both of you *instantly*.

What if you did that with your significant other and all your relationships? What if you did it with your children? What if you did it with the neighbor you are having a conflict with? What if you did it with the President? What if you did it with your perceived enemies or the government's perceived enemies? What if you did it with yourself?

Seeing the Divine in Yourself

Do this exercise as the first thing you do when you wake up in the morning. Why is this important? Because YOU CANNOT HONOR IN OTHERS WHAT YOU WILL NOT HONOR IN YOURSELF! Acknowledge your Divine essence. Say to yourself:

I honor the Divine essence in me.

Then see yourself as this being of golden light, radiating your light out for all to see. *Feel* yourself as this radiant light and bask in that warm radiance before getting out of bed each morning. *This is the transforming practice.*

It is not honoring the Divine in you as if you are better than everybody else. It is being that light within you so you can hold that vision of the light within others. It is there in everyone, sometimes submerged very deeply, but it is still there.

Being an Expression of the Divine

How would that change your relationship with your neighbors, with your community? As Gandhi said, "World change starts with you. World peace starts with you." You are transforming your world every time you honor the Divine within you and the Divine in your family members, your neighbors, your community, your state, your country and the world, and see the Divine in every situation.

Lots of people right now are focusing on all of the things that are wrong or could go wrong. I recently met a woman who was coming from a place of fear. I said to her, "The more you empower fear, the more fear will be empowered, and I'm not sure that's what you want."

I showed her all the different ways she could focus on the light, even though there is darkness there. For example, you can look at how horrific it was for my stepfather to be sexually inappropriate with me night after night as I was growing up or you can look at "Oh, my God, look at the gifts that I ended up having as a result of that. I am an incredibly more effective teacher because of those experiences."

Throughout our conversation I kept bringing it back to the light. Finally she said to me, "Don't you have any fear?" And I said, "My intention is to live my life in faith rather than in fear. That is what I focus on in all arenas of my life."

If we are afraid of our neighbors, if we are afraid of what is happening in the world, then we are empowering fear. Just as with horses and most animals, if you are fearful, even unconsciously, the horse is going to feel like you are not in control and it will react badly because it can feel your fear.

Instead, if you just take a deep breath, and remind yourself that you are the embodiment of the Divine and tune into the Divine flowing through you, then you will receive the guidance of what to do. Remember, your intuition manifests through clairsentience in your *second* chakra, through clairaudience in your *fifth*, through clairvoyance in your *sixth* and through clear knowing in your *seventh* chakra, so you can easily be guided to handle any situation that may appear fearful. You will be guided how to shine your light into the situation to transform it. We are definitely going to change our world with light, not with darkness. And we are definitely going to change it with faith, rather than fear.

Speaking as the Divine Self

As you develop the quality of hearing the compassionate words of the Divine, you become the voice of the Divine. How would allowing the unlimited Divine Self to speak through you change your relationships? The way to help another begin to change is to hold that light for them that they are not able to hold for themselves right now. By honoring the Divine within another with your words, no matter what they are doing, they can begin to see it within themselves.

How will that change your family environment and your home environment if you spoke from this place? You are holding the higher vision for the family so that they can become it. Communicating the Divine you see in your family is the greatest way to help them access this higher vision and to open more and more to it within themselves. If you see the worst in people and speak it, you are going to get the worst from people. If you see the best in people and you hold that vision for them and reflect it back to them in your words, you will get the best from them.

That does not mean do not set clear boundaries. Yet seeing the Divine in them and reflecting that back to them stimulates their goodness and best choices.

Time to Speak Up

How can we change the conditions in the world? If we all communicated from our Divine Self, rather than feeling either we do not have a voice or bad things are going to happen if we speak up, then the truth would start to flow from us rather than living in fear. And *our collective voices would transform our world.*

How is it going to be transformed unless we do that? How is it going to be changed unless we speak up? We can do it energetically, yet as we know speaking something gives it even more power. That's the way we create a new way.

You were born with a voice, even if you were born mute, you still have a way to communicate. Time to put your fears or issues aside and allow the Divine to flow through you. Being the voice of the Divine is your birthright. If you do not do it now, when are you going to do it? We are all born to be expressions of the Divine. And we are born to be vessels of the Divine flowing through us.

Living Our Life's Purpose

It was during my on-going state of Oneness non-duality and merging with the Cosmic Mother that I received the information about the chakra lifetimes and that karma was a thing of the past. I was shown that the new way to transform our lives is by evolving to higher levels of awareness and awakening to who we really are and why we are here, so we can rise out of pain and suffering into joy and return to unconditional love, acceptance and compassion.

I was provided a map of the chakra lifetimes so we can see where we have been and where we can go. Instead of judging ourselves for not being somewhere different, we can see how far we have come. And we can see where our children and significant others are so we can lovingly encourage them to take their next step.

Immediately I knew that I was shown a clear path to living in Oneness with everything, consciously creating our world around us and living in enlightenment. Being a spiritual teacher for thirty-nine years, I knew I was meant to share it with others.

We are all part of the same Divine Source of Creation and all of us are here to tap into that unlimited, unbounded energy and use it to fulfill our life's purpose and service in the world. I am not anything different than you. What I have done, you can do too.

I have personally watched my students go through the steps I have just given you of clearing the chakras and removing the cords and transforming into living in the Divine flow of grace and finally going into Oneness non-duality. So I know you can do this too.

It is my deep heartfelt desire that sharing my journey and what I have learned will make yours easier. One of my students said, "You have the way back to our Divine Self wired, so we don't have to figure it out for ourselves."

I know in my heart of hearts if you use the tools provided in this book and the wisdom I received from the Cosmic Mother, you will transform your life and excel on every level. That is my wish and prayer for you.

Pass It On!

Once you have learned the powerful steps in this book, please pass this book on to your loved ones, friends and co-workers, so they too can learn how to transform their lives.

Appendix: Guidelines for Book Study Group

Guidelines for Book Study Groups

It is suggested that you form a Book Study Group with others to deepen and augment your experience of working with the book and doing the exercises yourself. When you gather together with others with the same intent, the energy and transformational power of this book are increased and expanded exponentially.

The following guidelines are suggested to enhance your transformation.

Week 1 – Finding the Hidden Key

After choosing a Book Study Group Facilitator, have the participants arrive at the first meeting having read the Introduction and Chapter 1 prepared to discuss it.

Discussion Points:

1. How has learning about the End of Karma given you new understanding?

2. How has learning about Chakra Lifetimes expanded your understanding? How has it expanded your understanding of yourself? How has it expanded your understanding of others?

3. Play "Name the Chakra Lifetime" game.

Facilitator: Ask the participants, "What chakra lifetime do you think _____ (person in question) is on and why? Example: Oprah? The President? Arnold Schwarzenegger? Mother Theresa? Then ask, "For bonus points, what layer of that chakra lifetime do you think each of the above is working on?

4. How has what you have learned about Chakra Countries enhanced your understanding and tolerance?

Facilitator: Lead the participants through the questions in "Discovering Others' Chakra Lifetimes" in Chapter 1.

Participants share their experience.

Week 2 – Uncorking Your Ability to Excel

Discussion Points:

1. What new understandings have you received about your survival chakra?

2. What transformations are you beginning to see in your own life?

3. What are the Divine qualities you are in the process of developing?

Facilitator: Lead the participants through the Exercises at the end of Chapter 2. Begin by having them close their eyes and take some deep breaths to go into a relaxed state and then take them through each step of the following exercises.

- Identifying All the Ways You Have Kept Yourself From Being Divine in the First Chakra

    Releasing the Blocks

- Returning to Your Divine Essence

- Returning to Divine Feelings Throughout the Day

Participants share their experience.

Week 3 – Activating Your Feelings of Well Being

Discussion Points:

1. What new understandings have you received about your emotional, sensual and sexual chakra?

2. What transformations are you beginning to see in your life?

3. Are you now making choices that allow you to feel more loving toward yourself rather than out of fear?

4. What are the Divine qualities you are in the process of developing?

Facilitator: Lead the participants through the Exercises at the end of Chapter 3. Begin by having them close their eyes and take some deep breaths to go into a relaxed state and then take them through each step of the following exercises:

- Identifying All the Ways You Have Kept Yourself From Being Divine in the Second Chakra

- Releasing the Blocks

- Returning to Your Divine Essence

- Returning to Divine Feelings Throughout the Day

Participants share their experience.

Week 4 – Unleashing Your Ability to Manifest Abundance

Discussion Points:

1. What new understandings have you received about your will, willpower and manifesting chakra?

2. What transformations are you beginning to see in your own life?

3. What are the Divine qualities you are in the process of developing?

Facilitator: Lead the participants through the Exercises at the end of Chapter 4. Begin by having them close their eyes and take some deep breaths to go into a relaxed state and then take them through each step of the following exercises.

- Identifying All the Ways You Have Kept Yourself From Being Divine in the Third Chakra

- Releasing the Blocks

- Returning to Your Divine Essence

- Returning to Divine Feelings Throughout the Day

Participants share their experience.

Week 5 – Opening Your Ability to Love and Be Loved

Discussion Points:

1. What new understandings have you received about your giving and receiving love chakra?

2. What transformations are you beginning to see in your own life?

3. What are the Divine qualities you are in the process of developing?

Facilitator: Lead the participants through the Exercises at the end of Chapter 5. Begin by having them close their eyes and take some deep breaths to go into a relaxed state and then take them through each step of the following exercises.

- Identifying All the Ways You Have Kept Yourself From Being Divine in the Fourth Chakra

- Releasing the Blocks

- Returning to Your Divine Essence

- Returning to Divine Feelings Throughout the Day

Participants share their experience.

Week 6 – Optimizing Your Communication Abilities

Discussion Points:

1. What new understandings have you received about your communication chakra?

2. What transformations are you beginning to see in your own life?

3. What are the Divine qualities you are in the process of developing?

Facilitator: Lead the participants through the Exercises at the end of Chapter 6. Begin by having them close their eyes and take some deep breaths to go into a relaxed state and then take them through each step of the following exercises.

- Identifying All the Ways You Have Kept Yourself From Being Divine in the Fifth Chakra

- Releasing the Blocks

- Returning to Your Divine Essence

- Returning to Divine Feelings Throughout the Day

Participants share their experience.

Week 7 – Uncapping Your Psychic, Perception, Creativity and Healing Abilities

Discussion Points:

1. What new understandings have you received about your psychic, perception, creativity and healing chakra?

2. What transformations are you beginning to see in your own life?

3. What are the Divine qualities you are in the process of developing?

Facilitator: Lead the participants through the Exercises at the end of Chapter 7. Begin by having them close their eyes and take some deep breaths to go into a relaxed state and then take them through each step of the following exercises.

- Identifying All the Ways You Have Kept Yourself From Being Divine in the Sixth Chakra

- Releasing the Blocks

- Returning to Your Divine Essence

- Returning to Divine Feelings Throughout the Day

Participants share their experience.

Week 8 – Deepening Your Spiritual Connection

Discussion Points:

1. What new understandings have you received about your spiritual chakra?

2. What transformations are you beginning to see in your own life?

3. What are the Divine qualities you are in the process of developing?

Facilitator: Lead the participants through the Exercises at the end of Chapter 8. Begin by having them close their eyes and take some deep breaths to go into a relaxed state and then take them through each step of the following exercises:

- Identifying All the Ways You Have Kept Yourself From Being Divine in the Seventh Chakra

- Releasing the Blocks

- Returning to Your Divine Essence

- Returning to Divine Feelings Throughout the Day

Participants share their experience.

Week 9 – Reclaiming Your Freedom and Your Power to Manifest the Life of Your Dreams

Discussion Points:

1. What new understandings have you received about cords?

2. What transformations are you beginning to see in your own life?

Facilitator:

    a. Lead the participants through the following Exercises in Chapter 9:

- Identifying the Cords to be Removed

- Identifying the Cords You Placed in Others

    b. Play the recorded audio meditation that you can download by emailing audio@transformyourlifenow.net.

    c. After listening to the audio meditation, lead the participants through the "Deepening Your Connection with Your Loved One" Exercise at the end of Chapter 9.

Participants share their experience.

Week 10 – Living in the Divine Flow

Discussion Points:

1. What would your life be like living from the unlimited Divine and excelling on all levels?

2. What does living in the Divine flow look like to you?

3. What would that look like on a daily basis?

Facilitator:

    a. Lead the participants through the 7 questions at the beginning of Chapter 10.

    b. Then guide them through "Living in the Divine Flow in All Aspects of Your Life" in Chapter 10.

Participants share their experience.

Facilitator: Lead the participants through the "Daily Checklist to Ensure Living in the Divine Flow" from Chapter 10.

Participants share their experience.

Week 11 – Staying in the Divine Flow

Discussion Points:

1. What are the ways you have learned to stay in the Divine Flow?

2. What are some of the creative ways you have used to allow yourself to be unconscious or to be distracted from your spiritual growth?

Facilitator:
    a. Lead the participants through "Focusing on Where You Want to Go Exercise" from Chapter 11 applying this to an area of their life where they feel they have backslidden.

    b. Next lead them through the "Letting Go of Everything That is Not You for Your Highest Good" Exercise.

    c. Then lead them through the "Returning to the Divine Flow" checklist at the end of the chapter.

Participants share their experience.

Week 12 – Living in Oneness

Discussion Points:

1. What have you learned in these past 11 weeks?

2. How has your life transformed in all 7 areas of your life?

Facilitator: Lead the participants through the "Oneness with Everything" Exercise in Chapter 12.

Participants share their experience.

Facilitator:

    a. Lead the participants through a discussion of how they can live in Oneness using the "Living in Oneness" checklist from Chapter 12.

    b. Lead the participants in answering the final question:

As Gandhi said, 'World change starts with you. World peace starts with you.' You are transforming your world every time you honor the Divine within you and the Divine in your family members, your neighbors, your community, your state, your country and the world, and see the Divine in every situation. Ask each participant: *How will you do that in your own life?*

Facilitator: Pass out Oneness Cords. (You can obtain Oneness cords and instructions of how to perform the Oneness Commitment Ceremony by sending a self-addressed stamped envelope to: Oneness Cords, Laurie Grant, P.O. Box 843, Wailuku, HI 96793). Lead the participants in the Oneness Ceremony and have each state their commitment to remember Oneness.

About the Author

Laurie URI Grant is an internationally known spiritual teacher and leader with over 18,000 students and thirty-nine years of experience. She is a popular radio and television guest as well as a frequent keynote speaker at Expos and conferences throughout the country and abroad. Laurie teaches a wide variety of courses all over the world designed to develop healing and intuitive abilities, self-empowerment, spiritual growth, enlightenment and oneness.

The author received her Masters Degree in the form of counseling known as Art Therapy. She has studied many different holistic disciplines. Laurie is a Reiki Master Teacher, and the Founder of ARCH (Ancient Rainbow Conscious Healing), I'O (Infinite Oneness Enlightenment), Cosmic Source Healing, Oneness Ascension, and Transform Your Life NOW! Trainings.

Laurie discovered her metaphysical and healing abilities at an early age when she spontaneously began receiving clear, accurate premonitions. Founder and Director of three holistic health centers, she was booked a year in advance for appointments. Grant worked with MDs, NDs, chiropractors and acupuncturists as a medical intuitive discovering the causes of their patients' illnesses with a hundred percent accuracy.

In 2003 she went into Oneness non-duality. That same year she was initiated into the ancient Hawaiian tradition as a Kahuna of Oneness. In 2010 she merged into Oneness with the Divine Mother. Laurie's mission is to empower people to remember that they are One with the Divine and can live in love, peace and abundance.

The author currently lives on the Hawaiian island of Maui.

**To attend a Laurie Grant Seminar and
continue to Transform Your Life NOW!**

**visit: www.TransformYourLifeNow.net
for the latest schedule and registration information.**

Seminars: *The Path to Oneness Enlightenment*

I.   Level One: Awakening and Healing on a Physical Body Level – The ARCH (Ancient Rainbow Conscious Healing) Series

II.   Level Two: Awakening the Emotional and Mental Bodies and Learning the Tools to Enlightenment – The Kaula Program (Ho'oponopono, Intuition, Medical Intuition, Past Life Integration, Voices of the Ancestors)

III.   Level Three: Awakening Your Spiritual God/Goddess Self in this Body – The I'O (Infinite Oneness Enlightenment) Series

IV.   Level Four: Awakening Cosmic Consciousness and living in cosmic consciousness – The Cosmic Source Series

V.   Level Five: Awakening Oneness Ascension Consciousness and living the path of a Spiritual Master – The Oneness Ascension Series

Live Teleconferences/Webinars – Transformative life changing simulcasts. Tune in from the privacy of your own home to receive live transmissions of energy.

Personal Divine Oneness Blessings to activate the Divine within you, available at most live events.

Divine Mother Empowerments to empower you to awaken to your own Divinity.

Playshops – *Transform Your Life NOW! The Spiritual Key to Excelling on All Levels:*

I. Transforming Your Life and Excelling on: survival, emotional, sexual, will, willpower and manifesting levels
II. Transforming Your Life and Excelling on: love of self, love of others, communication, psychic, perception of things, creativity, and healing abilities levels
III. Transforming Your Life and Excelling on spiritual levels
IV. Living in a State of Mastering and Excelling Your Life Now on All Levels.

Lectures and teleconferences available on CD and DVD, visit: www. TransformYourLifeNow.net

Newsletter – Sign up for a FREE monthly newsletter at: www. TransformYourLifeNow.net

To book Laurie Grant as a Keynote Speaker at Expos and Conferences or as a guest on TV, radio and webcasts, contact:

808-757-9306
www.TransformYourLifeNow.net

CPSIA information can be obtained at www.ICGtesting.com
Printed in the USA
LVOW010920021111

253179LV00001B/14/P